BRAZIL

On Your Own

BRAZIL

On Your Own

by Arnold Greenberg

Harriet Greenberg
Series Editor

Published by Passport Books in conjunction with
Alive Publications

 **PASSPORT BOOKS**

Trade Imprint of National Textbook Company
Lincolnwood, Illinois U.S.A.

Acknowledgments

To my friend Bram Gunther – heartfelt thanks for your help in researching and writing this book – I couldn't have done it without you.

Muito Obrigado

Published by Passport Books, Trade Imprint of National Textbook Company.

© 1988 by National Textbook Company,
4255 West Touhy Avenue,
Lincolnwood (Chicago), Illinois 60646-1975
and Alive Publications Ltd.

Library of Congress Catalogue Card Number: 87-61395
Manufactured in the United States of America.

8 9 0 ML 9 8 7 6 5 4 3 2 1

Dedication

To the memory of my mother – who before every trip I ever took invoked "Go B'Sholom – and come B'Sholom."

My love and wish that you always be at peace.

Contents

The "On Your Own" Travel Guides

In a series of essays written in 1597, Francis Bacon penned, "When a traveller returneth home, let him not leave the countries where he hath travelled altogether behind him." Although we might phrase it rather differently, we wholeheartedly second that sentiment, and with it in mind, we have launched the "On Your Own" travel series.

These unique guides were created for the traveler who wants to be immersed in a different culture for a length of time. And for the adventurous independent traveler, curious and open minded, young and not "as young as they feel," who is eager to explore new travel horizons or yearns for a fresh approach to visiting those beloved familiar places.

For the individualistic traveler, a guidebook can be the key ingredient in a delightful travel experience. The "On Your Own" guides were designed to increase your knowledge of the destination before you depart by offering detailed information about the country today, the faces and faiths of the people, their foods and mores. Because the "past is prologue" we offer a concise glimpse into the country's history.

Travel has become a vital part of peoples' lives, but for most of us, travel time is limited by work or family commitments. We must make each vacation-minute count.

We have kept this firmly in mind when preparing these guides. Each author visited scores of places that are not included in the guide. Rather than merely offering a list of hundreds of sights or an alphabetical dispassionate report about a site, we have focused on those with unique features. We have visited each site, hotel, restaurant, and shop personally. Our choices are subjective, but recognizing that a person should "travel to his own drummer," we offer many options. These allow you to plan a trip to fit your style, interests, pace, and pocketbook.

The heart of the "On Your Own" guides is the designation of "base cities"—each interesting in its own right, located in an area of major tourist interest, and offering the region's best accommodations, restaurants, and nightlife. From the base, we offer exciting excursions that allow you to explore the surrounding area at your leisure and return to a comfortable bed, hot bath, and delicious dinner each night. A time saver, base cities permit you to spend your precious time seeing and experiencing—rather than packing and unpacking.

The guides are designed to be carried with you each day as every base city and major excursion is explored in depth and detailed walking tours lead you through the most important sights.

Aren't there plenty of guidebooks available already? Yes there are, but those old familiar names are just that—old and familiar. Having carved out comfortable niches for themselves thirty or more years ago, they have merely added new destinations while maintaining a pre-set format.

How can identical guidebooks work for destinations as disparate as Paris and Bali? Just as destinations vary so does our coverage, in an effort to present the information in the way it will work best for you. Guides with the most detailed sightseeing have inevitably been written for the low-budget backpacker who has several months to roam the destination's backroads.

Why do most guides assume that more affluent travelers require only superficial information? Other guides have remained static while American travelers, more of whom traveled abroad last year than ever before, have become increasingly confident, adventuresome, eager to explore, and involved. Travel is a hands-on experience.

If travel is your passion and you are curious, open minded, and willing to strike out on your own, you are an "On Your Own" Traveler. Welcome aboard!

Harriet & Arnold Greenberg

Introduction

Brazil is larger than life—it is a country of superlatives. Nearly as large as the United States, it covers half the land mass of South America. It has large cities, large jungles, large rivers, and large waterfalls. Its monuments and celebrations are large as well. Subtlety is not common here. The only things small about Brazil are the micro-bikinis, called *tangas*, worn on the country's beaches by some of the world's most shapely women. Many things combine to make Brazil different and, since you are reading this, we assume that you want to experience something different. South America is consistently overlooked in American travel plans. The continent is untapped in many ways but its tourism potential is phenomenal. Brazil at some point will become its main attraction; for now it remains almost a new frontier for tourists.

The common images most Americans hold of Brazil come from three sources: Rio and its beaches, Carmen Miranda, and the jungle. Indeed, Rio is equivalent to Brazil in most people's minds.The country suffers from the "Tarzan syndrome." For decades, the only image the average American received of Africa was of Tarzan, Jane, Boy, and Cheetah. Since few Americans traveled to Africa that image perpetuated. For Brazil, Rio is its Tarzan.

That is not to say that the concept is wholly wrong. Rio does have fabulous beaches, some of the greatest in the world, Carmen Miranda was Brazilian, and there are vast jungles here. But Brazil is a vibrant country with many cosmopolitan cities, scores of picturesque towns, and a fascinating mix of three distinct cultures—European, African, and Indian. Within its boundaries lie some fabulous natural phenomena.

Because the country is so large, you are probably anticipating great variety in topography and you won't be disappointed. We have selected our base cities with an eye to the country's topography and you will be able to explore each distinct region from a comfortable base.

Here are just a few Brazil highlights:

Rio is of course the main event and well it should be, for this is a city that moves to its own beat—that of the samba. Physically stunning, set between the waters of Guanabara Bay and a string of purple-hued mountains, Rio combines a total resort atmosphere with all the amenities of a cosmopolitan city: deluxe hotels, delightful restaurants, and terrific shops. Languid by day, the city explodes at night, when scores of clubs, catering to all appetites, open late and stay open later. Carnaval, a five-day pre-Lenten celebration, reaches a frenzy here unequaled anywhere else in the world.

The denizens of São Paulo like to say that they work while Rio's cariocas play and that is true enough, for this metropolis of eleven million (and still growing) is Brazil's industrial heartland. Peopled by large numbers of Orientals, São Paulo's Japan Town is larger than many small cities.

Brasília, the country's capital, just twenty-six years ago a dream in a president's eye, is now a modern—nay futuristic—city carved out of a vast wilderness. Designed in the form of a jet airplane, with public buildings in the most avant-garde architectural style, the city is striking.

Salvador is where Brazil was born and this delightful city has remained faithful to its colonial heritage and has retained its religious fervor. The religion, a hybrid, combines a type of voodoo called Candomblé with a veneer of traditional Catholicism. A visit to a terreiro to see a Candomblé service is a must. Salvador is also where you'll savor the finest Brazilian food.

Recife, a picturesque city, is Brazil's Venice, for canals form the city's major thoroughfares. A delightful place to visit, Recife grew from a fishing village and has some of the country's most beautiful churches and museums. Nearby, the city of Olinda, with winding narrow streets, colonial houses, and quiet convents is also lovely to visit.

Nature has been kind to Brazil, for the country has been blessed with perfect weather year round and its long Atlantic Coast is studded with white sand beaches, stunning bays, and beautiful flora.

Iguaçú Falls, which sit on the border of Brazil and Argentina less than twenty miles from Paraguay, is a spectacular grouping of more than 275 thundering waterfalls. You can fly over them, take a boat ride nearby, or stand under one, the Garganta do Diabo. At night you can gamble at a Paraguayan or Argentinian casino.

Manaus is your door to the Amazon—both the river and the jungle. You'll want to explore the city and use it as your base for trips into the jungle with its unique animal life and the river which dominates it.

A visit to the Pantanal, the world's largest wildlife reserve, inhabited almost exclusively by birds, animals, and fish, will give you a close-up view of the harmony of nature.

And finally, the earthy gaucho is alive and well on the plains that surround the southern port, Porto Alegre, capital of the state of Rio Grande do Sol, while Curitiba, in the state of Paraná, is a European-style city with a touch of Brazilian seasoning.

Now, that is some vacation by any measure. Brazil is a new language and must be accepted that way. Its context is wholly different and the point of a trip here is its uniqueness.

Brazil — the Country Today

Brazil is a mixture of three cultures: European, African, and Indian. Its founders and colonizers were the Portuguese. Soon after Portuguese consolidation, slaves were brought over from Africa, mainly Northwest Africa and Nigeria. The indigenous people of Brazil are its Indians; the dominant cultures are European and African. The two have meshed in a unique way. Catholicism has joined in a subtle way with the African religion Orixia, called Macumba in Rio. Although Catholicism is the overlord, fidelity to Macumba is strong; the religion is practiced by over ten million Brazilians. Carnaval, Brazil's biggest event, is a cultural hybrid. Originally a Christian celebration, with roots going back to ancient Rome, Carnaval is mixed with Samba, the African-originated music and dance.

The handicrafts that come from Brazil are unique. Works all depict common cultural symbols; pieces will reflect an artist's affiliation with Catholicism, Macumba, or Indian myths. Some experts consider the handicrafts of the northern state of Pernambuco (its capital is the important port city of Recife) the finest in the world.

Brazil is based on the American model of democracy. In 1985, the military relinquished rule to the civilian sector; the president is José Sarnay. An unusual and sad event occurred at the return to civilian rule. President-elect Tancredo Neves fell ill and died before taking office. The country, which had rallied behind him and looked forward to his leadership, was shocked. His vice-president, Sarnay, has done a terrific job and Brazilians are once again proud of their government. One of Sarnay's initial moves was to stanch the two hundred percent inflation rate. He changed the currency and put a cap on prices and wages and, for the moment, has stemmed the continuous round of price increases.

There are twenty-three states in the country, and they too follow the American model. There are state capitals, with state assemblies, senators, and representatives. Brazil's model is American, but the actual substance of the country is greatly different. The gap between rich and poor is immense. Wealthy people pay less than one percent of their income and wealth to the state. There are a lot of poor people. *Favelas* (slums) are pervasive and unavoidable. There is a new welfare system and the state has set up free medical facilities for the poor. The awareness is here and change is on its way.

Brazil, a youthful country, is on the rise. Its economy is booming and it is moving away from a pure agricultural base. Hard industry is expanding and new businesses are opening. Brazil had the most rapidly growing economy of any country in the world in 1985. It is the world's fifth or sixth largest producer of cars, has fledgling industries in ships, trucks, computers, and electronics, and has the fifth largest weapons industry in the world.

Freedom of the press and speech is greater than in most South American countries, but not equal to America's. There is room for dissent, but because of the long years of military rule, people are less vocal. Caught between the first and third worlds, Brazil's political climate and economic structure are becoming more solidly western.

Brazil is not primarily a place for sightseeing; it is a place to experience. Seeing a church or visiting a museum is almost inconsequential here because it is out of context. Most museums are formulated on the European mold and don't reveal a great deal about Brazil's culture. What is important is to understand the Brazilian structure.

Visiting Europe for an American is like visiting your mother in another state; visiting Brazil is meeting a stranger. It is important to visit the churches in Salvador, the northeastern birthplace of Brazil, because churches here illuminate the city's culture and soul. A trip to the jungle and the jungle city of Manaus is like nothing ever experienced in the United States or Europe and can only be understood by being involved. The great waterfalls of Iguaçú Falls are completely foreign to us and can only be appreciated by seeing and hearing them. Brazil is a new language and must be accepted that way. Its context is wholly different, and the point of a trip here is its uniqueness. São Paulo is Brazil's most European city, yet it is very different from any European city we know. The sights of Brazil range from its intense and strange culture in Salvador to the uncharted jungles of the Amazon and Pantanal to the great waterfalls in Iguaçú to the modernity of its prefabricated capital, Brasília, to the wonders of Rio. The sounds of Brazil are loud, for lively music underscores everything. The wild and clear smells of Brazil remind you that you are in a virgin land.

The feel of Brazil is bronze. The climate ranges from tropical to warm; only in the south will there be any cold weather. Because it is a tropical coastal country, beaches are a major component of Brazilian culture.

Brazilians' devotion to *futebol* (soccer) is intense and loyal. There is no fighting in the stands, as there is in England, and futebol at the stadium—Rio has the largest stadium in the world—is like a half-day *Carnaval*.

Brazil, though not yet among the world's major industrial powers, is quickly closing the gap. Badly hurt by the oil crunch, its international debt soared and its economy suffered. The gap between rich and poor widened. However, there is a growing middle class of trained workers and management rising to fill that gap. There is a lot of crime, some people are hungry, and not everyone has a real home. *Favelas,* the poor shantytowns, are fantastic reminders of this condition.

The lure of Brazil is its size, its strangeness, and its jumble of influences. It is like a benevolent King Kong— massive, from the jungle and transported to the western world, confused, full of potential, foreign, and young.

The People

Brazil's indigenous people are its Indians, who numbered about one million at the time of the arrival of the first Portuguese. The second culture of people in Brazil were the Europeans; the Portuguese first in 1500, the French in Rio soon after, and the Dutch a bit later. The next contingent of people to arrive were Africans, brought here as slaves in the sixteenth and seventeenth centuries. In the early nineteenth century, a census calculated that there were about 920,000 whites, two million Africans, and one million Indians.

Modern immigration began after 1850, with an onslaught of Italians followed by more Portuguese, German, and Spanish people. Over the next decades Brazil welcomed many Japanese, Slavs, and Lebanese, and immigrants from many other countries as well. The southern part of the country is the most European, for many Germans and Italians went to the most southern states. By contrast, the northern states, the nation's birthplace, are very black and are dominated much more by African culture.

Today, whites dominate the economic structure of the society, but black culture is an extremely powerful force in the country's culture and mores. In fact, African culture has provided Brazil with its unique hue, and has given the country, in a lot of ways, its texture.

Art and Architecture

The art and architecture of Brazil resemble its cultural makeup—an odd mix of African and European ideas. Manaus, the jungle city, is probably the most condensed example of European imports. Its market was modeled after Les Halles in Paris, its opera house after the theater in Paris, its customs house has stones imported from Scotland, and its floating docks follow a concept imported from England.

Modern Brazilian architecture has come into its own, and its shining example is the prefabricated capital, Brasília. Laid out symmetrically, following the model of an airplane, the city is a modern wonder, with glass designs dominating the skyline. The House of Representatives of Brazil meets in a giant bowl and the Senate in a giant saucer. The foreign ministry meets in a building with artificial cascades pouring out of its columns. Its central church is shaped like a wine cup, with sixteen spires reaching toward the sky, its theater is shaped like an Aztec pyramid, and its crowning symbol is the soaring Television Tower. Brasília was a classroom for modern architecture, and its students got to experiment.

Most representative of common art are Brazil's handicrafts, which highlight the culture's fascination with religion and myths—Indian, Catholic, and African.

The fine arts of Brazil are mostly European-influenced; its writers and painters use the African and Indian strains of Brazil, but stick to western models.

The country's many phases can be traced through its architecture. Brazil's original architecture was, of course, influenced by the ideas coming from Europe, primarily from Portugal. The churches of Salvador reveal the different strains of the time. The churches combine baroque, classical, neoclassical, colonial, gothic, and other styles emanating from Europe. The church of São Francisco is all gold, and the other churches in the city used these styles to best fit their design. The old cities of Brazil are arrogant in their beauty, and stand as relics of the colonial period. The cities of Olinda and Ouro Preto are international monuments, given that title by UNESCO (many other towns and small cities in Brazil are either international or national landmarks). Olinda, specifically, highlights the subtle but radiant style used in the colonial period, and is unscathed in its antiquity. Brazil of the eighteenth century was soaked with classical European design. Rio's Municipal Theater is a direct copy of the Paris Opera House, and many of its structures were traced from the blueprints of the famous buildings of Europe.

Faiths of Brazil

The culture of Brazil is hybrid and atypical. A mixture of European, African, and Indian influences, the outcome is a jumble of institutions and rituals. Catholicism has fused with the African religion of Macumba, and the two provide a peculiar form of devotion. For most, the day-to-day religion is dictated from Rome; there are experiments, like Liberation Theology, the form of Catholicism that aligns itself with the suffering of the poor and was banned by the Pope. But outside the normal, Macumba is looked to for alternative solutions: mortal sickness, hope, rejuvenation. The New Year's festival of Macumba's water goddess Iemanjá is nationally practiced and followed. Catholicism and Macumba blend; they are not in competition. The people of Brazil are different hues, both white and brown. Intermarriage is accepted here, but is not that common. There is racism, but it is subtle here. Coming together is not superficially uncommon nor frowned upon. The people come together for Carnaval and for futebol.

The Taste of Brazil

The food of Brazil is imported, except for the original cuisine served at churrascarias and Bahian eateries. Churrascarias, which serve a hodgepodge of meats, developed from Brazil's abundance of *fincas* (farms) in the south. A typical dish in a churrascaria is an assortment of meats cooked in front of you: steak, veal, chicken, turkey, bacon, pork chops, sausages, etc. The rodizio style of churrascaria is basically a smorgasbord of meats that keep on coming until you can eat no more.

Bahian food is African-influenced, with touches of Indian and Portuguese ingredients. The food is rich, unpredictable, and hot. The common denominators of all dishes are the African ingredients of palm oil and pepper. From the Indians came the common use of manioc flour, with dishes like corn cereal and sweet potatoes. The Portuguese introduced meats and chicken, sweets, and the use of olive oil as opposed to palm oil.

Here are some sample recipes:

Vatapá is made of palm oil, coconut milk, peanuts, cashews, garlic, pepper, shrimp, and herring and has a soft bread center.

Caruru is a pasta dish made with okra, peanuts, cashews, dried shrimp, onion, salt, and palm oil.

Moqueca is a fish stew whose main ingredient is either oysters, crab, lobster, shrimp, or octopus. It also contains palm oil, coconut milk, tomato, onion, coriander, lime, and salt.

Sarapatel is made with pork giblets, mint, garlic, black pepper, bay leaf, salt, pork lard, blood, and peppers.

Xinxim de Galinha uses whole chickens, several pounds of dried shrimp, large onions, palm oil, salt, pepper, garlic, and lemon.

Palm Oil Farofa is a mixture of palm oil and manioc flour and also is made with onions and dried shrimp.

Acarajé is a bean dish with salt, onions, palm oil, peppers, and shrimp.

Brazil serves all kinds of international foods. The most popular dishes of Italy, China, and France are available in every city. In Rio and São Paulo all cuisines are available, from burgers to sushi to Wiener schnitzel.

Seafood is prevalent and very good, especially in the water-linked cities of Salvador, Recife, Manaus, and Iguaçú. Brasília is known mainly for its international dishes.

Brazilian beverages usually contain fruit juice, and there are many alcoholic drinks. The *batida* is small but potent, and is a mixture of fresh fruit, Brazilian rum (cachaça), sugar, and ice; originally the Indians made batida with manioc liquor. The drink is adaptable and subject to supply; it is widely experimented with and comes in many different forms. (One variation uses oryx milk.) It is also inexpensive.

Caipirinha is a blend of limes, sugar, and cachaça. Vodka (caipiroska) can be substituted for the cachaça. These drinks are most popular and are best for helping you relax. There are many good Brazilian beers. *Cerveja* is beer from a bottle and *chope* is beer from the tap.

Geography

Brazil, the largest country in South America, is the fifth largest in the world; it encompasses over 3,285,000 square miles. It covers half of the land mass of the continent and touches every country except Ecuador and Chile. It can be divided into five regions: the South, Southeast, Central-West, North, and Northeast. Each region comprises several states and has a distinct landscape, almost as if it were a separate country.

The South region is comprised of the states of Paraná, Santa Catarina, and Rio Grande do Sul. The biggest and most important cities in the region are Curitiba, the capital of Paraná, and Porto Alegre, the capital of Rio Grande do Sul. The most visited city is Foz do Iguaçú, the city of Iguaçú Falls in Paraná.

The topography is basically flat, with a lot of woods and fields. It is the coolest part of Brazil, with frost sometimes occurring.

Porto Alegre and Foz do Iguaçú are gateways to Brazil for people coming from the south. The two are also international cities because of their tourist attractions; Foz do Iguaçú for its falls, and Porto Alegre for its gauchos and folklore.

Curitiba and Porto Alegre are quite European in atmosphere and look; the people are very pale, and many are blond. The mid-nineteenth century saw great waves of European immigration, and these immigrants arrived with the intention of setting up European enclaves.

The state of Santa Catarina is also very European, dominated by German immigrants in the Itajai Valley and the city of Blumenau. The coast of Santa Catarina is beautiful, with some of Brazil's greatest undiscovered beaches.

Rio Grande do Sul is the Alamo state of Brazil. Proud and arrogant, it is the home of the gauchos, tough cattle farmers. Porto Alegre is the base for treks to the mountains nearby, where skiing and health clubs are the big attractions.

Paraná's biggest attraction is Iguaçú Falls. Located at the border of Brazil and Argentina and less than twenty miles from Paraguay, the city of Foz do Iguaçú is home to the world's largest dam, Itaipu Dam.

The Southeast region is Brazil's most productive area and the best known, for the cities of Rio de Janeiro and São Paulo are there. No other area can compare for importance, reputation, and wealth. A third city, Belo Horizonte, has grown tremendously over the last few years.

The region is made up of four states: São Paulo, Rio de Janeiro, Minas Gerais, and Espirito Santo.

São Paulo dominates the state of São Paulo, which is the most productive and wealthiest state in the nation. It is the industrial heartland, producing sixty percent of the country's total output.

The state of Rio de Janeiro is, of course, the home of *Cidade Maravilhosa,* Rio. The major tourist attraction in the country, Rio is famous for its beaches, its two mountains—Sugarloaf and Corcovado, its nightlife, its Carnaval celebration, and its beautiful women. Rio (the city) is on a coast known as Costa Verde (Green Coast), which is very beautiful and less developed than the coast north of it, which is called Costa do Sol (Sun Coast). The beach town, Búzios, on Costa do Sol is home to many of Rio's wealthiest citizens.

Minas Gerais is a foresty, hilly state and its capital, Belo Horizonte, is a rapidly growing city. There are gold mines and many health spas in the mountains of Minas Gerais.

The Central-West region is made up of the states of Goiás, Mato Grosso, and Mato Grosso do Sul. Brazil's most isolated region, the area is basically uncharted. Brasília, the country's capital, is in the state of Goiás; the Pantanal, a huge wilderness populated primarily by wildlife, is in Mato Grosso and Mato Grosso do Sul.

The Northeast region of Brazil is the location of the country's birthplace, Bahia. This region comprises nine states: Bahia, Pernambuco, Maranhão, Sergipe, Alagoas, Piauí, Ceará, Rio Grande do Norte, and Paraíba; the most important are Bahia and Pernambuco.

Bahia is the birthplace of the nation and one of the most culturally interesting areas, although it is one of Brazil's poorer states. With the working mixture of African, Indian, and European cultures, Bahia is very religious. African culture dominates, yet there are 365 Catholic churches there. Its beaches are stunning and the Bay of All Saints, off Salvador, the state's capital, is magnificent. Itaparica Island in the bay boasts a Club Med, the first in South America.

Recife, the capital of the state of Pernambuco, is the major gateway for travelers from Europe. Its wealth originated from sugar, but the city is now important for its port facilities. The third largest city in Brazil, Recife adjoins Olinda, which was declared an International Monument by UNESCO. The nation's finest handicrafts are produced in Pernambuco. The other states in the region are less important.

The North is Brazil's largest region and it is here that we find the Amazon jungle and river. This area is one-third the size of Europe and incorporates sixty percent of Brazil.

The jungle dominates. Probably one of the most important regions in the world, the rain forest and jungle provide one-fifth of its water reserves and replenishable oxygen. Containing ten of the world's twenty largest rivers, the Amazon is truly uninhabited.

The North has four states: Amazonas, Pará, Rondônia, and Acre. The region's two major cities are Manaus in

Amazonas, which is the gateway to the Amazon, and Belém, capital of Pará, at the river's mouth. Both have international airports; until recently Manaus' only other entry option was the river—now there is also a highway.

Manaus is the major tourist attraction. It stands on the banks of the Rio Negro River and is known for its classical European architecture, including an opera house where Caruso sang. The city is now a free zone for international goods.

Belém, on Guajara Bay, is a pretty city with colonial architecture and a small piece of Amazonian forest in its center.

A Capsule History

Brazil's history is in large part the history of Bahia and its city of Salvador, and Rio. It was founded in 1500 by the Portuguese explorer Pedro Álvares Cabral, who landed in Porto Seguro in the state of Bahia. Brazil's first three cities were São Vicente (1532), in the state of São Paulo, and Salvador (1549) and Olinda (1537), in the state of Pernambuco.

Brazil's first settlers were broken into two groups: the more wealthy Portuguese of Bahia and Pernambuco and the less wealthy settlers of São Vicente. The Portuguese settlers were initially interested in the export of Brazilwood (rosewood), but that economy was soon superseded by that of growing sugar and was dominated by the people in the northeast. With the rising importance of sugar, slaves began to be imported. During the second half of the sixteenth century and all of the seventeenth century, the provinces of Bahia, Pernambuco, and Paraíba were the world's largest suppliers of sugar. A wealthy elite arose from the sugar trade and in Olinda they were called the Sugar Lords.

To compensate for the northeast's coup of sugar money, the people of São Vicente began the quest for gold in Minas Gerais. Called *bandeiras,* the miners were finally successful toward the end of the sixteenth century. In 1572 a viceroy appointed from Portugal divided the country and set up two capitals: Salvador and Rio. The ruling class were the slave owners who ran the sugar industry. Brazil was dominated by the Portuguese except for the Dutch's successful invasion of Recife in 1630 and the French's initial rule over Rio.

The Dutch takeover of Recife hurt the sugar lords of Olinda. Using Recife's natural harbor, the Dutch were able to keep the elite of Olinda down and lessen the town's importance. The Dutch ruled Recife until 1654, and in that time Olinda became secondary to Recife. The departure of the Dutch sparked a war between the sugar lords of Olinda, who were trying to reclaim power, and the rising middle class of Recife, who were determined not to be quashed.

Rio had been claimed by French Huguenots in 1555, but in 1565 the Portuguese claimed it and ordered the Governor General of Brazil, Mem de Sá, to expel the French. He did so but they returned, and it wasn't till after a two-year battle that Rio became Portuguese in 1567.

The government that existed in Salvador was headed by Governor General Thomé de Souza. The branches controlled by the governor general were: ouvidor-mor (justice), capitão-mor (defense), provedor-mor (treasury), and alcaide-mor (military).

The seventeenth century saw great changes in the fledgling colony. Pulled in too many directions, the sugar lords of the northeast and the gold miners of São Paulo moved to consolidation. Brazil's dominance in the sugar field receded as islands in the Caribbean began to export. The gold market then rose to the surface. The original gold expeditions in Minas Gerais by the Paulistas now proved even more important. The gold rush sparked the rise of Ouro Preto, which is now an international monument. It also helped Rio.

Rio was the nearest coastal town from which the gold could be shipped and its rise was in direct relation to the discovery of gold. In 1763 the capital was moved to Rio from Salvador, and this cemented the city's wealth and importance. In 1825, though, a new source of income arose: coffee. Coffee was the catalyst of São Paulo's rise. Attracting great numbers of immigrants, primarily Italians, São Paulo became the country's leading producer of coffee and today it still produces one third of Brazil's coffee.

The country was expanding as more Europeans arrived. In 1789, an unsuccessful revolt against Portuguese rule was led by Tiradentes (Joaquim José da Silva Xavier) in Minas Gerais. The turning point in Brazil's political history was the rise of Napoleon.

In 1808, Napoleon forced the Portuguese king, Dom João VI, and 15,000 nobles to leave Portugal. For thirteen years, the king ruled from Brazil. During that time, he created a supreme military court, law courts, a naval academy, a medical school, and the Bank of Brazil.

Brazil became more European in nature. Its wealth increased, fostered by several successful treaties with Great Britain. Soon it became an equal partner in the United Kingdom of Portugal, Brazil, and Algarve.

Dom João VI returned to Portugal in 1821 and left his son Pedro in charge. Although opposed by the Portuguese parliament (the Cortes), Pedro stayed in power at the behest of the Brazilian people and in 1822 he became the Emperor of Brazil, Dom Pedro I.

On September 7, 1822, Dom Pedro proclaimed Brazil's independence. This was an unfortunate and unfavorable proclamation, for he faced a secession in the north, lost Uruguay, and had public marital problems. Dom Pedro I was forced to abdicate in favor of his five-year-old son, Pedro II. Dom Pedro II's reign was much more successful. He promoted education, increased the country's communication capabilities, and advocated immigration. It was during his rule that many European immigrants arrived— Italians, Germans, Slavs, etc.,—moving to the south of the country and into Rio and São Paulo. The turn of the century saw another great wave of immigrants, this time including Japanese. São Paulo now has a huge Japanese population. The last large wave of immigration was before World War II, when many Jews arrived, followed by Germans.

Dom Pedro II's rule ended with his daughter Isabel's declaration of emancipation for the slaves. Although this had been discussed many times during his reign, the fatal flaw of her declaration was that it provided no compensation for slave owners. Almost spontaneously the country revolted. People demanded full independence and on November 15, 1889, Brazil became a republic.

The turn of the century witnessed Brazil's last boom: the rubber boom in Manaus. With the discovery of rubber in the jungle, Manaus swelled in size and wealth, becoming an international city almost overnight. Importing stones and architecture from Europe, the city became a mini-Paris and was the symbol of overheated western capitalism. Its heyday was classical and opulent; but soon the Manaus rubber market was replaced by Asian markets, and the boom vanished.

In 1930 the Governor of Rio Grande do Sul, Getulio Vargas (Father of the Poor) led a revolt for advanced social institutions and ousted President Washington Luis. Vargas assumed the presidency and dictatorship. In 1945 he was forced to resign and the republic was restored. In 1960, President Juscelino Kubitschek's dream of a capital city in the interior was realized when Brasília, a city carved out of the wilderness, was proclaimed the new capital of Brazil, replacing Rio.

At that point the political climate of Brazil took a downturn. Unstable and corrupt, the government was overthrown by a military coup in 1964. The military ruled Brazil with varying results until 1985, when the first civilian president in over twenty years, Tancredo Neves, was elected. Neves took ill, was sworn in while hospitalized, and died soon thereafter. His vice-president, José Sarnay became leader of a democratic Brazil. President Sarnay, a recent visitor to the U.S., has proven to be an able leader and Brazil once again is moving forward.

Brazil's Hotels

Brazil offers visitors a whole range of accommodations. There are fabulous deluxe resort hotels as well as chic big-city establishments. Hotels come in all sizes and there is one, probably a lot more than one, to suit every pocketbook.

The government rates all hotels with a star system. Deluxe stops are five-star hotels; those with the fewest amenities rate just one. Our selections will advise you of the hotels' ratings.

In Brazil's large cities you will find five-star hotels that offer all the comforts of deluxe establishments in New York; an added plus here is an outdoor pool which can be used year round. Most hotels of this class are on or quite near the beaches. Rio's beach strip, from Copacabana to Barra, has some of the world's finest hotels.

Most international hotel chains are represented here— Meridien, Hilton, Sheraton, Inter-Continental, Tropical, and Novotel; fine Brazilian chains include Othon, Nacional, and Luxor.

Deluxe hotels offer private baths and the rate includes a hearty breakfast of fruit, eggs, cheese, rolls, pastry, and coffee or tea. Many hotels now have health clubs, and special services are provided for business travelers, including use of the hotel's computers. Many pick up U.S. TV and it is common to pick up CNN or the Armed Forces Network twenty-four hours a day. I've watched the Super Bowl while sipping a carpirinha on my terrace.

Hotels in Rio and São Paulo are more expensive than those in other parts of the country. To give you a ballpark figure to work with, we have noted a price estimate after each hotel write-up. Keep in mind that prices do rise for Carnaval and during peak holiday times like Christmas.

Our scale, based on double room prices, is as follows:

> Expensive—in Rio and São Paulo $100+
> a night
> elsewhere $80–$100 per night
>
> Moderate—$60–$80 per night
>
> Inexpensive—under $60

The Restaurants of Brazil

Restaurants in Brazil range from those serving gourmet foods to fast-food eateries found on or near the beaches. Brazil's sophistication is mirrored in the vast numbers of restaurants in the cities and in the enormous varieties of foods served. Each immigrant group contributed its native cuisine and today restaurants serving Italian, Japanese, French, Spanish, and Mexican foods are commonplace here. First-class restaurants in Brazil are excellent; some of the hotel restaurants in Rio and São Paulo are on the same level as fine restaurants of New York and Paris. The finest restaurants usually serve French or Continental cuisine.

Brazil's indigenous cuisine is the churrascaria—a variety of meats—and Bahian food, African-influenced and dominated by seafood. The most common restaurants could only be defined as international and serve a mixture of dishes; nothing will be unfamiliar. The average cost of a meal at a top restaurant in Brazil will average between $10 and $15 depending on the city, Rio and São Paulo being at the upper end, Manaus and Iguaçú at the lower.

Brazil is cattle country and its beef is excellent, second only in the world to Argentina. Even inexpensive restaurants serve good food just because of that; the meat is always delicious.

Brazilians, especially Cariocas (the Indian and common word for Rio's residents) and Paulistas (the common name for residents of São Paulo), eat late, after 9 P.M. If you must eat before that time, expect to be alone.

Only in French or Continental restaurants are reservations a must—except at Carnaval, when you should reserve anywhere, if you eat at all. If you feel more comfortable reserving, by all means do so. We have included phone numbers for all restaurants in this guide.

The unique foods of Brazil are its meats as served in churrascarias and Bahian food. As previously mentioned, Bahian cuisine is an amalgam of African and Indian influences mixing with the Portuguese. Hot palm oil, manioc flour, and pepper are standard. The most social of Brazilian drinks is *cafezinho,* which is a small cup of thick black coffee served with lots of sugar. It will suddenly and endlessly appear at any business or social gathering. Drinks like *guarana,* a sweet, fruit-based carbonated soda, *batida,* a sugarcane-based, powerful alcoholic drink, and *caipirinha,* a cachaça cocktail, are very common and popular. The two best-selling Brazilian beers are Brahma and Skol.

Brazilian wine is tasty and inexpensive, but does not compare to Chilean or Argentinian wines. The white wine is better than the red, which is the converse of those from Chile and Argentina. Imported whiskey is very expensive; domestic versions of internationally known whiskeys are much cheaper and not much different in taste. By U.S. standards, restaurants in Brazil are less expensive and also more flexible. It is not uncommon or unexpected for one to ask for a change of dish, a change in ingredients, or for a dish to be prepared that is not on the menu. The dress code is casual even in posh places. A tie is a rarity. There is a cover (*couvert*) charge (usually very small) for a celery, olive, and carrot plate along with bread and butter, which you can decline if you wish. You can also ask to share a dish with your dining companion if you're not that hungry. Just ask the waiter for an extra plate. No problem. Shrimp is the most expensive dish you'll find in almost any restaurant. It can be as much as fifty percent more expensive than meat dishes.

Shopping in Brazil

Shopping can and should be a highlight of your trip—and your return. Shopping exists on many levels but without doubt your best buys are in gemstones and folk art.

Gemstones

Brazil has practically every type of gem and precious metal. The most popular gemstone is the aquamarine, one of the loveliest members of the beryl mineral family, to which the emerald also belongs. The finest aquamarines in the world are mined in the states of Minas Gerais, Espirito Santo, and Bahia. Emeralds, the famous "green stones," are found in several regions, particularly in the states of Goiás and Bahia. Tourmaline, another well-known stone, is mined in Brazil in several colors, especially green but also red and pink. A unique topaz, which is highly prized and rare, is called Imperial Topaz or Ouro Preto Topaz, and is found only in Brazil. Although the country's diamond production presently accounts for three to five percent of the world production (Brazil used to be the world's major producer before the beginning of diamond exploitation in Africa), the superior beauty and hardness of Brazilian diamonds places them among the world's most desired gems. More recently, Brazil has begun the mining and processing of minerals belonging to the corundum family (rubies and sapphires), found respectively in the states of Bahia and Mato Grosso.

Folk Art

Brazil's folk arts and crafts are a natural consequence of the country's immense size and varied cultures. The diversity of Brazilian popular art, based on traditional techniques, reflects the country's different influences—Indian, African, European. Among the crafts are ceramics from Bahia (which resemble pre-Columbian artifacts), laces from the north and from Santa Catarina, and the embroidery work of the women from the northeast. These handmade crafts demonstrate the art and beauty that simple techniques can produce.

Beyond folk art and gemstones, you will want to shop for bikinis, tangas, leather goods, and maybe even some Macumba items. You can shop for handicrafts at city markets and hippie fairs all over Brazil, and many shops stock handicrafts as well.

The handicrafts and folk art of Recife, Manaus, and Belém are the finest in the country and worth seeking out. The art and Macumba and religious items are best in Salvador.

When shopping for fine leathers or gemstones it's best to shop in Rio or São Paulo. Many well-known jewelers have shops throughout the country. The best known is H. Stern, an international jeweler with shops all over the world.

There is a free zone for international goods in Manaus, but you might not get a fantastic buy because high-tech goods are cheapest in America. The cheapest places to buy native goods are the many fairs each city has, and at the hippie fair in Manaus on Sunday.

The other side of Brazilian shopping is its international western contingent. All big cities have fantastic shopping centers, similar to the U.S.

Getting There

The only practical way to get to Brazil, whether from North America, Europe, or Asia, is to fly. Cruise ships do ply Brazil's Atlantic ports but the time involved does not make this a viable alternative. Of course, if you do have the time it is a relaxing way to travel; several cruise companies operate from Miami.

Many airlines fly to Brazil. The two major carriers from the United States are Varig, the Brazilian airline, and Pan

American. Major U.S. gateways to Brazil are New York and Miami, but there are flights from Los Angeles and San Francisco too. Over thirty cities hook up with the flight network into Brazil. Varig has a wonderful reputation and it is well deserved. It has the most up-to-date equipment, planes are spic and span, the food is first-rate, and the staff is polite and considerate. Children are promptly served to avoid overtiredness. Whatever section of the plane you are in, whether it be first class or economy, every effort is made to make your trip an enjoyable one. I can still recall a stewardess bringing me a fresh cup of cafezinho—without my asking. She sensed, when I left the first untouched, that I did not like it with sugar. A touch of class! Varig has daily flights from New York, Miami, and Los Angeles to Rio and on to São Paulo. Direct flights, less frequent however, do exist from Miami to Manaus, Belém, Recife, and Salvador.

Pan Am is the major U.S. carrier with service to Brazil. A dependable airline, Pan Am's service in Latin America is top-notch. Here too, expect on-time landings and good food. Pan Am flies to Rio and São Paulo.

Flight time from New York to Rio is about eight and a half hours, an hour less from Miami. West Coast flights make the trip in thirteen hours.

Many European flights set down in Recife. Varig flies from Brazil to Europe and several European carriers make the run as well.

Getting Around in Brazil

Domestic Airlines

Brazil's domestic carriers offer a great deal which will help you see this vast country. It's called the Air Pass. Flying from one point to another is virtually a given if you intend to see several parts of Brazil. The country's size is comparable to that of the U.S., and you wouldn't dream of touring the U.S. by car on a two- or three-week holiday. Brazil's size and varied terrain makes flying a must, particularly if you visit the Amazon.

The Air Pass, offered by all of Brazil's carriers—Varig/Cruzeiro, Transbrasil, and Vasp—is basically a reusable one-priced ticket good for travel throughout Brazil. Comparable to Europe's Eurail Pass, the Air Pass must be bought outside Brazil and comes in two different forms: at this writing, twenty-one days of travel and fourteen days. No segment can be flown twice. The benefit of the pass is that it allows cheaper and more efficient travel throughout the country; the pass would be unnecessary if you were just visiting Rio and Salvador. (See Varig route map on page 385.)

An MCO (miscellaneous charge order) is issued in the U.S. which upon entry is transformed into tickets for the routes desired. Refunds are available if for some reason you don't use your pass.

Touring by Bus

Touring Brazil by bus is possible through Soletur bus company. Several package tours are offered, and their tours are intensive. The company is based in Rio and offers multilingual tours in air-conditioned buses. Tours can cover up to 115 towns and last up to thirty days. Soletur is located at Rua Visconde de Pirajá 550 (Suite 1708) 22410, Rio de Janeiro, RJ Brazil (phone 213-0237).

Car Rental

The infrastructure of Brazil is good and more and more paved highways are being completed; a highway connecting Recife and Manaus was just opened. The roads along the coast and through the southern region are excellent. Car rental prices are equivalent to those in the U.S. Hertz, Avis, and National are ubiquitous at airports and throughout Brazil. All you need is a valid driver's license and a major credit card; you must be 23 years of age.

Getting Ready

Documents Required

A valid passport and a visa are required for U.S. citizens (no visa is necessary for British or Canadian citizens). Tourists' visas are usually processed within one day and can be obtained through a Brazilian Embassy or Consulate. A passport-size photo, a signed and completed application form, and a round-trip ticket are necessary to receive the visa, which is good for ninety days and allows multiple entries within that period.

Vaccinations

No inoculations are necessary for travel to Brazil; however, malaria is present in the Pantanal and pills for the disease should be taken and carried. Be cautious when out of large cities—avoid drinking tap water and do not eat uncooked vegetables or unpeeled fruit.

Money Matters

Currency

Inflation has for decades been a fact of life for Brazilians and visitors. Because Brazil is caught between the third world and the world's industrial powers, an annual inflation rate of two to three hundred percent was the rule, rather than the exception. When I first visited Brazil in 1965, the local currency, the cruzeiro, was valued at six to each U.S. dollar. With the passage of time, the cruzeiro weakened and almost daily the number of cruzeiros a dollar could buy would increase. With each visit, my dollar purchased more and more cruzeiros. You had to read the daily newspaper to know what your money was worth. By February of 1986 you could purchase more than 17,000 cruzeiros for a dollar. At the same time there were two separate markets for currency exchange—the official and the parallel market, with a variance of as much as fifty to sixty percent. The parallel is not quite a black market, since it is quoted in the papers and prices at shops are based on the parallel market price. With soaring inflation and a steadily weakening cruzeiro, rents, wages, bank accounts, and loans are indexed so that if in one particular year there was a one hundred percent inflation rate, your salary and rent would increase by a like amount.

With the election of Tancredo Neves in 1986 and the assumption to the presidency by his vice president, José Sarnay, a bold new economic plan was initiated. The cruzeiro was replaced by the cruzado, one cruzado being worth one thousand old cruzeiros. Prices, wages, rents, etc., were to some extent frozen and as of this writing, inflation has been lowered to a respectable level. Old cruzeiro notes are being stamped by the central bank with new cruzado prices so that a 100,000-cruzeiro bill has a 100-cruzado stamp. Not all bills have been stamped, so be careful. Eventually, new bills will be printed and hopefully by our next edition this paragraph will not be necessary.

In March of 1986, when the new cruzado was inaugurated, it was valued at about seventeen per U.S. dollar on the parallel market, and by the end of the year, it had risen to over twenty-two. The official rate was twelve.

What will the future hold? *Quem sabe?* (Who knows?) Economists, even Brazilian economists, must wait until the following year to evaluate the year before. Our advice? Check your newspaper or bank prior to departure for the latest information. Remember, where and how you exchange your dollars or pounds for cruzados can determine to a great extent the cost of your Brazilian adventure.

Don't exchange your money at a bank or hotel, for you will receive the official rate. Instead make every effort to get the parallel rate or as close as possible to it. It is not difficult to obtain as long as you are aware of the situation. Obviously your best bet is restaurants and shops where you make purchases. Your concierge will be able to offer assistance. All credit cards are acceptable in Brazil, but since you will be charged at the official rate, it is desirable and intelligent to pay for everything in cruzados. Contrary to Madison Avenue hype, in Brazil it's better to leave your credit cards at home.

Tipping

Tips are usually included in the price of your restaurant bill, but if not, fifteen percent is commonly acceptable. The last item on your bill reveals whether the tip has been included or not. Tipping the bell captain, bellboys, chamber maids, and other hotel employees is usual. Cab drivers expect a ten percent tip, and so do barbers, hairstylists, and messengers.

Customs

Going through Brazilian customs is to play red light—green light. After you retrieve your bags you must push a button as you enter the Customs area. If the light flashes green, as it does eighty percent of the time, you go right through. A red light means your bags will be checked. This is a random thing.

Brazil permits clothing and personal belongings, including one radio, one tape deck, one camera, one Walkman, and one typewriter, without any problem. More than that number or goods not personal valued over $300 will require additional inspection. The government is concerned about electronic equipment brought into the country; they do not want you to sell it here.

An unusual feature in Brazil is the duty-free shop in the arrivals area. Here you can buy whiskey, perfume, cigarettes, and cameras at duty-free prices, so there is no reason to buy them at your embarkation point.

Traveling within Brazil

As previously mentioned, the Air Pass is probably the most efficient way of traveling throughout the country.

From the airport to your hotel, the most efficient means of transportation are taxis. Buses are available, but don't have a lot of room for luggage. The safest taxis are government taxis, for which there is a fixed price.

Moving around within cities, especially Rio and São Paulo, is best done by taxis also. Parking is a problem and the traffic is insane, so it is not worth driving yourself. Bus systems are efficient and clean, but slower. São Paulo and Rio have subways.

Renting a car is not worthwhile for either traveling through the country or for driving around in the city. Prices are comparable to those in the U.S., but, as mentioned, traffic is heavy in the cities and distances are long in the country. You might consider renting a car for day trips outside your base. Fuel is expensive and some cars now run on alcohol (called álcool in Brazil). The country's highways are very good and widespread.

Business Travelers

Business travelers will usually go to São Paulo, the country's business area, but many will visit Rio, Recife, and Brasília too.

Business travelers must have a signed letter from their company, on their letterhead, stating the purpose of the trip, and assuming full responsibility for their employee's conduct.

Staying in the downtown section of a city (for Rio, Copacabana is probably the choice) is efficient because of proximity to the commercial areas and because the better hotels will be in that area.

A majority of the top hotels offer business facilities that include secretaries, interpreters, computers, telexes, direct dial phones, and meeting space. São Paulo, Salvador, and Recife have first-class convention centers. Many of these hotels have health clubs and most large Brazilian cities have business-oriented hotels.

The holidays to avoid are Carnaval, which is right before Lent; Tiradentes Day on April 21; Labor Day on May 1; Independence Day on September 7; All Soul's Day on November 2; Proclamation Day on November 15; Christmas; and New Year's Day. Also avoid Good Friday (two days before Easter).

The general etiquette in Brazil is indirectness and diplomacy; Brazilians don't like conflict. There is also a tradition of gift-giving and voiced appreciation. Business hours start at 8:30 A.M. and may last until 6 P.M., with a lunch break of one and a half hours. Banks are open from 9 A.M. to 4:30 P.M., but are closed on Saturdays or Sundays.

An excellent book about business protocol world-wide is *Global Edge* by Sondra Snowden (Simon and Schuster, 1986).

Traveler's Potpourri

Churches

Brazil has members of all major religions and unless you are a member of an esoteric sect, there should be no problem finding a place to pray. Rio and São Paulo have large Jewish communities with synagogues.

Climate

Most of Brazil lies between the Equator and the Tropic of Capricorn; hence the country is generally hot. The weather is basically static, with warm to hot temperatures—65 to 85 degrees—in most places (Manaus is the hottest) and nice sea breezes along the coast. The only place it gets cold is the far south, in the mountains around Porto Alegre.

Clothing

Summer weather is common year round and you should plan your clothing accordingly. Formal attire is rare here, so unless you will be attending a specific function, leave furs and gowns at home. Ties are rarely worn, but jackets are common in the better restaurants. Cotton dresses in pastel shades are usual here, as are men's lightweight suits. If you are headed south, bring a warm sweater and a raincoat.

Cosmetics

U.S. cosmetics are readily available. You can buy shaving cream, toothpaste, and more personal items day or night. Don't become a walking drugstore.

Electric Current

Rio and São Paulo work on 110 or 120 volts. Salvador works on 127 volts. Recife, Brasília, and a number of other cities work on 220 volts. Bring a convertor and adapter plugs.

Embassies

There is an American Embassy in Brasília, the capital, and consulates in all the major cities. Canadian and U.K. consulates are also in those areas.

Holidays

The major public festivals are Carnaval, New Year's Day, Christmas, Independence Day, and Proclamation Day. There are also religious holidays, for Brazil is the largest Catholic country in the world. Macumba festivals are also celebrated.

Language

The primary language of Brazil is Portuguese with English (not Spanish) in second place. I have conversed here for over twenty years, using an impromptu language affectionately called Porunhol. This is the language used by people who know more Spanish (español) than Portuguese and use a Spanish word in place of an unknown Portuguese word. If you speak Spanish, don't be bashful; say it the best you can, throw in a Portuguese word here and there, and you will be understood with a smile. Brazilians are lovely people.

Mail

The mail system in Brazil does not have a good reputation, but it works—slowly. There are convenient post offices in every city.

Pharmacies

Drugstores are open Monday through Saturday from 8 A.M. to 8 P.M. In each district there is a 24-hour pharmacy, signaled by a sign reading *Turno* on the door.

Phones

There are public phones throughout Brazil. A *ficha* (token) must be used to get a connection. (Fichas can be bought in banks, hotels, and stores.) Phone booths are identified by big yellow ears. There is direct-dial service to the U.S. from many deluxe hotels.

Reading Material

The Brazilian English-language newspaper, the *Daily Post*, is printed every day except Monday. There are Latin American editions of *Time* and *Newsweek*. The *New York*

Times, Miami Herald, and *Wall Street Journal* are available in Rio and São Paulo a day or two late. They are very expensive.

Time

Brazil is two hours later than Eastern Standard Time. When it is 10 A.M. in New York, it is noon in Rio. When New York switches to Daylight Saving Time, the difference reverts to one hour. Manaus, far west of Rio, is on Eastern Standard time (one hour earlier than Rio).

Toilets

Public bathrooms are usually found in hotels or restaurants.

Important Caveats

Brazil is a poor country (the average wage is less than $70 per month) and there is a crime problem. Don't carry anything valuable to the beach. Pickpocketing is common, especially during Carnaval. Use the same common sense you would when traveling in poor areas anywhere. Leave all your valuables, including your passport, in a safety-deposit box at your hotel.

When swimming, pay attention to the lifeguards and to the colored flags. A red flag means that the current is strong, so don't swim. In the afternoon, currents are often strong, and there is a strong undertow as well. Swim near the beach and don't panic if you are caught in the undercurrent. Just wave your arm to get the lifeguards' attention. Needless to say, swimming in an area where there are no lifeguards is a big mistake.

Rio de Janeiro

The Main Event

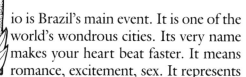io is Brazil's main event. It is one of the world's wondrous cities. Its very name makes your heart beat faster. It means romance, excitement, sex. It represents and fulfills every person's fantasy. Brazil's international magnet, it attracts the citizens of its own country and lures visitors from the four corners of the world. None are disappointed, for Rio's nickname, *cidade maravilhosa* (marvelous city) is right on the mark.

Physically stunning, the city is unique, for within its borders lie eight sugar-sand beaches and the sparkling waters of the Atlantic and Guanabara Bay. Two landmark mountains dominate Rio's skyline. Thimble-shaped Sugarloaf guards the bay while Corcovado, inland, is home to the city's most photographed sight, Christ the Redeemer. Between the ocean and the mountains lies a shimmering lagoon.

Rio's neighborhoods, linked by a series of tunnels, vary. The older downtown area, which retains a colonial flavor, is the commercial center—bustling, noisy, and fast-moving. The newer areas, built around the beaches, are residential and offer deluxe hotels, fabulous restaurants, and an intriguing nightlife. Scattered throughout the city are delightful shops where you can buy sparkling gemstones, soft leathers, and unusual handicrafts.

Probably Rio's most powerful image is that of Carnaval—a rousing pre-Lenten celebration that is more exciting here than anywhere else in the world. The streets are crowded and insane, the beat of the samba is everywhere, and the city is the site of fancy costume balls and frenetic beach parties. The city molds into one swaying unit and

35

dances for four days. Carnaval allows amnesia; it takes the poor of Rio away from their poverty and puts them in the limelight. It also allows rich and poor to mesh without bitterness.

The samba music and dance that underline Carnaval is taken very seriously. The Sunday-night parade of samba schools is a competition that is planned for and practiced for through the year. The designs are elaborate, the choreography precise, and the music original. If you aren't here for Carnaval, make sure to see a samba school rehearsal.

Samba reflects Rio's African heritage and influence. Basically a western city, Rio, and the country for that matter, is heavily affected by the culture that former slaves brought over. The odd mixture that the African Macumba and Catholicism have produced give Rio another unique hue.

Rio's famous beaches and its stunning women have been immortalized in song. Copacabana in its twilight still shines and the string includes Ipanema, Leblon, and the ever developing Gavea and Barra. That strip of the Atlantic has produced some of the finest and most sought-after beaches in the world.

History

Rio (the name comes from a mistaken identity; the original founders believed Guanabara Bay, Rio's entry port, was the mouth of a river) would have been much different if the original settlers had been able to keep it. Rio, it is suspected, was first seen by André Gonçalves and Amerigo Vespucci in 1502 as they inspected, for the king of Portugal, Pedro Alvares Cabral's finding of Brazil in the northern state of Bahia. What is for sure is that Rio's first residents were French Huguenots in 1555.

Under the command of Admiral Villegagnon, some 1,000 French settled in Rio and built a fort in 1557. When the Portuguese found out, the governor general of Brazil,

Mem de Sá, went to expel them and in two days, starting February 21, 1560, his fleet had expelled the French. Yet he left with no garrison and the French soon came back.

It wasn't until 1565 that the Portuguese returned to fight the French once again. Estácio de Sá, the governor general's nephew, now led the fleet. A two-year battle ensued and was won only after Mem de Sá sent reinforcements. Shot by an Indian on January 18, 1567, Estácio de Sá is credited with founding Rio.

The Portuguese began to build up Rio at Morro do Castelo (Castle Hill), an area adjacent to Guanabara Bay.

During the remaining part of the sixteenth century and most of the seventeenth century, Rio was left unattended to. The most important structures were the churches and there were three roads in 1648, the primary one being Rua da Misericordia.

The catalyst for Rio's growth was the discovery of gold in the state of Minas Gerais, just west, in the 1690s. As the closest port, Rio became the center for the expeditions. Rio's importance grew tremendously as gold continued to be found.

The news spread and the French, once again, attacked the city in 1710, this time led by Du Clerc. Repelled, the French attacked again in 1711 with an even larger force and were able to sack the city and extract a ransom.

With the city's growth, the infrastructure was enlarged. In 1724 the Aqueduto da Carioca (Carioca Aqueduct) was begun. It was built to transfer water from Santa Teresa forest to the public fountain. (Today the aqueduct is used for bondinhos (streetcars) traveling from Santo Antônio to Santa Teresa.)

Rio's future was cemented in 1763, when it became the capital of Brazil, taking that title away from Salvador, the city in Bahia. Largo da Carioca was built and the city's streets were expanded to reach Botafogo and Tijuca, south of Rio's birthpoint.

In the early part of the nineteenth century, Europe was being ravaged by Napoleon, and his might forced Dom

João VI to flee Portugal for Brazil. His presence in Rio immediately changed its texture and secured Rio's importance. He instituted the Supreme Military Court, law courts, a naval academy, a school of medicine, and the Bank of Brazil.

Giving the city a western hue, Dom João made Rio the economic, political, and cultural center of Brazil. In 1821 Dom João returned to Portugal and left his son Pedro in charge. On September 7, 1822, Pedro declared the country independent and became Dom Pedro II. In 1826 he was pressured to step down and he eventually relinquished his throne to his five-year-old son, Dom Pedro II.

In 1854 Rio was lit by gas; in 1858 its first railway was built; the first tramway was completed in 1868. The later part of the nineteenth century saw many changes in the country and the city. On May 3, 1888, Dom Pedro II's daughter declared slaves independent and this led to Brazil's becoming a republic on November 15, 1889. Dom Pedro II was exiled and Deodoro da Fonseca became interim leader.

Rio's geographical growth was directly linked to the building of the tunnel to Copacabana in 1892 and the tunnel to Leme in 1904. The city began to take its present shape when Avenida Rio Branco was completed in 1904. Home to Rio's elegant Municipal Theater, which was modeled on the Opera House in Paris, Avenida Rio Branco became the city's major thoroughfare.

During the 1940s two important landfills were begun. The first was the little peninsula where Santos Dumont airport was completed in 1944, and the second was the creation of Flamengo Park out of twelve million square feet of land reclaimed from the sea, finished in 1960. Rio's third important reclamation project was the widening of Copacabana beach in 1970.

Brazil's history is saved in certain parts of the city. Many of its historical buildings are centered around Praça 15 de Novembro, the square on the docks. Three important buildings from Rio's earlier age still stand: Igreja Matriz de São José (St. Joseph's Church), Palácio Tiradentes

(House of Representatives), and Nossa Senhora do Bonsucesso Church.

In downtown Rio there are several ancient buildings, most of them from the sixteenth and seventeenth centuries. They are: Santa Lúzia's Church, Ordem Terceira de São Francisco da Penitência Church, Convento do Carmo, and Arco do Teles.

Nossa Senhora do Carmo da Antiga Sé was built in 1752 and later became Rio's cathedral. The cathedral too is downtown.

While Rio is not nearly as large nor as wealthy as São Paulo and it has been replaced as the country's capital by Brasília, it remains in reality Brazil's first city both to Brazilians and to people in far corners of the world.

It is the capital of the state of Rio de Janeiro and its citizens, called cariocas, are the friendliest people in the world.

The large European immigration at the turn of the century and again during World War II has dominated Rio's culture but has not sequestered the singular culture of the Africans. Macumba, the African religion, is practiced by some ten million Brazilians, and its rituals are a large component of Rio's life.

African culture has also given the city and the country samba, an integral part of Brazilian society.

Futebol dominates Rio, and its loyal spectators fuel the city with a spirit close to Carnaval.

Rio has given the world the bikini and nobody belittles that gift. Highlighted on the beaches, the bikini, mixed with the drink caipirinha, made out of lemon and cachaça, and the bronze people of Rio make the city the darling of the country.

Arrival

Galeão, the international airport serving Rio, is modern and the largest in the country. If you have flown here from the United States your flight will have taken about nine and a half hours and chances are that you will arrive just as the sun rises. The landing pattern takes you over the bay, which is stunning; you're sure to spot Sugarloaf. Have your passport and visa handy.

You'll see the baggage claim area right ahead; twenty percent of incoming passengers will have their bags examined. This is done randomly and works on the red light—green light system. As you move through the customs area, you must push a button. If the green light appears you go right through, but if a red light shines your bags will be checked. There are no additional forms to fill out. Apart from personal items, you must declare goods totaling over $300 and any pets, foods, plants, or chemicals.

An unusual feature is the duty-free shop in the baggage area. You can purchase up to $300 of liquor, cigarettes, and perfumes here; officially, it is before your entry into the country. No need to buy these items at your embarkation point.

The government tourist office, Flumitur, will help with hotel arrangements and provide information. There is a place to change money and a restaurant at the airport.

Two taxi companies run from the airport: Transcoopass, red cars, and Cootrama, blue cars. The fare is prepaid, and the taxi, which is air-conditioned, will take you right to your hotel. The ride will take about thirty minutes. Alvorada buses make the run to the beach areas in one and a half hours.

Orientation

Downtown (Centro) Rio's central avenue is *Avenida Rio Branco,* one of Rio's older streets. Downtown, as in any big city, is made up of tall office buildings, traffic, and a massive number of people. There are special crossing lanes.

Av. Rio Branco runs north and south through the entire downtown, from Praça Mauá to Av. Beira Mar, near Guanabara Bay and its beaches. On the avenue are some famous landmarks—the Municipal Theater, modeled on the Opera in Paris, the Library, and the Museum of Art.

Av. President Vargas runs east and west, perpendicular to Av. Rio Branco. A wide, busy thoroughfare, Av. Presidente Vargas is the location of the Guanabara Palace Hotel and the Candelária Church.

Rua Gonçalves Dias is a narrow shopping street that is closed to cars during the day.

Rua Senador Dantas is the major street in Rio's movie district of Cinelândia. It is near the Hotel Ambassador and its main square is Praça Mahatma Gandhi.

At the eastern tip of Centro, on the bay, is *Santos Dumont Airport,* on island made of landfill and originally held by the French.

Swinging south out of downtown and hugging Guanabara Bay is *Av. Beira Mar,* which soons turns into *Praia do Flamengo* in the section of *Flamengo.* On the avenue are the Museum of Modern Art and the Gloria Hotel, as you reach Flamengo. Praia do Flamengo turns into *Praia de Botafogo* when it reaches *Botafogo,* where the yacht club is. All along the route arc beautiful views of Sugarloaf.

Passing through the tunnel you reach *Leme,* where *Av. Atlântica* starts. The main street beyond the beach is *Rua Gustavo Sampaio.* On the beach stands the Meridien Hotel, the dividing line, with *Av. Princesa Isabel,* between Leme and *Copacabana.*

Copacabana was originally divided in six posts, but that system is no longer in operation, although people still use the dividing lines as references. *Av. Atlântica,* the beachfront promenade, is paved with tiles and mosaics. Marking points are the Rio Othon Palace Hotel, in the middle, and Rio Palace Hotel, at the end. The beach is usually packed and there are many restaurants and cafés off it. Avenida Copacabana, one block away, is the area's busy shopping street. Many restaurants and cinemas are here too. Rua Barata Ribeiro, two blocks away, has fine budget hotels, small restaurants, and shops.

Arpoador Beach separates Copacabana from *Ipanema,* which is just west and almost at a right angle. The beach street here in Ipanema is *Av. Vieira Souto* and that is followed by *Rua Prudente de Morais.* The restaurant/nightclub Caligula-Le Streghe is here. Ipanema's main street, *Rua Visconde de Pirajá,* houses some of the city's chicest boutiques and its two major plazas. Praça General Osório, site of the Sunday Hippie Fair, is nearer to Copacabana; Praça Nossa Senhora da Paz is beyond it and is the heart of the commercial area. The fourth street in Ipanema, Rua Barão da Torre has many of our nightclub and dining choices.

A canal divides Ipanema and *Leblon,* the wealthiest district of Rio. The beachfront street is *Av. Delfim Moreira* and the street behind it is *Av. General San Martin.* The main shopping street is *Av. Ataulfo de Paiva.*

Av. Visconde de Albuquerque marks the end of Leblon and the beginning of *Vidigal,* whose main street is *Av. Niemeyer.* Vidigal is now in the midst of being built up, taking some of the slack of the three other beach districts. The Sheraton, the best hotel in Vidigal, is just beyond Leblon. Its stone structure overlooks Leblon and Ipanema beaches.

Heading farther out, you come next to São Conrado, home of the Intercontinental and Nacional hotels. A fine shopping center and the golf club are here.

Ten to fifteen mintues from São Conrado is *Barra da Tijuca,* another beach section that will eventually be like Leblon. Less developed than Leblon now, Barra is the chic place of the future, with branches of many of Leblon's and Ipanema's well-known shops opening up here. It is the site of many of our restaurant and nightlife suggestions. It is one of the nicest sections of Rio and the site of the largest shopping center in Rio. The main street is *Av. Sernambetiba.*

The section of *Lagoa,* inland from Leblon and Ipanema, borders the huge Lagoa Rodrigo de Freitas, a reservoir. It is as fancy as Leblon and its main street, running around the lagoa, is *Av. Epitácio Pessoa.* There are tall condominiums overlooking the bay. At Av. Leblon, Epitácio Pessoa becomes *Av. Borges de Medeiros*. The race track, *hipodromo*, and botanical gardens are just beyond this area. The Tivoli Amusement Park is also on the lagoa on Av. Borges de Medeiros.

Just north of Lagoa is Corcovado mountain, with Christ the Redeemer on top, and Tijuca Forest, which sits in the middle of Rio.

Climate

Roughly on a latitude (relative to the Equator—but south) with the Caribbean, Rio is truly tropical with only slight seasonal variations. Spring and summer run from October to March (the reverse of the Northern Hemisphere) with temperatures 85 to 95 degrees and sometimes humid. Short bursts of tropical rainstorms break up the heat on occasion. No matter how hot it gets, cool breezes sweep over the beach areas, making them comfortable. The winter and fall—running from April to September—are slightly cooler and much less humid, particularly in the evenings. Yes, there's year-round swimming. By the way, Rio is free of hurricanes and typhoons. There is no time of the year to avoid; the weather is always a plus.

Hotels

As you might expect, Rio has an enormous number of hotels and the range of accommodations works to your advantage. There is a hotel to suit everyone's style and all budgets. You can choose a downtown location, but you shouldn't, because the beach areas have the nicer hotels and are where the action is.

Surprisingly, most Rio hotels are not resort-style; only a few in the newer beach areas have large grounds. Most, even the most elegant, resemble classy in-city hostelries and many actually look like apartment buildings. Location is important, so if you want to save money, choose a hotel a few blocks off the beach. It will still be clean, comfortable, and most important, air-conditioned.

As throughout Brazil, hotels are rated by the government on a five-star basis as to services and quality of facilities, with a five-star rating at the top. Although not perfect, this rating system is a good guide to all-around quality.

Several hotels belong to the Leading Hotels of the World reservations system and you can book through them for the Rio Palace and Caesar Park. The Sheraton and Intercontinental have stateside reservation systems too, and these are two of the hotels with spacious grounds, large pools, and tennis courts. The other, the Nacional, is farthest from Copacabana.

While prices are not low, they are certainly far less than prices for comparable accommodations on Caribbean islands. Remember too that rates here, as throughout Brazil, include breakfast which may be anything—from continental style (juice, rolls, and coffee) to a four-course meal featuring Brazilian cheeses, fruit, rolls, and that fabulous Brazilian coffee.

Major hotel chains in Brazil include Othon (Leme Palace and Othon Palace, among others); Horsa (Nacional and Excelsior); Luxor (Regente, Luxor, and Continental); Veplan (Rio Palace); Sheraton; and Intercontinental.

Rio Palace 5[x]
Av. Atlântica, 4240
Copacabana
Phone 521-3232
Telex 021-21803

The Rio Palace offers the ultimate in excellence. Located in Copacabana, it has two small swimming pools and 418 rooms that offer air conditioning, color TV, radio, minibar, and refrigerator. The hotel is equipped with two restaurants, two snack bars, and a discotheque, as well as the his and her health clubs that are adjacent to the pools. The hotel is connected to the *Cassino Atlântico* shopping center, with 189 new shops and boutiques. Rooms are decorated with Brazilian hardwoods, marble, and tiles, and terraces offer spectacular views of the beach and the ocean. A kitchenette on every floor speeds room service, and a special lounge is set aside for arriving and departing guests. There is even a telephone in your bathroom. Expensive.

Caesar Park Hotel 5*
Av. Vieira Souto, 460
Ipanema
Phone 287-3122
Telex 021-21204

Located in Ipanema, the Caesar Park has 226 rooms on twenty-three floors, all decorated with the newest furnishings. The hotel has two excellent restaurants: Petronius, which specializes in seafood, and Tiberius, which offers a great view from the twenty-third floor. The hotel has extensive convention and meeting rooms for business travelers. Its facilities also include a swimming pool, a sauna, a beauty parlor, and a barbershop. Under the same management as Caesar Park in São Paulo, this is a popular hotel with businesspeople. The service is incredible; any reasonable request will be honored. Expensive.

Hotel Rio Sheraton 5*
Av. Niemeyer, 121
Vidigal
Phone 274-1122
Telex 021-21206

The Hotel Rio Sheraton, with its almost private beach, is located in Vidigal, a community on the shoreline not far from Leblon. There are 617 rooms with air conditioning, TV, and radio. Renovated in 1986, the hotel now has a new bar in addition to its two pools, tennis courts, health club, and sauna. At the pool, Brazilian drinks are served by Casa da Cachaça. The Top Bell health club, with gym, sauna, and masseur, is the best in town. The lobby is sumptuous, with floor-to-ceiling columns. On the second level is a small museum of antiques. There are two great restaurants on the premises; the churrascaria, O Casarão, serves a delicious buffet lunch. A new restaurant, Valentino, is one of our top recommended restaurants. The Sheraton also has airline offices, book shops, an H. Stern branch, and a nightclub and discotheque. Expensive.

Hotel Intercontinental 5*
Av. Litorânea, 222
São Conrado
Phone 322-2200
Telex 021-21790

Hotel Intercontinental takes luxury to the point of decadence with its cocktail bar that projects out onto the waters of its pool. All 500 rooms have balconies and authentic Brazilian furnishings. The restaurants here are good, and the Papillon discotheque draws young locals en masse. Tennis is a bargain and sauna and massage are available after the game. Private buses leave every twenty minutes to Leme via Copacabana. It is one of the few hotels with grounds, just off the ocean. Expensive.

Hotel Nacional (Horsa chain) 5*
Av. Niemeyer, 769
São Conrado
Phone 322-1000
Telex 021-21238

Designed by Brazilian architect Oscar Niemeyer, who gained international fame with his avant-garde design of Brasília and the U.N., the Nacional is a mammoth structure on Rio's beachfront. Dramatic against its mountain backdrop, the perfectly round glass building offers panoramic views of the Atlantic. Two pools (one for children), a sauna, and golf privileges at a nearby country club make up their facilities. There are 520 fully equipped rooms on twenty-six floors. Adjacent to the Intercontinental. Expensive.

Marina Palace Hotel 5*
Av. Delfim Moreira, 630
Leblon
Phone 259-5212
Telex 021-30224

A comfortable beachfront hotel, the Marina Palace has 160 rooms and a pool with a sundeck. The Bistro da Praia restaurant is outstanding. There are also a coffee shop, a bar, a sauna, and a beauty parlor, as well as extensive executive meeting rooms. Expensive.

Rio Othon Palace Hotel 5*
Av. Atlântica, 3264
Copacabana
Phone 255-8812
Telex 021-23265

With a superb location, the Rio Othon Palace towers over Av. Atlântica, and is the giant of the Othon chain. There are 606 rooms on thirty floors with air conditioning, TV, refrigerator, and minibar. There is a pool and a bar on the roof. Guest rooms are done in bright oranges, reds, and browns. Expensive.

Hotel Meridien 5*
Av. Atlântica, 1020
Av. Princesa Isabel (Leme-Copacabana border)
Phone 275-9922
Telex 021-23017

Home to Regine's, the posh disco on the street level, the Meridien is luxurious and chic. There's a pool with a bar, and superb French food at Café de la Paix on the main floor and St. Honoré on the top. Breakfast, which ends at 11 A.M., is worth getting up for. Expensive.

Copacabana Palace Hotel 5*
Av. Atlântica, 1702
Copacabana
Phone 257-1818
Telex 021-22248

This old-world hotel has fourteen-foot ceilings and a huge second-floor lobby, fully appreciated by a faithful following of customers who return regularly to enjoy the luxury of a 1920s-style resort hotel. Recently the hotel was completely renovated. In the heart of the beach district, the hotel is also adjacent to the Teatro Copacabana. Rooms, which have terraces, are light and airy. A good English bookshop on the premises sells the *International Herald-Tribune*. Expensive.

Leme Palace Hotel 4*
Av. Atlântica, 656
Leme
Phone 275-8080
Telex 021-23265

The beachfront Leme Palace, with a beauty parlor, a barbershop, a nightclub, a bar, a sidewalk café, and a highly regarded restaurant, Le Cordon Bleu, is on a par with a European hotel. Its 194 plush rooms on seventeen floors look out on the water. A well-stocked refrigerator in your room will cost you only what you consume. The exterior is white; there's a small lobby. Moderate.

Hotel Regente (Luxor chain) 4*
Av. Atlântica, 3716
Copacabana
Phone 287-4212
Telex 021-23887

Located in the liveliest beach area of Rio, the Regente emphasizes comfort. Its 254 rooms are modern, with music, TV, and refrigerator. You can dine outdoors and enjoy the street scene, or if you prefer, try Forno e Fogão restaurant, adjoining. Moderate.

Hotel Sol Ipanema 4*
Av. Vieira Souto, 320
Ipanema
Phone 227-0060
Telex 021-21979

This hotel has ninety rooms, all decorated with brilliantly colored Bahian tapestries and jacaranda furniture. There are swimming pools, a sauna, a barbershop, and a beauty parlor. Although the hotel is quiet, Copacabana is only ten minutes away by cab or bus. Moderate.

Hotel Gloria 4*
Rua do Russel, 632
Flamengo
Phone 205-7272;
245-8010
Telex 021-21683

The Gloria, with seven hundred rooms, has been the traditional class hotel of Rio. It's within five minutes of downtown and has a full view of Sugarloaf. You may swim in either Guanabara Bay or the pool. The meticulous parquet floor in the lobby and the large rooms with TV and carpeting, furnished in the Brazilian colonial style, are worth a look, even if you don't stay here. Expensive.

Everest Rio Hotel 5*
Rua Prudente de
Morais, 1117
Ipanema
Phone 287-8282
Telex 021-22254

A modern hotel with twenty-three floors and 176 rooms, the Everest has the advantage of its location in Ipanema, a quiet district of Rio that is only ten minutes from Copacabana. The Casserole Restaurant on the mezzanine is a popular stop, and adjacent to the pool on the top floor are a bar and a coffee shop. Expensive.

Marina Rio Hotel 4*
Av. Delfim Moreira,
696 Leblon
Phone 239-8844
Telex 021-30224

Small and quiet compared with the large luxury hotels of Rio, this one has the beaches of Leblon at its doorstep. There are seventy-three rooms on twenty floors, with air conditioning, TV, and radio. The continental restaurant also offers some excellent Brazilian dishes. The piano bar is good for a nightcap. Moderate.

Ipanema Inn 4*
Rua Maria Quitéria, 27
Ipanema
Phone 287-6092
Telex 021-22833

Not well known, this small, modern hotel offers all comforts at reasonable prices. There are fifty-six rooms on nine floors, with air conditioning and radio. Just one block from the beach. Inexpensive.

Arpoador Inn 3*
Rua Francisco
Otaviano, 177
Ipanema
Phone 247-6090

The Arpoador Inn, with fifty rooms, is under the same management as the Ipanema Inn. Expensive.

Other Hotels

Besides these more-well-known luxury hotels, there is an abundance of hotels that offer good value throughout the districts of Rio. The list below begins in Copacabana, moves to Leme, and then south to Ipanema, Leblon, and Gávea, ending finally in Flamengo Beach and downtown Rio.

Hotel Excelsior (Horsa chain) 3*
Av. Atlântica, 1800
Copacabana
Phone 257-1950
Telex 021-21076

A room at the front of the hotel will give you stunning views of the ocean and Av. Atlântica. Accommodations are plush, as is the sitting room. The American bar and outdoor tables are especially pleasant. Rear rooms are less expensive. Moderate.

Ouro Verde Hotel 4*
Av. Atlântica, 1456
(at Rua Duvivier)
Copacabana
Phone 542-1887
Telex 212-3848

A handsome circular stairway and white-gloved elevator operators set the tone for this Swiss-type hotel. There are twelve floors; sixty-six spacious rooms. The hotel boasts one of Rio's best continental restaurants. The reading room on the second floor is right out of old Europe. Moderate.

Hotel Trocadero (Othon chain) 3*
Av. Atlântica, 2064
(at Rua Paula Freitas)
Copacabana
Phone 257-1834
Telex 021-23265

Trocadero has an attractive lobby and a beautiful beach right in front, where you can enjoy a drink at sunset at their outdoor bar. The rooms are fine, and moderately priced; there are 121 rooms on twelve floors. One of Rio's best native restaurants is the Moenda, located here. Moderate.

Hotel Lancaster (Othon chain) 4*
Av. Atlântica, 1470 (near Rua Duvivier) Copacabana
Phone 257-1840; 541-1887
Telex 021-23265

The Lancaster is an intimate hotel with only twenty-four rooms (it used to be a luxury apartment house). Rooms are charming and spacious and most have separate sitting areas; front rooms have terraces overlooking the beach. The hotel has a regular and devoted following of customers. Moderate.

Savoy Othon Hotel 4*
Av. Copacabana, 995
Copacabana
Phone 257-8052

One block from the beach, the Savoy Othon features 156 elegantly furnished rooms, fully carpeted, with air conditioning and TV. Its main restaurant is of gourmet quality and its executive meeting rooms make this a good choice for the business traveler. There's a pub bar and a coffee shop, as well as the Savoy Grill for larger meals. Moderate.

Luxor Copacabana 4*
Av. Atlântica, 2554
Copacabana
Phone 257-1940
Telex 021-23971

With 123 rooms on eleven floors, the Luxor uses jacaranda wood most effectively to complement its modern design. The beachfront café is recommended. Moderate.

Hotel Praia Leme 3*
Av. Atlântica, 866
Leme
Phone 275-3322

Small, with two floors and twenty-two rooms, but extremely clean and tastefully furnished, the Praia Leme is highly recommended. Because of its low rates, it tends to attract long-term guests, so write well ahead for reservations. Inexpensive.

Miramar Palace Hotel 4*
Av. Atlântica, 3668
Copacabana
Phone 247-6070
Telex 021-21508

This is one of Copacabana's most comfortable and cozy hotels, moderately sized with fifteen floors and 140 rooms. From the roof bar, there is a panoramic view of Rio. Moderate.

Hotel Debret 3*
Av. Atlântica, 3564
(corner of Rua Almirante Gonçalves, 5)
Copacabana
Phone 521-3332
Telex 021-30483

Deocrated in the Brazilian colonial style, this is a good traditional hotel with a restaurant and a barbershop on the premises. Inexpensive.

Hotel Olinda 3*
Av. Atlântica, 2230
Near Siqueira Campos
Copacabana
Phone 257-1890
Telex 021-23265

Part of the Othon chain, this beachfront hotel has 102 rooms and a sidewalk bar, as well as a good restaurant. Inexpensive.

Riviera Hotel 3*
Av. Atlântica, 4122
Copacabana
Phone 247-6060
Telex 021-21076

Close to the Rio Palace, this is a small, simple hotel of ten floors, one hundred rooms. Inexpensive

California Hotel 4*
Av. Atlântica, 2616
Copacabana
Phone 257-1900
Telex 021-22655

The California, with 121 rooms equipped with air conditioning, TV, radio, and refrigerator, is another fine member of the Othon chain. Moderate.

Continental Palace Hotel 3*
Rua Gustavo Sampaio, 320
Leme
Phone 275-5252

At Continental Palace, one block from the beach, a heaping breakfast of eggs, ham, and cheese is included in the rate. There are 150 rooms on eight floors. Moderate.

Hotel Castro Alves 3*
Av. Copacabana, 552
Copacabana
Phone 257-1800

Another Othon Hotel, the Castro Alves is one block from the beach in Copacabana. Its 76 rooms have air conditioning, TV, and stocked refrigerators. Inexpensive.

Praia Ipanema 4*
Av. Vieira Souto, 706
Ipanema
Phone 239-9932
Telex 021-31280

Most striking for its location right on the beach at Ipanema, the Praia has a swimming pool and sundeck with a bar and a good restaurant, La Mouette. There are 105 rooms. Moderate.

Hotel Vermont 3*
Rua Visconde de Pirajá, 254
Ipanema
Phone 247-6100

A small, 38-room hotel on the main shopping street, the Vermont is quite comfortable and affordable. Look for the sign (pink) and the red and white canopy. Inexpensive.

Hotel San Marco 2*
Rua Visconde de Pirajá, 524
Ipanema
Phone 239-5032

On the same street, Hotel San Marco has small but clean rooms, some without air conditioning but with large ceiling fans. More expensive doubles with air conditioning are available. Inexpensive.

Hotel Carlton 3*
Rua João Lira, 68
Leblon
Phone 259-1932

The Hotel Carlton in Leblon, four stories high with forty-six rooms, is perfect for families. Two-room suites with sitting rooms are available, with TV and air conditioning. The Carlton, under the same manage-ment as the Vermont and the San Marco, is quite similar to them. Two blocks from the beach. Moderate.

Flamengo

Hotel Novo Mundo 3*
Praia do Flamengo, 20
Flamengo
Phone 225-7366

Offering great views of Fla-mengo Park and Sugarloaf, the Novo Mundo, once one of the best-known luxury hotels, has retained its charm. In Flamengo near the center of Rio, it's one block from the Hotel Gloria and the beach, near the Museum of the Republic. There are two hundred air-conditioned rooms in twelve stories. In-expensive.

Downtown

Ambassador Hotel 3*
Rua Senador Dantas, 25
Downtown
Phone 297-7181
Telex 021-21796

On the main street of Cinelân-dia, the Ambassador is noted for its service. The hotel is well cared for and offers moderate rates. Its 130 air-conditioned rooms on eighteen floors, with TV and refrigerator, repre-sent good value.

Grande Hotel OK 3*
Rua Senador Dantas, 24
Downtown
Phone 292-4141

Across the street from the Ambassador is the Grande Hotel OK, with seventeen floors, 174 rooms. Inexpensive.

Aeroporto Hotel 3*
Av. Beira Mar, 280
Downtown
Near Santos Dumont Airport
Phone 262-8922

If airport proximity is important to you, you may want to consider the Aeroporto Hotel, with nine floors and eighty rooms. Rooms have refrigerators, but no air conditioning. Inexpensive.

Restaurants

Cariocas love to eat and Rio is tailored to that expectation. The city's sophistication is accurately mirrored in the enormous number and variety of first-class, elegant dining spots that thrive here. Located throughout the city, on the beach strips, overlooking the lagoon, and hugging the mountainsides, these eateries offer French, Italian, Japanese, Chinese, Polish, and Mexican specialties, each authentically prepared yet subtly Brazilian. The diversity in ambience will please you as well. The city's French and continental restaurants are as formal and posh as those in New York or Paris but far less expensive. The majority of Rio's dining spots are casual, like the cariocas, and you can relax under a star-filled sky and breathe the salty sea air.

As you stroll through the city, you will notice that every block has its hangout—a small restaurant-bar where locals stop for a beer or a cafezinho before heading home or a nightcap before retiring. Some blocks have as many as four or five and they are all crowded.

The restaurants that are indigenously Brazilian are churrascarias, which specialize in barbecued meats, Brazilian style, and Bahian, which serve the typical foods that emanated from that northeast state where Brazil was founded. Churrascarias are Rio's most popular eating spots and if you aren't careful you'll get hooked, too. It may be the beef, which comes from the southern region. The cattle here are specifically fed to produce meat with little fat. Of course, it may be the barbecuing technique, where the meats are skewered and slowly grilled over an open hearth. At any rate, one meal at a churrascaria and you'll get the picture.

There are two kinds of churrascarias in Rio: standard and rodizio. The standard churrascaria has the client choose the type of meat and what he wants with it. The rodizio is basically a smorgasbord of meats, where everything is tried and the food doesn't stop until you are full. There is one set price and the meats are usually filet mignon, rib of beef, brisket, pork, ham, turkey, and chicken. Beef, the mainstay of the Brazilian diet, is usually served rare. If you want your *bife* better done, specify *ao ponto* for medium or *bem passado* for well done, in which case be prepared for a baleful glance.

Bahian food is a mixture of many influences: African, Indian, and Portuguese. Hallmark ingredients are hot palm oil, pepper, and manioc flour. Some dishes are: *feijoada,* a mixed platter of pork and sausage, with black beans over white rice and slightly cooked with manioc powder (a tropical vegetable root, traditionally served on Saturday); *xinxim de galinha,* pieces of chicken or shrimp in a mild sauce; *vatapa,* a mishmash of fish, meats, pepper, onions, and coconut milk. *Badejo* is a popular flounder-like fish; another popular dish is *frango com arroz,* which is chicken, rice, vegetables, hard-boiled eggs, and olives. *Caruru* is a pasta dish made with okra, peanuts, cashews, garlic, pepper, shrimp, and herring, with a soft bread center. *Sarapatel* is made with pork giblets, mint, garlic, black pepper, bay leaf, pork lard, and blood. *Bife de panela* is a thin steak served with onions and tomatoes, and is very common.

The most social of Brazilian drinks is *cafezinho*, which is a small cup of thick black Brazilian coffee served with lots of sugar. Drinks like *guaraná*, a sweet, fruit-based carbonated soda, a *batida*, a powerful sugarcane-based alcoholic drink, and *caipirinha*, a cachaça cocktail, are very popular. The two best-selling Brazilian beers are *Brahma* and *Skol*.

Brazilian wine is decent and inexpensive, but does not compare to Chilean or Argentinian wine. Brazilian white wine is better than the red—the converse of Chile and Argentina. Imported whiskey is very expensive. Domestic versions of internationally known whiskeys are much cheaper and not much different in taste.

Restaurants in Rio are cheap by U.S. standards, and also more flexible. One may unfearfully ask for a change of dish, a change in ingredient, or for a dish to be prepared that is not on the menu. Many restaurants do not list such international foods as hamburgers and fries on the menu. They assume you will ask for it irrespective of the menu.

Cariocas eat late, starting about 9:00 P.M. Dinner, though, can be eaten as late as 3:00 A.M. in many places. What is uncommon is to eat dinner at about six. Lunch is served from noon to 3 P.M. Many restaurants in Rio are closed on Monday.

The dress code is casual, even in the fanciest places. A tie is rarely worn. There is a nominal cover (*couvert*) charge for a celery, olive, and carrot plate and bread and butter. You can decline the couvert is you wish. Shrimp is probably the most expensive dish you'll find in any restaurant; it's sometimes more than fifty percent more expensive than the other dishes. Many menus are bilingual. It is not uncommon or frowned upon to share a plate, so don't be bashful if that's how you feel.

French

The French restaurants are considered the best on an international scale. That is not to say that all French restaurants in Rio are automatically excellent, but a majority of them are first-class places.

Ouro Verde
Av. Atlantica, 4240
Copacabana
Phone 542-1887
Noon–4 A.M.
Expensive

Ouro Verde is an excellent restaurant located in the hotel of the same name. Not nouvelle cuisine, but classic French, the restaurant's specialty is chateaubriand. Designed in classic European style, the restaurant has a trilingual menu—English, French, and Portuguese. The Swiss chef is world-famous and Ouro Verde is considered by many upscale cariocas as the best restaurant in Rio.

Le Pre Catalan
Rio Palace Hotel
Av. Atlântica, 4240
Copacabana
Phone 521-3232
7:30 P.M.–1 A.M.
Expensive

This nouvelle cuisine restaurant is in the Rio Palace Hotel, overlooking the water. Serving excellent food that is imaginative, Le Pre Catalan is the sister of the restaurant of the same name in Paris. The decor is elegant, the waiters professional, and the food is served on fine china and silver trays. The restaurant is successful in its attempt to maintain a Parisian atmosphere. There is an English menu.

Monsigneur
Hotel Intercontinental
Av. Litorânea, 222
São Conrado
Phone 322-2200
7–11:30, Sunday–
Thursday
7–1 A.M., Friday,
Saturday
Expensive

The restaurant in the Hotel Intercontinental was refurbished recently and Monsigneur has since become an excellent haunt. Its food is thoroughly French; some outstanding dishes are the chateaubriand, the lobster bisque, and the coeur du filet mignon. The restaurant invites different restaurants from around the world to take over for short periods. There is also a set of roving musicians to do serenades.

Le Saint Honoré
Meridien Hotel
Av. Atlântica, 1020
Leme
Phone 275-9922
Noon–3; 11 P.M.
Expensive

On the thirty-seventh floor of the Hotel Meridien, with a wonderful view of the ocean, Le Saint Honoré is run by the famous chef Paul Bocuse. The food is fantastic and the place elegant. The luncheon special, at one price excluding drinks, is very popular, but dinner is the lure. A sister restaurant is in Salvador at the Meridien Hotel there.

Cafe De La Paix
Meridien Hotel, Lobby
Level
Av. Atlântica, 1020
Leme
Phone 275-9922,
275-1122
7:30–10 A.M.;
noon–1 A.M.
Moderate

Also in the Hotel Meridien is another fine French restaurant, separated from Le Saint Honoré by thirty-seven floors and by formality. Brasserie in style, the restaurant also serves an excellent tea from 3 P.M. to 6 P.M. Try l'omelette bataille and les mignonnettes de boeuf aux trois poivres.

Le Bec Fin
Av. N. S. de
Copacabana, 178
Copacabana
Phone 542-4097
7 P.M.–3 A.M.
Expensive

Featuring more traditional French cuisine, the restaurant is very elegant and covered with mirrors. Founded in 1948, Le Bec Fin is unpretentious and hard to find, with its small brass sign. There is also a bar.

Churrascarias

Churrascarias are typically Brazilian, but not to be mistaken with Bahian food, also an indigenous Brazilian cuisine. Churrascarias are restaurants serving a variety of barbecued meats. There are two styles of churrascarias. *Rodizio* style means the food is served as a smorgasbord, but brought to your table. The food does not stop until you request it to. Standard churrascarias have menus like any other restaurant, and you choose the combinations of meats desired. All churrascarias are inexpensive.

Marius
Av. Atlântica, 290
Leme
Phone 542-2393
11 A.M.–2 A.M.
Inexpensive

Rodizio in style, with one fixed price, Marius is one of the best churrascarias in the city. A large place, seating 350, the restaurant will serve drinks while you wait. There is always a lot of food. It's always crowded; on Sunday expect to wait a full hour. Remember, this is usually the maids' day off.

Porcão
Rua Barão da Torre, 218
Ipanema
Phone 521-0999
11:30–3
Inexpensive

Also rodizio in style, the set price is similar to that at Marius. With about five locations, this one is the best, and its tile floors are interesting if they don't put you off. There is another branch of Porcão in Barra da Tijuca at Av. Armando Lombardi, 591 (phone 399-3355).

Carreta
Praça São Perpetuo, 116
Barra da Tijuca
Phone 399-4055
Inexpensive

Not rodizio in style, Carreta is an old-fashioned churrascaria with the cooking meat visible and an extensive menu. The restaurant serves excellent food in a large wood-paneled room. It recently moved from Ipanema, where it was my favorite for years.

Rincão Gaúcho
Rua Marques de Valenca, 83
Tijuca
Phone 264-6659
11 A.M.–3 A.M.
Inexpensive

This is a huge restaurant that can seat up to a thousand people, with music nightly and great food. Not a rodizio, but the menu is extensive and the restaurant is gaucho in style. There is dancing.

Churrascaria Jardim
Rua República do Peru,
225
Copacabana
Phone 235-3263
11 A.M.–2 A.M.
Inexpensive

With two dining rooms, Churrascaria Jardim is a traditional churrascaria, with a wide selection of meats. The French fries are fantastic and the cover generous. (The sausage with tomato and onion salad is fabulous.) There is an English menu. I have frequented this restaurant since 1966; it's a favorite of mine.

Churrascaria
Copacabana
Av. Copacabana, 444
Copacabana
Phone 255-7849,
247-8257
11 A.M.–2 A.M.
Inexpensive

Popular among residents, the restaurant has both typical churrascaria and international cuisine. Gaucho in style, the dining room is rustic and brick-walled.

Roda Viva Churrascaria
Av. Pasteur, 520
Urca (near Botafogo)
Phone 246-7205
10–2 A.M.
Inexpensive

Here is a restaurant in an art gallery—paintings are for sale—that has a bar. The chefs cook under a thatched roof and the food is cheap. English is on the menu.

Rodeio
Av. Alvorado, 2150
Barra da Tijuca
Phone 325-6166
Noon–3 P.M.; 7–1:30
Inexpensive

This excellent churrascaria, not a rodizio, is extremely popular; its one drawback is its distance. More elegant than the normal churrascaria, there is a main dining room and an outdoor area for beer and snacks. Near the Barra Shopping Center.

Continental

Continental food, of course, can take in many different styles and tastes. The term is almost generic, but has no bearing on the quality that can be found at any of these restaurants.

Antonino
Av. Epitácio Pessoa, 1244
Lagoa
Phone 267-6791
Noon–2 A.M.
Moderate

With a totally French menu, Antonino, although international in its dishes, has a classic French orientation. The surroundings are formal and there is a wonderful view of the Lagoa from the windows. Piano bar downstairs. Jacket and tie are not uncommon here.

Petronius
Av. Vieira Souto, 460
Ipanema
Phone 287-3122
Moderate

In the Caesar Park Hotel, and next to the sushi bar Mariko, Petronius is fashionable and tasteful, and specializes in seafood. Looking out over Ipanema beach, the restaurant, on the second floor, has a peaceful feel with its marble floor and quiet piano with romantic songs.

Negresco
Rua Barão da Torre, 348
Ipanema
Phone 287-4842
Noon–3; 6–2 A.M.
Moderate

Located next to Ipanema's main plaza, N.S. da Paz, Negresco is very small, with only nine well-spaced tables. There is a large bar and a thoroughly international menu. Two dishes are recommended: spaguetti do vongoli and fettucine Alfredo.

Sal & Pimenta
Rua Barão da Torre, 368
Ipanema
Phone 247-7178,
521-1460
Noon–4; 8–midnight
Moderate

Set in a private house, with a mixture of Brazilian and Italian (but predominantly Italian) dishes, Sal & Pimenta is a fashionable haunt, with large mirrors and large flowers. The Alo-Alo piano bar is downstairs and features jazz and Brazilian music. Bilingual English and Portuguese menus. Tables are a precious commodity and are competed for.

Del Mare
Rua Paul Redfern, 37
Ipanema
Phone 239-7842
Noon–2 A.M.
Moderate

The entrance to Del Mare is a spiral wood staircase and inside are old maps, wine bottles hanging on walls, paintings of sailors, and a general nautical design. Across the street from the Mediterraneo (to come), Del Mare specializes in Italian and seafood dishes. Recommended are pesce bollito and the steak. Excellent food and decor.

Valentino's
Rio Sheraton Hotel
Vidigal
Phone 274-1122
7–midnight
Expensive

Upgraded with the Sheraton's refurbishment, Valentino's is comfortable and has plenty of space. There are stars on the walls and the dishes center on northern Italy. Try the slices of quail breast in morel sauce. The service is impeccable; there is a pianist.

Antiquarius
Rua Artistides Espínola, 19
Leblon
Phone 249-1049
Noon–2 A.M.
Expensive

In this restaurant designed and styled like a private house, you will find antique furniture, beamed ceilings, a garden, and fine china. Antiquarius is one of Rio's best. The relaxed atmosphere is heightened by the restaurant's antique collection (for sale upstairs) next to more seating. There are a bar and private alcoves. Dinner is usually packed; lunch much less so.

Florentino
Rua General San
Martín, 1227
Leblon
Phone 276-6841,
274-6240
Noon–2 A.M.
Expensive

A two-story house in Leblon, Florentino was once a popular artists' hangout. The walls are Scotch plaid and the wall mirrors have wood frames and are fronted by wine racks. Try the poulet aux amandes and the chateaubriand. Florentino has a sister restaurant in Brasília, which I find to be even better.

Le Flambard
Av. Epitácio Pessoa
Lagoa
Phone 259-1041
7–1 A.M.
Expensive

Although classified international, Le Flambard is French in style and serves excellent nouvelle cuisine in a fancy but relaxed atmosphere; there is a bar with paintings on the walls. Try to be seated near the windows for a good view of the Lagoa. Upstairs is for private parties. The menu is in French.

Equinox
Rua Prudente de
Morais, 729
Ipanema
Phone 267-2895
Noon–3; 7–1 A.M.
Expensive

Equinox, a fine first-class restaurant, is in a private house, with a piano bar downstairs. With a truly international menu—the food is from all over the world—the restaurant is slick; the owners are experienced, one of them is the former food and beverage manager at the Rio Palace. Called Equinox because the menu changes on September 23 and March 21 (on the equinox). Lunch and traditional feijoada are served on Saturday.

Terraço Atlântico
Av. Atlântico, 3432
Copacabana
Phone 521-1296
11 A.M.–3 A.M.
Moderate

A huge place, with outdoor and indoor seating, Terraço Atlântico has a piano bar and is next to the disco Help. There is a great view of the beach and Copacabana.

Antonio's
Av. Bartolomeu Mitre, 297
Leblon
Phone 294-2699
Noon–midnight
Moderate

An artists' hangout that is small and quiet, Antonio's has wood paneling, floor-to-ceiling wine racks, and seating on a veranda. The menu is only in Portuguese; we recommend the camarões a bordaleza (shrimp in bordelaise sauce), the fettucine Alfredo, the scaloppine marsala, or the filet mignon a pizzaiola.

La Tour
Rua Santa Lúzia, 651
Downtown
Phone 240-5795
Noon–midnight
Expensive

On the thirty-seventh floor of an office building, La Tour is Rio's only revolving restaurant, and that is its attraction, of course. The food is average, and mainly international. The restaurant makes a complete rotation about every hour, so that the entire city is served up to you as you dine.

Café do Teatro
Av. Rio Branco
Phone 262-4164
11:30 A.M.–3:30 P.M.
Closed weekends
Expensive

In Rio's Teatro Municipal, Café do Teatro is just as elegantly classical as the theater itself. A special experience the Café makes you feel plugged into the glamour class while you're there. Part of the Nino Antonino group, Café do Teatro is open only for lunch, serving continental food.

Nino
Rua Domingos Ferreira,
242
Copacabana
Phone 255-9696
Noon–3; 7–2 A.M.
Moderate

A comfortable restaurant with a long tradition, Nino has lovely paintings and murals on the walls and serves good "asperges" vinaigrette. There is also a Nino in Barra da Tijuca on Av. Sernambetiba, 330.

Seafood

A coastal city, Rio of course has great seafood and an abundance of restaurants serving fish. Seafood can be a real treat here.

Grottamare
Rua Gomes Carneiro,
132
Ipanema (at the beginning)
Phone 287-1596
6 A.M.–2 A.M.; noon–2 A.M. on Sunday
Moderate

Suitably nautical, the restaurant has dark etched wood panels over brick, wine bottles perched atop wooden shelves, and an upstairs dining room and terrace. Although Grottamare is large and noisy, the lure is the food (the fish are caught by the restaurant's own fishermen),

which is predominately seafood with some Italian dishes. Try peixe ao Grottamare (almost enough for two, with a spectacular sauce) or any of the spaghetti dishes.

Farol da Barra
Av. Sernambetiba, 1700
Barra da Tijuca
Phone 399-1143
Noon–1 A.M.
Moderate

With large windows overlooking the ocean, a terrace, and two levels, Farol da Barra has both seafood and Bahian food. The lighthouse is next to the restaurant (*farol* means "lighthouse"). The restaurant is a landmark.

Bahian and French food are served upstairs; downstairs is seafood. Upstairs has a nautical decor and a great view of the sea. Waitresses are in typical Bahian dress. Drinks are served outside.

A Marisqueira
Rua Barata Ribeiro, 232
Copacabana
Phone 237-3920
11 A.M.–1:30 A.M.
Moderate

A Marisqueira has dining on two levels and very good seafood. As at most of the fish restaurants, fine Italian platters appear on the menu.

Alba Mar
Praça 15 de Novembro
Downtown
Phone 221-3261
11 A.M.–10 P.M.
Moderate

Located in the downtown dock area, Alba Mar is in a circular building with a turret top. There's a cocktail lounge below the dining area, which has a good view of the water and the departing ships. We recommend the camarões baiana and the peixe á Brasileira.

Sole E Mar
Av. Nestor Moreira, 11
Botafogo
Phone 246-1529
11:30 A.M.–midnight
Moderate

Sole E Mar is known for its mussels, squid, octopus, assorted shellfish, and view. There are cocktails below on a lower terrace that faces Sugarloaf, and the restaurant itself is near the Rio yacht club. The views of Guanabara Bay are spectacular.

Principe Real
Av. Atlântica, 974
Leme
11 A.M.–2:30 A.M.
Inexpensive

Part of the chain, the Real is not overly impressive physically, but it has marinated crab that is sensational. The menu is in both Portuguese and English. It is located near Marius, beyond the Meredien Hotel overlooking the ocean.

Italian

Rio's and therefore the country's large Italian population leads to many good Italian restaurants.

Mediterraneo
Rua Prudente de
Morais, 1810
Ipanema
Phone 259-4121
Noon–3 A.M.
Moderate

In a private house with a relaxed, friendly, and communal atmosphere, Mediterraneo has dining inside under wood-beamed ceilings or outside on a terrace; it is basically a neighborhood haunt. From a plethora of dishes, we recommend pesce al forno and paella al frutti di mare. Popular and crowded on weekends.

Le Streghe
Rua Prudente de
Morais, 129
Ipanema
Phone 287-1369
7:30–2 A.M.
Expensive

Romantic, overlooking Praça General Osório, Le Streghe has excellent food and fun service. Located on the top floor of its own house, the restaurant can seat seventy comfortably. Below is the bar/disco Caligula, which is recommended in our nightlife section.

Chinese

Mr. Zee
Av. General San Martin, 1219
Leblon
Phone 294-0591
7:30–midnight
Closed Monday
Expensive

Owned by David Zee, formerly of Chase Bank, who was born in Hong Kong and educated at Cornell, Mr. Zee has one large, mirrored dining room and a bar. The waiters are in kimonos. A nice touch are the vegetables designed in certain figures like swans.

New Mandarin
Rua Carlos Góis, 344
Leblon
Noon–2; 6–midnight
Moderate

Considered by some the best Chinese restaurant in Rio, New Mandarin specializes in soup. Try the shark fin, the shredded beef, the butterfly shrimp, the

Szechuan duck, and frango con nozes (chicken with nuts). There are three dining rooms in this converted private house.

The China Town Restaurant
Rua Barão da Torre, 450
Ipanema
Noon–3; 6–midnight
Moderate

Owned by a native of Nanking, the restaurant is divided into several sections from one large dining room. We recommend fried chicken, shredded beef, shrimp with green peas, and sweet and sour pork.

Oriento Restaurant
Rua Bolivar and
Av. Copacabana
Copacabana
Noon–3; 6–midnight
6–2 A.M. weekends
Inexpensive

Oriento serves huge portions, the best of which are diced chicken with bean sprouts, shredded beef with green pepper, and shrimp in curry sauce. Head up one flight of stairs, look for the orange sign.

Japanese

Mariko
Av. Vieira Souto, 460
Ipanema
Phone 287-3211
6 P.M.–1 A.M.
Moderate

In the Caesar Park Hotel, Mariko is next to Petronius, on the second floor. There is an excellent sushi bar; try the selection of nine rice balls in raw fish.

Akasaka
Av. Copacabana, 1391
Copacabana
Phone 287-3211
Noon–3 P.M.; 6 P.M.–
midnight
Moderate

With both a conventional western dining room and a typical Japanese one, Akasaka features chawanmushi, soup, sukiyaki, teriyaki, and batajati. I ate here on my first visit to Rio in 1965. It was good then and it still is today.

Portuguese

Brazil, being an ex-Portuguese colony, is very influenced by Portuguese cuisine and does not really need to have a Portuguese restaurant. But for typical European Portuguese cooking we recommend two.

A Desgarrada
Rua Barão da Torre, 667
Ipanema
Phone 239-5746
8 A.M.–1 A.M.;
closed Sunday
Moderate

Popular with locals, A Desgarrada has a show. Fado music and traditional food keep this restaurant usually crowded.

Adega de Evora
Rua Santa Clara, 292
Copacabana
8 P.M.–2 A.M.,
closed Sunday
Moderate

Adega de Evora features a show and requires a cover. The seafood is good here.

German

Bar Haus Alfred
Rua da Passegem, 171
Botafogo
Phone 541-6598
Moderate

A small place with an open-air deck, travel posters of Germany, and wooden chairs, Alfred offers many typical and excellent German dishes, from Weiner schnitzel to salsicha; there are also German wines.

Alpino
Av. Epitácio Pessoa, 40
Lagoa
Phone 247-1854
6 P.M.–1 A.M.,
closed Monday
Moderate

By the ocean, with outdoor terrace dining, this restaurant serves good food, with the marinated herring a particularly good appetizer. Lunch on Sunday is most popular. The bratwurst is one of my favorites.

Lucas
Av. Atlântica, 3744
Copacabana
Phone 247-1606
Noon–2 A.M.
Inexpensive

In a re-creation of a Bavarian restaurant, Lucas serves typical German fare, and has sausages and wine bottles hanging everywhere. The best dishes are the Wiener schnitzel (here called escallop a Vienese) and steak Leipzig.

Bahian

Bahian food may be the only truly authentic Brazilian cuisine. Its mixture of African, Indian, and Portuguese ingredients represents the three original cultures in the country.

Maria Thereza Weiss
Rua Visconde Silva, 152
Botafogo
Noon–midnight
Moderate

The owner and cook, Maria Thereza Weiss, is well known for her books on Bahian cooking and experiments. Her restaurant is in a private house, with several dining rooms, a sweeping staircase, couches and tables along the wall, and a baby grand. Dishes recommended are moqueca, xinxim, vatapá and bobó de camarão. Highly recommended.

Chalé
Rua da Matriz, 54
Botafogo
Phone 286-0897
7 P.M.–midnight
Moderate

Inside an 1884 home, Chalé establishes a Bahian atmosphere, with waitresses in traditional Bahian garb. There is a marvelous selection of pastries, especially banana and apple. Other dishes to try are the moqueca de peixe, chicken or shrimp in tomato sauce, and xinxim.

Oxalá
Rua Francisco Serrador, 2
Downtown
Phone 242-0256
11–1 A.M.
Inexpensive

With only counter service, Oxalá is good for a light dinner before theater. Resembling a native Bahian hut with polished stone walls, Oxalá features vatapá and frigideira de camarão, a casserole of egg and shrimp.

Restaurant Tabefe
Rua da Matriz, 62
Botafogo
Phone 246-7791
Noon–3; 7–10
Inexpensive

A small one-room restaurant with Indian artifacts on the walls, Tabefe is quite popular; there is usually a wait. Located a few steps from Chalé.

Mexican

Café Pacífico
Rua Visconde Silva, 14
Botafogo
11–3; 7–2:30 A.M.

One of Rio's two Mexican restaurants, Café Pacífico is in a private house, has a bar, beamed ceilings, and pictures of Mexico. It also has good old Mexican food: nachos, guacamole, tacos, enchiladas, burritos, etc. Photos and license plates of Mexico abound.

Lagoa Charlie's
Rua Maria Quitería, 136
Lagoa
Phone 287-0335
7 A.M.–2 A.M.

A bilevel restaurant, with outdoor and indoor dining, Lagoa Charlie's has strolling Mexican musicians. The food is typically Mexican and the menu is in three languages. The location is fabulous. Same spot since 1973.

Spanish

El Cordobes
Av. Borges de Medeiros, 3207
Lagoa
Phone 246-7431
6–2 A.M.; Sunday 12–2 A.M.
Expensive

A large restaurant, with a red tile roof, indoor and outdoor dining, and a mirrored-ceilinged bar, El Cordobes is very large (holds three hundred) and serves Spanish and seafood dishes. The restaurant offers free cab to and from your hotel—ask

Jacques—and has the same owner as Grottamare. Try the cazuela de mariscos a la Catalona and paella a la Valenciana. You'll enjoy the exterior—it's in a gorgeous old Spanish house.

English Pubs

Lord Jim
Rua Paul Redfern, 63
Ipanema
Phone 299-3047
4–1, Tues.–Sat.
11–1 Sunday
Moderate

Genuinely British in style, Lord Jim is the hangout for Rio's English-speaking community. The ground floor is a typical English pub, complete with a dartboard. The restaurant, taking two floors above the bar, has typically English food, such as roast beef and Yorkshire pudding, shepherd's pie, and fish and chips, as well as curry on the weekend. With rugby plaques and pictures of the Queen, Lord Jim is England transported.

Piccadilly Pub
Av. General San Martin, 1241
Leblon
Phone 259-7605
6:30–1 A.M.
Moderate

In a private house, with a spiral staircase, Piccadilly is English in name, intimate in feel, and international in terms of the food it serves: French, German, and even Mexican food. Try médaillon of pork.

American

Neal's
Rua Sorocaba, 695
Botafogo
Phone 266-6577
11–4; 7–3

A New York bar and grill (owned by a Canadian), with videos, barbecued ribs, and show posters. There are also, of course, hamburgers and roast chicken. This restaurant, popular and crowded, is a good place to meet fellow gringos.

Swiss

Le Mazot
Rua Paula Freitas, 31
Copacabana
Phone 255-0834
Noon–2 A.M.
Moderate

In the heart of Copacabana, one block from the beach, Le Mazot has carriage lamps and wood paneling. The restaurant is small, and there is a bar at the left of the entrance, as well as one downstairs. Try the fondue bourguignonne, osso buco de veau, and the duck (canard). Fantastic desserts.

Le Chalet Suisse
Rua Xavier da Silveira, 12
Copacabana
Phone 255-3320
7 P.M.–2 A.M.
Moderate

Owned by the people of Le Mazot, Le Chalet Suisse is a perfect reproduction of a Swiss chalet, with beamed ceilings, rosewood panels, Swiss bells, and Alpine murals. Try the fondue fromage and the soufflé glacé Grand Marnier. There are two floors.

Danish

Helsingor
Rua General San Martín, 983
Leblon
Phone 294-0347
Noon–2:30; 6–1 A.M.

As in many Copenhagen restaurants, Helsingor, set in a private Scandinavian house with two indoor dining rooms and a terrace, specializes in large open sandwiches on Danish buns. Helsingor also serves filet mignon with sour cream and potato, roast beef with bacon and onions, chicken with tomato, and smoked salmon with asparagus. There is an endless smorgasbord Saturday and Sunday for lunch.

Polish

A Polonesa
Rua Hilário de Gouveia
Copacabana
Phone 237-7378
7 P.M.–1:30 A.M.
Inexpensive

Here since 1940, tiny and simple, A Polonesa is the place to get stroganoff, borscht, herring, and gefilte fish.

Confeitarias

Confeitarias, fancy coffee shops, are quite prevalent in Rio and very popular for late-afternoon pastry or cocktails.

Confeitaria Colombo
Rua Gonçalves Dias,
32
Downtown
Av. Copacabana, 890
Copacabana
Inexpensive

Extremely well known and packed, Colombo has a charming shop downtown, broken into a take-out, stand-up eatery, and a dining room and balcony. Colombo is designed with towering ceilings and huge chandeliers. They serve meat pies, pastries, and candy that is lined up around the place in glass jars. For dinner try breaded drumsticks, stuffed crabs, and meat pies. The Copacabana branch has none of the pleasant amenities, but is otherwise similar.

Tiberius
Av. Vieira Souto, 460
Ipanema
Phone 267-3122
Noon–3 P.M.; 6 P.M.–
midnight

On the twenty-third floor of the Caesar Park Hotel, Tiberius is more than a coffee shop, with an excellent menu, offering everything from snacks to breakfast and dinner. The view is wonderful, highlighting Ipanema and Leblon beaches.

Sidewalk Cafés

Castelinho
Av. Vieira Souto, 100
Ipanema

The Castelinho is a comfortable place for an outdoor cocktail or snack. Sandwiches are very reasonable. Crowded always.

Barrill 1800
Av. Vieira Souto, 100
Ipanema

Enjoy live music most evenings at Barrill 1800, next door to Castelinho, where you can order a snack or a full dinner. There's a bar too, with a whiskeria next door. A late-night espresso stop, with good sandwiches and cakes. It's a block from the beach, with outdoor seating on bright yellow tables and chairs.

Garota da Ipanema
Av. Vieira Souto
Ipanema

Across the street, Garota da Ipanema is more renowned. Vinicius de Morais composed "The Girl from Ipanema" while seated here. Nearby is *Varanda de Ipanema,* very similar.

In Copacabana there are numerous outdoor cafés on the Avenida Atlântica. You'll spot their colorful umbrellas immediately. Stop for a chope (beer from the tap) and watch the passing scene. Endless shoeshine boys, lottery salesmen, and hookers are all part of the backdrop.

Fast Food

La Mole
Rua Dias Ferreira, 147
Leblon
Rua Armando
Lombardi, 175
Barra da Tijuca
399-0925
11 A.M.–2 A.M.

La Mole is a popular and prevalent (there are five other locations) sophisticated fast-food restaurant. The prices are great, the menu is extensive, and the restaurants are convenient. Open-air tables.

Chaplin
Visconde de Pirajá,
189
Ipanema

Charlie Chaplin is still a draw in Rio, and this restaurant is testimony to the eternal allure. Murals of Chaplin in various film scenes dot the walls. Buy a ticket from the cashier in front, pick up your food, and find a seat in the rear. Waffles, hamburgers, and ice cream are good.

McDonald's
Rua Hilário de Gouveia
Near Av. Copacabana
Copacabana

The golden arches have arrived in Rio and can be found in Copacabana. The Big Mac and the quarter pounder (Quarterão) taste and cost exactly the same as back home.

Pancake Bar
Rua Rainha
Quilhermina, 95C
Leblon
Rua Rainha Elizabeth
85D
Copacabana

A Brazilian version of I-Hop. This is a popular stop for families. Prices are reasonable.

Rock Dreams Café
Almirante Pereira
Guimarães, 79A
Copacabana

This is yet another hamburger stop.

Bob's
Rua Garcia D'Avila
Ipanema

Bob's is a chain that serves crêpes, egg platters, and chicken at modest prices. It's a stand-up eatery.

Gordon's
Visconde de Pirajá
(facing Pl. General
Osorio)
Ipanema
Av. Copacabana,
Copacabana

Sandwiches, such as hamburgers with tomato, ham and onion, and hot dogs, are specialized at Gordon's. Another house specialty is cappuccino (made with cognac).

Bonis
Rua Siqueira Campos
(at Av. Copacabana)
Copacabana

Good pastries and crêpes.

There is also an American-style coffee shop at the Hotel Savoy Othon, and boardwalk vendors proffer tasty hot dogs (cacchoro quente).

Rio – Sunup to Sundown

Rio's fabulous weather makes sunning, swimming, and other water-based activities definite possibilities year round. It is a rare day in August when the sun doesn't shine here. You will want to spend many of your daylight hours enjoying the fine weather and swimming, water skiing, surfing, or sailing. You can explore a new beach each day of your stay or you can find one that fits your mood and then stick with it. Rio has more beautiful beaches than any other city in the world.

The city has more to offer than beaches, however, and you will want to spend some time exploring Rio's other faces.

Two mountains dominate Rio's skyline: Sugarloaf and Corcovado. Sugarloaf (Pão de Açúcar), thimble-shaped and reached by cable car, offers terrific views of the city from its place beside Guanabara Bay. At night lively clubs operate on the summit. Several action-packed scenes from a recent James Bond movie were shot on Sugar Loaf and its cable car, but your ride will be a lot tamer.

More sedate Corcovado, part of the inland mountain range, is home to Rio's most photographed sight, the towering, 125-foot-high Christ the Redeemer statue.

You will also enjoy a boat ride around Guanabara Bay and a stop at one of the picturesque islands found there. These offer water sports, bicycle riding, and privacy.

Over ninety percent of the world's gemstones are found in Brazil, some of which are delicately cut, polished, and set in stunning 18-carat gold settings, while others are roughly cut and shaped into ashtrays, jewelry boxes, and paper holders. Great for gifts! Here in Rio you have an opportunity to see how an ugly rock becomes a beautiful swan—er—jewel. H. Stern, Brazil's largest jeweler (and one of the most widely known jewelers in the world) has organized a tour of his museum and workshops. Here you can follow the entire process. It's a fascinating, educational experience, it's free, and you are under no obligation to buy a thing. Of course, your willpower will be sorely tested.

Since the common perception of Rio is strictly Hollywood hype—lithe women in tiny bikinis lolling on a sun-drenched beach or dancing to the samba beat—you might be surprised to learn that Rio has museums, twenty-one of them in fact, and some will be of interest to you.

While Rio's beaches make it hard to do, if you pull yourself away from them you will find many other interesting things to do in *Cidade Marivilhosa.*

Rio's Beaches

Less than a century ago, Copacabana and the Atlantic stretch were almost unreachable. The beaches of prominence were on Guanabara Bay to the east. Not until the construction of Tunel-Velho (old tunnel) in 1892, linking Botafogo to Copacabana, was the Atlantic easily accessible. The building of the Copacabana Palace Hotel cemented both the move away from the bay and Copacabana's fame.

Copacabana, Ipanema, and Leblon are now the most famous beaches in Rio, and for that matter Brazil, but Barra, a bit past Leblon, is the beach of the future, with development going on at a quick clip. Barra and the adjacent São Conrado are experiencing a real influx of wealth and development, and because of its relative isolation, the beach is wonderful and unspoiled.

When venturing out to the beach, there are a few safety measures to keep in mind. The first rule of thumb is not to bring valuables with you. If you must bring them, keep them well hidden in a bag. Never leave anything alone. If you are approached by a group of boys, keep your hands on your belongings. Chances are that they will try to pull a con job of some kind on you. Also keep in mind that the water gets rough during the afternoon and that a red flag is warning of just that, while a green flag means that the water is fine for swimming.

There are approximately fifty miles of beaches in Rio, from Guanabara Bay in the east to Sepetiba Bay in the west.

Beaches on the Bay

Four beaches are on Guanabara Bay. *Flamengo Beach*, which fronts the Gloria Hotel and the Santos Dumont airport, is closest to downtown and is adjacent to Flamengo Park. With the park's grass paralleling the sand, Flamengo's beauty is heightened, but the beach itself is not a popular one and is used mainly for sunbathing and sports. Flamengo offers a great view of Sugarloaf, and the sunsets from here are fantastic.

Botafogo Beach, adjacent to Flamengo Beach, is home to the Rio de Janeiro Yacht Club and is the departure point for the Bateau Mouche boats, which make day trips into the bay. The beach is perfect for sailing.

At the foot of Urca Hill, where there is an excellent view of the city, is *Urca Beach.* The beach is small and the fort of São João is here.

Dividing the bay from the Atlantic is *Praia Vermelha* (Red Beach). At the foot of Sugarloaf, Vermelha, a small beach with thick, dark sand, is popular with swimmers.

Beaches on the Atlantic

The official start of Copacabana and the Atlantic beaches is Leme, which is the eastern part of a six-kilometer beach strip. It is quieter and less crowded than its neighbor. Leme is often referred to as "Posto I." There are six posts along Copacabana (they are one kilometer apart) and each is marked by a lifeguard stand.

Copacabana is synonymous with *beach*. It is probably the most famous, most photographed, and most exciting beach in the world. If you are anticipating a Miami Beach-like hotel strip, you are mistaken. A solid row of buildings of all sizes and styles does line the beachfront street, Avenida Atlântica, but most of them are apartment houses. The hotels are understated and not readily apparent. The cariocas did not build Copacabana for tourists but for themselves. Recently upgraded by landfill, the beach is wider than ever but is still very crowded on weekends. The mosaic sidewalk is full of people, seeing and being seen, and the small streets nearby have bars, restaurants, and shops that are also filled. Swimming, sometimes an afterthought here, is more fun than on the bay, for the waves are often high. Copacabana draws cariocas from every walk of life.

Copacabana stretches for more than two miles, ending at Copacabana Fort in the west. It houses 300,000 middle-class cariocas. The hotel landmarks here are the Meridien in the east (at Leme), the Othon Palace (mid-beach), and the Rio Palace (at the western tip).

Just beyond Copacabana surfers reign at *Praia do Diabo* (Devil's Beach) and *Arpoador*. With obviously rougher waters, Arpoador is on the other side of Copacabana Fort and begins, after Copacabana's curve, the stretch of Ipanema and Leblon.

Ipanema, enshrined in song as in "The Girl from . . . ," is a more affluent area. The community is very residential and is rather upper class with newer buildings and some nice private homes. The beach is almost as crowded as Copacabana on weekends, but it is a more homogeneous group—chic, young, and fit. No one sits still here. They jog, play volleyball and soccer, or swim. Ipanema has fewer hotels on the beachfront (only Caesar Park and the Ipanema Sol) and restaurants and shops are two blocks away. Because most swimmers leave early, Ipanema quiets down earlier. The beach is wide and the water just rough enough to enjoy.

Just beyond Ipanema, a canal crosses the beach strip. It is the link between the Atlantic and Rio's stunning lagoon mid-city. The beach beyond the canal is Leblon.

Leblon, Rio's wealthiest area, has fewer hotels (only the Marina Palace and Marina Rio front the beach) and fewer restaurants and shops as well. Leblon has posh apartment houses, tree-lined streets and plazas, and almost a suburban atmosphere. Smaller in length than Copacabana and Ipanema and less crowded, Leblon ends at Avenida Niemeyer. Here the city changes and the areas beyond are less developed.

Gávea, the next beach community, has grown rapidly. The first sand strip here is *Vidigal*, which fronts the Sheraton Hotel and has topless bathers. It is quiet and rarely gets large numbers of cariocas. Beyond Gávea is the beautiful *São Conrado* (also called Pepino), which is one kilometer long and has two luxury hotels, the Intercontinental and Nacional. Home to a special breed, the hang glider, this beach is almost deserted during the week. On weekends it draws a local crowd.

The rapid development in this area will certainly make it an even more popular beach in the near future.

The next stretch of beach is in *Barra* and at nine miles is the longest. Reached by Joá Road or Lagoa-Barra Highway, Barra is in the midst of becoming more developed and an upscale Copacabana. The first few miles already have many restaurants and nightclubs. The construction and development are obvious. Barra is the Leblon of the future; many of the famous institutions of Leblon and Ipanema are opening branches and shaping Barra's future now. The western end of Barra is remote and sparsely developed. The clear green water and cooling ocean breezes make this area very attractive.

The end of Barra is marked by a large rock and *Recreio dos Bandeirantes*. Quiet, less crowded, and good for swimming, Recreio is a pleasant change from crowded Copacabana. There are people here only weekends.

Grumari, thirty minutes from Ipanema on Barra is almost deserted on weekdays and only slightly less so on weekends. It is almost entirely untouched by man and has just a few nice little restaurants.

Touring the Beach Strips

You'll want to spend many of your daylight hours on these delightful beaches and everyone will have a personal favorite. But the beaches are such an integral part of life here that to understand how the city has grown, you should follow the beach strip from Flamengo, an older, established community, to Barra, a new, growing one. En route you will pass many of Rio's new, affluent neighborhoods and see some beautiful scenery. Leave it to the cariocas to come up with a novel way to see the beaches and have fun too.

Jardineiros, open-sided buses, ply the beach routes daily. The stops are marked by wooden posts and the round trip will cost about twenty-five cents. Of course, if you bring a bathing suit along you can stop for a swim en route.

Rio's Mountain Landmarks

Corcovado

Corcovado (the word means "hunchback") is topped by a statue of Christ the Redeemer, which stands 125 feet tall. Because of the statue the mountain is world famous, but the view the mountain gives of the city and ocean is as great a phenomenon. The mountain top is 2,326 feet high and towers over the city.

One of the first people to climb the mountain was Dom Pedro I, but it was his son, Dom Pedro II, who gave permission, on January 7, 1882, for a railroad to be built to the top. The entire ride to the top was first completed in 1885.

The idea for the statue of Christ was first proposed in 1921, the country's centennial. Between 1926 and 1931 the statue was erected, with costs covered by donations given in churches.

Construction on the statue began in Paris, with the French sculptor, Paul Landowski. The statue weighs 1,450 tons, and the reach from fingertip to fingertip is 75 feet. It is made of concrete and granite and done over in soapstone.

The view from in front of the statue is an overview of the entire city, except for the north view behind Corcovado. Guanabara Bay is to the left and Copacabana, Ipanema and Leblon to the right. Sugarloaf is directly in front of Corcovado. Below the mountain is the Lagoa (lagoon), Joquei Club, and Botanical Gardens.

At 1,300 feet is *Vista Chinesa,* an observation point marked by a green pagoda. Two hundred feet higher is the Mesa do Imperador (emperor's table), which offers slightly different angles and views of the city below.

The top can be reached in several ways. There is a train or, the mountain can be ascended by car or, if you prefer, with an organized tour. Taking a tour relieves you of the feeling that you are missing something. The guide will point things out and the tour should be reasonably priced.

Riding the train is fun in and of itself. As the train climbs, the view slowly widens. A lot of the mountain is pure greenery and the train ride reveals its beauty and abundance. New Swiss trains have just been installed and can be taken from their own station at Rua Cosme Velho, 513, from 8 A.M. to 8 P.M. The station on Ladeira dos Guararape can be reached by cab or by car.

Going up the mountain by car (or taxi) is also a possibility. The mountain can be reached by Rebouças Tunnel from the Lagoa. There is a toll at the Paineiras Hotel.

Sugarloaf

Corcovado's sister peak, Sugarloaf (Pão de Açúcar), which is shaped like a giant bent knee, is Rio's other landmark. Located on the water, Sugarloaf is more commercial than Corcovado, but provides no less spectacular a view.

First scaled in 1817 by a British woman, the mountain from that point became a dueling ground between British and Brazilian climbers competing for territory. Climbing is still practiced on weekends.

You are better off taking the cable car. The idea for the cable car first surfaced in 1908. The first run, reaching 650 feet, was on October 9, 1912, for fifty members of the press; three days later the cars were open for the public. The whole mountain was finally spanned by cable car on January 18, 1913.

The old cars, German-made, were used for sixty years. In 1972, new cars were introduced to fulfill the extraordinary demand. Italian-made, they can carry up to seventy-five passengers in a car.

The first run of the cable car is from Praia Vermelha Station to Morro da Urca, about 700 feet high. The peak at Urca has a restaurant, a disco, a museum, and a playground and is host to a terrific Carnival ball. There is always live music outside. Urca offers a great view of Guanabara Bay.

The second run on a different cable car rises almost vertically to a point of nearly 1,500 feet. The view from atop Sugarloaf is as sprawling and as magnificent as the one from Corcovado, but from an entirely different vantage point.

The cable cars run from 8 A.M. till 10 P.M., and the disco is open till 1 A.M. The samba clubs have shows starting at 9:30. The mountain is easily reached by cab, by bus 511 from Copacabana, or by bus 107 from downtown.

Other Daylight Possibilities

On Water

Bateau Mouche Boat Rides

For an in-depth tour of Guanabara Bay, with its many islands and islets, Bateau Mouche is a solid boating tour company sailing out of Botafogo. The company has morning cruises leaving at 9:30 and returning at 1:30. This tour takes in the lower half of the bay and includes lunch and a stop at Piratininga Island.

The afternoon cruise sails the top half of the bay and leaves at 2 P.M. The tour includes Niteroi Bridge and a stop at the island of Paquetá. The boat returns at 6:30. A combination of the two tours is also available.

Bateau Mouche is located at Av. Nestor Moreira in Botafogo (phone 295-1997, 295-1947, 295-1896).

Paquetá

Guanabara's loveliest island, Paquetá, is only one square kilometer large. The attraction is its beauty and the fact that there are no cars.

Known as the Isle of Love, Paquetá has many beaches: José Bonifacio, Tamoio, Moreninha, and Praia das Gaivotas (beach of the gulls). Located in the top part of the bay, farther from the mainland, the water is clear and the sand soft and white.

To explore the island, there are three options—one can walk, take a horse-drawn carriage, or bicycle. The island is romantic and secluded, although on weekends it can be crowded with tourists.

Boats leave for Paquetá regularly from Praça XV and take about one and a half hours, costing about 50 cents. Departures are at 5:30 A.M., 7:10 A.M., 10:15 A.M., 1:30 P.M., 5:30 P.M., 7 P.M., and 11 P.M.

A hydrofoil also goes to the island in about twenty-five minutes. Departures are from 7 till 4 weekdays and 8 till 5 weekends and cost about $1.

The Bateau Mouche also stops there.

There are three modest hotels on the island: Fragata, Lido, and Cabana.

On Land

Botanical Gardens
Founded in 1808, the Botanical Gardens cover 340 acres and have over 5,000 types of plants and trees, as well as an abundance of birds and animals.

Located behind the Jockey Club at Rua Jardim Botanico, 1008 (phone 274-3896), it is open from 8 A.M. till 6 P.M. On the premises are the Kuhlmann Botanical Museum and the Museum of Dry Plants.

Jockey Club (race track)
Behind the Botanical Gardens, the race course is also on the Lagoa and makes for a beautiful view; Corcovado is starkly clear from the track.

Races are held Saturday and Sunday at 2 and Monday and Thursday at 5, all year round. The grandstand, which costs less than $1, holds 35,000 people. There are five other stands, two private, three for the public.

There is a grass track one and a third miles long, a sand track one and a quarter miles long, and a training sand track. There are stalls for 1,600 horses. Brazil's most important race is the Brazilian Grand Prix, which takes place on the first Sunday in August.

Tijuca Forest

The largest park in Rio is Tijuca National Park, which is made up of eight different forests, Tijuca being the best known.

Dense, but well paved, Tijuca's most mountainous part is the Alto da Boa Vista, which can be reached by Lopes Quintas to the Botanical Gardens and the Estrada Dona Castorina. This route passes the Chinese View and the Emperor's Table. The park has a 100-foot waterfall in its midst and several restaurants. The park is open from 7 A.M. till 9 P.M.

The Hippie Fair

Held every Sunday at Praça General Osório in Ipanema, the Hippie Fair is popular with both cariocas and tourists. The fair has nothing to do with hippies as Americans know them, although some of the artists exhibiting here are Bohemian looking. The Hippie Fair is actually an extensive flea market.

With goods from tapestries to belts to bags, sandals, wallets, masks, trays, jewelry, and instruments, the fair is a veritable department store in the sun.

Vendors set up anywhere in and around the plaza and there are many young and unestablished artists here selling their paintings. At times, Indians from the Amazon attend the fair and sell some of their crafts. One can spend from one dollar to hundreds. The fair is the perfect place to buy a gift or souvenir. Bargaining is taken for granted and expected; don't buy it at the initial price. The fair is held from 9 till six.

Maracanã Stadium

The largest stadium in the world, Maracanã can hold close to 200,000 people. It was built for the 1950 World Cup and still holds the crowd record.

Although the crowd seldom reaches the full potential, it does consistently pass 100,000 for heated matches between local rivals and big World Cup matches, if Brazil is the host country.

Games are played Sunday at 5 p.m. and Saturday at 9 p.m. There is a tour of the stadium during the week from 9 till 5 with entry through Gate 15 on Rua Prof. Eurico Rabelu. The tour takes in the museum in the stadium, a view from the presidential box, the locker rooms, and other points of interest.

The stadium is connected to a smaller stadium, Maracazinho, seating 20,000, that is used for basketball, volleyball, and concerts. An Olympic pool is also on the premises.

Maracanã has a perimeter of 944 meters and a distance of only 375 feet from the field to the farthest seat. It is located near Quinta da Boa Vista, downtown. Make every effort to see a match. Check for schedules in the *Daily Post* or ask at the hotel desk.

Streetcar Touring

Santa Teresa, a hilly, picturesque residential section, has been bypassed by the age of technology. A *bonde* (streetcar) trolley runs through the area. Unfortunately Santa Teresa has not been bypassed by crime, so if you take this enjoyable ride, leave your valuables behind.

Gemstone Tour

Brazil is the foremost producer of gemstones in the world, with ninety percent of the earth's supply. Emeralds, aquamarines, tourmalines, the yellow-gold citrine topaz, amethysts, and now some diamonds are almost solely the natural possession of Brazil.

The many gemstones are buried in various parts of the country. Emeralds are uncovered in the states of Goiás and Rio de Janeiro. Aquamarines are found in Rio Grande do Norte, Bahia, and Espírito Santo. Tourmalines are unearthed in Goiás, Ceará, and Minas Gerais. Citrine topaz is found in Mato Grosso, Ceará, and Rio Grande do Sul. Amethysts, finally, are found in Ceará, Bahia, Minas Gerais, and Espírito Santo. The Brazil earth also turns up such gems as opals, garnets, sky-blue turquoises, and tiger-eye beryls.

A very intricate process, requiring precision and skill, is involved in taking what looks like a big rock with blue or yellow parts and removing the gems. Brazil's largest jeweler (as you might expect, Brazil and especially Rio has lots of jewelers), *H. Stern,* offers an informative and fascinating peek at this process. The company, which by the way has shops (over 150 of them) in thirteen countries, has arranged a tour (in English) of its workshops and has even opened a gem of a museum (pardon the pun). You can watch every step of the process—how gems are found, cut, shaped, faceted, polished, and set in an 18-carat gold setting. The tour, which is free, is self-paced and you can linger at the museum, which exhibits the world's largest uncut gemstone—a sparkling aquamarine. A gift shop and handicraft store are here too. You are under no obligation to buy anything, but you will have to exert all your willpower to resist. Jewelry is customs free upon returning home and of course is tax free here. Tours from 8:30 till 5:30 daily. Free transportation to the H. Stern Building at Rua Visconde de Pirajá 490, corner of Rua Garcia d' Avila, Ipanema, is available from many hotels.

Planetarium
Completely remodeled in 1976, the Planetarium is on Rua Padre Leonel Franca, Gávea. Why go? Because you've probably never seen the southern sky before and the constellations are so different, it is astonishing. Look for the Cruzeiro do Sul (Southern Cross), which is to every Brazilian what the Big Dipper is to us.

Parks
Rio, a city already engulfed in greenery and forest, is also park-filled. The largest is Tijuca National Park (previously mentioned), where Corcovado is located. The Botanical Gardens exist, like any prefabricated garden, as a sampling and an exhibit.

    Flamengo Park, though, is the most famous. Reclaimed from Guanabara Bay, Flamengo Park is 1.2 million square meters and has 13,000 trees. Located right in the midsection of the city and crisscrossed by a major highway, the park has on its premises Santos Dumont Airport, the Museum of Modern Art, the Carmen Miranda Museum, the Museum in Honor of the Dead of World War II, the monument to the Dead Soldiers, a skating rink, and space for sports such as tennis, football, basketball, and volleyball.

Rio has many other parks worth seeing. *Campo de Santana* has many animals that roam free and many lakes. Relaxing and quiet, the park is located on Av. Presidente Vargas, in front of Dom Pedro Training Station. This park is where the Republic was proclaimed in 1889.

Quinta do Boa Vista is home to the National Museum and Zoo.

Parque Lage, Jardim Botanico, 414, is a small wooded area with serene lakes, gardens, and coves.

Parque da Cidade, Estrada Santa Marinha, at the end of Gávea, has ten acres of lawns and ponds and is in sight of the City Museum.

Parque do Cantagulo, Av. Epitácio Pessoa, on the Lagoa, is pretty and has tennis courts, cycle tracks, and playgrounds.

Tivoli Amusement Park

Located on the Lagoa near the Jockey Club, Tivoli Park, although named after the one in Copenhagen, is more American in style and substance. With many rides for kids of all ages, Tivoli, like its American counterparts, has many fast-food counters. Closed Monday, Tivoli is open Tuesday through Friday from 2 till 8, Saturday from 3 till 11, and Sunday from 10 till 10. Tivoli is on Av. Borges de Medeiros Sul.

Museums

Rio has twenty-one museums in all. The range is like that of any big city, from art to culture to history to science. Entrance fees are modest.

The *Museum of Modern Art,* Av. Infante D. Henrique, 85 (Flamengo), is just that. Destroyed by fire in 1978, it has no permanent collection, but is host to a rotating schedule of exhibitions. Open Tuesday through Sunday, 12:15–6 (phone 210-2188).

Chácara do Céu, Rua Murtinho Nobre, 93 (Santa Teresa), has a varied collection of Brazilian and foreign paintings, sculptures, ceramics, furniture, and engravings. In an old mansion, the house is worth seeing for itself. Open Tuesday through Saturday, 2–5; Sunday 1–5.

The *National Museum, Quinta da Boa Vista* (São Cristóvão), has more than one million items, including Brazil's botanical, ethnological, mineral, and classical antiquity collections. The actual building of the museum was done in 1803 and it was given, as a gift, to Dom João VI, who lived in it, then turned it into a museum in 1818. Both Dom Pedro I and Dom Pedro II lived in the house near the zoo and Fauna Museum. The National Museum is open Tuesday through Sunday, 10–4:45.

Museum of the Republic, Rua do Catete, 179 (Flamengo), is dedicated to Brazil's history since it became a republic in 1889. The building was erected between 1858 and 1866, and was previously the presidential palace, Catete Palace, until 1954. The museum has 2,700 different items dating from the Republic era. The ground floor has furniture and paintings; the second floor is in the original palace style; the third floor has the bedroom of President Getulio Vargas, who committed suicide there. Open all week from 9–6 (phone 225-4302).

The *Natural History Museum,* Praça Marechal Âncora (Centro), contains items from Brazil's discovery in the fifteenth century to the establishment of its republic in 1889. It houses historical treasures, colonial furniture and sculpture, paintings, maps, and other artifacts. The building itself was once São Tiãgo Fort and dates back to the early seventeenth century. It is considered Brazil's most important historical museum. Open Tuesday through Friday, 10–5:30; Saturday and Sunday 2:30–5:30.

The *National Fine Arts Museum,* Av. Rio Branco, 199 (Centro), has paintings by Brazilian and foreign artists. Broken into the Brazilian Art Gallery and the Foreign Art Gallery, the museum also has furniture, porcelain, crystal, and engravings on exhibit. There are 10,000 items. Open Tuesdays and Thursdays 10–6:30; Wednesdays and Fridays noon–6:30; Saturdays and Sundays 3–6.

The *Museum of the City,* Estrada Santa Marinha (Gávea), is located in the Parque da Cidade. The museum traces Rio's past in chronological order. Occupying the house of the Marques de São Vicente, it has been there since 1948. Open Tuesday through Sunday, 12–4:30.

Itamarati Palace (Diplomatic Museum), Av. Marechal Floriano, 196 (Centro), was the headquarters for the Foreign Ministry until 1960. The building was constructed in neoclassical style, and dates back to 1954. Recently renovated, the 21-room museum has works from Brazil's best artists and also furniture, porcelains, and silverware. Open Tuesday through Friday, 11–5.

The *Indian Museum,* Rua das Palmeiras, 55, is devoted to the history of Brazil's native residents—their culture, art, rituals, economics, and survival. It is the only museum in the country devoted solely to Indians. Open Monday through Friday 10–5; Sunday 1–5.

Carmen Miranda Museum, in Flamengo Park on Av. Rui Barbosa, is devoted to the belongings, trivia, memorabilia, and history of famous Brazilian star and singer Carmen Miranda. Open Tuesday through Saturday, 12–5. Nostalgia buffs will love this one.

Rio's other museums are devoted to such subjects as the military, music, movie personalities, movie history and arts, sports, and the police.

Municipal Theatre

Modeled after the Paris Opera, and opened July 14, 1909, the theater now offers guided tours. But if you can, see a ballet or concert here. It is located on Av. Rio Branco, downtown.

Sports

To say soccer is the national pastime is to miss the point completely. It is the national passion. Soccer (called *futebol* here) is to Brazilians what baseball, football, and basketball *together* are to Americans. It is the World Series and the Super Bowl. It is watched obsessively and played everywhere by men and boys of all ages.

Games played on the beaches and park lawns are taken seriously and played fiercely with amazing grace and expertise.

Brazil's national teams have won the World Cup several times and have played in the finals more than any other country. Pele, a hero in Brazil, is the most widely recognized athlete in the world. But the national teams are just the highest point of a soccer network that exists throughout the country and is made up of local teams.

Rio's several local teams are excellent and play as relentlessly as the national. Flamengo, Fluminense, and Vasco are probably the best local teams, with Bangu, Botafogo, and America added in. The teams compete for the regional title. There is also a national title to compete for.

The clubs play in huge Maracanã stadium on Saturday night and Sunday. Watching them is highly recommended.

Rio also has other sports. Many parks have recreational facilities for tennis, basketball, volleyball, and riding. Jogging on the beach is popular. The city has facilities for boating, sailing, fishing, gymnastics, hang gliding, ice skating, cricket, skydiving, squash, windsurfing, and surfing. The Jockey Club has horse racing. Car racing can be seen at the Autodromo, with the big race the Grand Prix. Sailing and fishing can be arranged through the Yacht Club (265-0797) on Botafogo Beach. Golf can be played at a course in Gávea, private, but welcoming visitors (phone 265-0797). It's next to the Hotel Intercontinental. Itanhanga Golf Course (399-0507) in Barra da Tijuca also allows guests. Basketball and other sports can be seen at the stadium next to Maracanã, Maracanãzinho.

Shopping

Whether you are a dedicated shopper or a casual one, whether you want to buy a memorable gift or an inexpensive one, you will enjoy shopping in Rio. Shops, some elegant and others very rustic and casual, are located in the downtown commercial area and in Copacabana and Ipanema. New shopping centers are springing up throughout the city as well.

Rio's best buys are gemstones and the jewelry pieces they are set in. Because most of the world's gemstones are found here, the city offers a wide variety of stones; styles range from highly traditional to the avant-garde. Important factors to keep in mind are that there is no tax on jewelry here and that jewelry made in Brazil is not subject to customs duty.

Brazilian handicrafts and folk art are colorful and will really add zip to your kitchen or living room. Primitive paintings of Brazilian life are good buys and very attractive. Craftsmen here produce beautiful ceramics, tapestries, and many items made of jacaranda (rosewood) wood. Small gift items such as papagaio kites, wall masks, and *figas* (good-luck charms) are always well received back home.

Clothing boutiques stock mostly sportswear, for even middle-class Brazilian women have their dress clothes made to order. In keeping with Rio's cosmopolitan image, imports are widely available, but Brazilian-made goods are still the best values. Clothing prices are roughly equivalent to those in the U.S. Free alterations can be made in one or two days.

When shopping, you will find English spoken widely. Browsing is permitted, but you will find salespeople waiting to help you.

Main Shopping Areas

Deluxe hotels have good shopping arcades. Shops are representative of those found elsewhere and prices are comparable although at the upper end of the scale. Good shops also have branches near hotels. Major shopping areas are:

1. Copacabana: Look for boutiques, crafts, and leathers on Av. Nossa Senhora de Copacabana and Rua Barata Ribeiro.

2. Ipanema: The city's finest boutiques are on or near Rua Visconde de Pirajá. Don't forget the Sunday Hippie Fair in Praça General Osório.

3. Downtown: Many handicraft stores are located on Rua Gonçalves Dias from Largo da Carioca to Rua Buenos Aires. This is an interesting area to walk around in too.

4. Leblon: A smaller but upscale shopping area is centered around Av. Ataulfo de Paiva.

Gemstones and Jewelry

Brazilian soil is rich in minerals, and the country produces ninety percent of the world's gemstones. The country's jewelry stores also outnumber those of any other country in the world. Jewelry is less expensive here than anywhere in the world.

The aquamarine is a member of the beryl family of stones (emeralds are in this group too). These stones are found in varying shades of blue, with the darkest shades the rarest.

Tourmalines come in green, red, pink, and blue, with the green hue the most popular. Lighter-colored gems are most costly.

A gold-yellow precious stone, the topaz is one of the rarest gemstones. There is also a citrine category of topaz, which comes in yellow and is found in Bahia, Rio Grande do Sul, and Goiás.

Amethysts are purple stones and the darker the better.

Other gemstones commonly found in Brazil are cat's eye, opal, and agate. Emeralds sold here now compare with those sold in Colombia and Africa.

H. Stern, with a thirteen-story building in Ipanema (Rua Visconde de Pirajá 490, at Rua Garcia d' Avila) and shops in deluxe hotels throughout the city, is Brazil's largest jeweler. Jewelry and typical charms come in all price ranges and utilize every variety of stone imaginable. Styles vary and there is something to suit every taste and most budgets. Very nice service too. With a year-long, worldwide guarantee as to quality and repair, how can you lose?

Another reputable concern with shops throughout Copacabana and Ipanema (often near Stern shops), *Amsterdam Sauer* also specializes in fine Brazilian gemstones set in 18-carat gold settings. All prices.

Folklore Shops

Handicrafts in the form of jewelry and good-luck charms are very popular with cariocas. The most commonly seen charm is the *figa,* a clenched fist with the thumb extended between the second and third fingers. They are often made of jacaranda wood, but more elaborate figas of gold, sometimes enhanced by a gemstone, may be seen. They are available in sizes as large as a carved paperweight. Figas were originally worn by black male slaves and were considered to be fertility symbols. They are thought to bring good luck, and they are considered by some as essential for warding off evil spirits.

The *penca* is a necklace or bracelet that holds a variety of charms designed in the shapes of fish, coconuts, bananas, or other foods. This object is another vestige of the era of slavery, when the penca was given to a slave by his owner for good behavior. Each act of good behavior earned another charm to add to the bracelet, and with numerous charms the slave became more valuable. Large-size pencas are often hung on the kitchen walls of homes.

The *saci* (soss-ee) is a statuette of a one-legged black boy who wears a stocking cap and smokes a pipe. A nineteenth-century legend has him an imaginary trickster who plays practical jokes on travelers. Usually the saci is a charm, but larger versions will be found in people's homes.

Another popular charm is made from the polished tusk of a wild boar and trimmed with gold, silver, and/or gem-

stones. Besides jewelry, there are papagaio kites (pronounced papa-gayo), wax shrunken heads, and numerous
household objects carved from jacaranda wood, including
trays, bookends, and masks.

Casa do Folclore   A casual shop with English-
Rua Garcia d'Avila, 113 speaking salespeople (easy on
Ipanema   the tourist), it has a good selec-
                          tion of figas, pencas, papagaio
kites, wax shrunken heads, and objects carved in
rosewood. Particularly interesting are pins and pendants
fashioned from the workings of antique watches. Raw
mineral fragments, as well as cut and polished gemstones
to be purchased and set at home, are available. Prices are
moderate.

Thompson   This shop has a Chinese owner
Av. Copacabana, 371-A who sits at the back near the
Copacabana   cash box. Prices here are the
                          lowest in Rio (for the quality).
The boar-tusk charms are reasonable and a good value.
There are fine figas and jacaranda wood dishes and trays.

E. Simon   There are jacaranda salad bowls
Av. Copacabana, 339-C for $24 and up, and superb ice
Copacabana   buckets at $60. Carved figures
                          of Bahian women are $18 and
                          up, and there is also a jewelry
                          section.

Siri   The store has some unique ob-
Av. Atlântica, 1536   jects, including a paperweight
Copacabana   fashioned from lucite with a
                          pretty butterfly mounting. The
jacaranda wine server and salad bowl set (six pieces) and
the serving platters are handsome and a good buy.

Minas Souvenir
Rua Fernando Mendes, 28-C
Copacabana

There are Bahian costumed dolls sold here that make great gifts. English-speaking salespeople will show you the boar-tusk charms, wood trays, and tapestries. Good, inexpensive costume jewelry.

Eskada
Av. General San Martín, 1219
Leblon

Eskada and the shops that follow mix folklore with a variety of other objects of interest. Eskada sells planters and brilliantly colored ceramic lamp bases. The three-room shop is filled with brightly colored paintings and ceramics and wood items that make the shop eye-catching and fun to visit.

O Sol
Rua Corcovado, 213
Jardim Botanico
Phone 294-5099

A tiny shop in a private house in the Jardim Botanico, O Sol has rows and rows of linen, basketry, and ceramic products, handcrafted. The knitted shoulder bags are $12 and up. Brightly colored end tables and painted floor chests are lined up here too.

Star Jewelry
Rua Duvivier, off Av.
Copacabana

The shop has a stone chess set and natural grain wood tables, along with other items of interest.

Tapestries

The finest tapestries to be found in Rio are made by Patrick Kennedy, son of an Irish doctor and a Bolivian mother, who developed his skill in tapestry weaving while recovering from malaria in Salvador. Kennedy continues to produce tapestries with strictly Bahian motifs that hang in the homes of wealthy cariocas as well as in restaurants and hotels. He has remained in Bahia and operates an art gallery and a studio there.

**Rei dos Gobelinos Tapecaria
Rua Santa Clara, 50
Shop 202
Copacabana**

This shop holds a large selection of fine handmade tapestries in Brazilian and French motifs. There is a wide price range.

**Blue-Bay
Rua Prudente de Morais, 1286
Ipanema**

Blue-Bay is another shop worth browsing in.

**Galeria Irlandini
Rua Teixeira de Melo, 31
Ipanema**

A small and versatile gallery in Ipanema, Irlandini exhibits styles ranging from primitive to modern abstracts.

**Galeria Bonino
Rua Barata Ribeiro, 578
Copacabana**

A converted barn, Bonino retains an informal atmosphere that is a draw to local collectors.

**Galeria Rachid Belas Artes
Av. Rio Branco, 156
Downtown**

This gallery is worth investigating for its primitives.

**Solo Espaço de Arte
Rua Visconde de Pirajá, 547
Ipanema**

Another gallery worth visiting is Solo Espaço de Arte.

Galeria Rio
Rua Barão de Ipanema,
43
at corner of
Av. Copacabana
Copacabana

Good primitives can be found at Galeria Rio, with a large assortment of paintings by Silvio Pinto, a fine local artist. It's open 9 A.M. till 11 P.M. and is halfway off the street, so you'll have to look for it.

Boutiques

Most of the good boutiques are found on Rua Visconde de Pirajá on the seven blocks between Praça General Osório and Praça Nossa Senhora da Paz. Sportswear is emphasized in most of these tiny shops, including pants, tops, suits, and bikinis. Denim is popular.

Les Griffes
1702 Ave. Atlântica
(Copacabana)
486 Rua Visconde de
Pirajá (Ipanema)

Very nice costume jewelry and fine leathers and linens are sold here. You'll also find such designer names as Cartier, H. Stern, Louis Ferand, and Pierre Cardin.

Centro Commercial
General Osório
Rua Visconde de Pirajá
Ipanema

This is a miniature shopping center with three floors of boutiques. *Love Love,* on the first floor, has denim goods. Also on the first floor, *Lib Boutique* and *Fruto Prohibido,* with embroidered jackets and sweaters; bikinis at *Avant-Premiere Boutique.* Upstairs, *Maria Cebola* has tops and costume jewelry. There are chic dresses and nice jackets and pants at *Não and Sim.*

Forum de Ipanema
Praça Nossa Senhora da
Paz
Ipanema

The small gallery of shops here includes *Marisa,* where you'll find quality handbags and belts at good prices. For shoes, try *Cantão.*

Galeria 444
Rua Visconde de Pirajá
near Galeria Beco de
Ipanema
Ipanema

Another arcade, where the shops to look into are *Aujourd'hui Boutique,* with a good choice of house dresses and skirts, *Sorry* for Indian-style tops, *Res do Chão* for bikinis, and India House.

Michel, an elegant and expensive boutique on Rua Visconde de Pirajá, has a good women's department.

For bikinis, there is one shop to try especially: *Bum Bum Bikinis,* which has an entire arcade at Rua Visc. de Pirajá devoted to two-piece bathing suits, in every size, shape, and color imaginable. Bum Bum was recommended by local friends. Another shop to try is *Ki Tanga,* on the Rua Visconde de Pirajá. There's another branch in the Rio Sul shopping center.

Along the Rua Garcia d'Avila, there are some other clothing boutiques to try: *Drishna, Elle et Lui,* at number 124, *Company,* at number 56, and *Bee,* at number 83.

For Men

A good place to shop for men is *Michel,* which is expensive but will give you a feel for Brazilian fashion even if you don't buy anything. The emphasis here is on trousers, shirts, and sweater-type jackets. There are shoes and belts as well. Open till 7 P.M.

Dom Vicente
Rua Visconde de Pirajá,
233
Ipanema

This is a good shop for shirts, some with lots of ruffles.

For offbeat clothing, try *Elle et Lui,* with some wild shoes and boots as well, and *Mau Mau,* near Rua Farme de Amode. Try *Jopar* (Galeria Beco de Ipanema) for a wide selection of shirts.

For Children

You can pick up a T-shirt with a cute slogan for your children at the *Malhas Herring* shops around town.

Leather

Brazil owes its abundance of leather to a thriving cattle industry in the south.

Copacabana Couros E Artesanatos
Rua Fernando Mendes, 45-A
at Av. Copacabana
Copacabana

An impressive array of objects in leather includes folding leather chairs, leather hassocks, lampshades made of tooled leather, and a handsome mirror with a leather frame; there are leather wallets and belts as well. All items sold are handmade on the premises. This is a popular shop and is usually crowded.

Badalhoka Artesanato
Av. Copacabana, 455-B
Copacabana

A wide selection of handbags, belts, and wallets, all in hand-tooled leather.

Victor Hugo
Av. Visc. de Pirajá, 507
Ipanema

For fine leathers, you may also want to try Victor Hugo, across from the San Marco Hotel in Ipanema. There's another branch in Rio Sul shopping center. Find wallets, handbags, luggage, belts, cases, and more. The store is open from 9 A.M. till 6 P.M.; closed Sunday.

Art

In Brazilian primitive art, realistic Bahian scenes predominate. The style employs a broad stroke, and most work is done in oils or water colors. Gildemberg is one of the best known primitive artists here, along with Chatel, who until recently was living in Rio.

Brazilian artists have achieved international notice for their contemporary abstract paintings, which come in as broad a range as the work that can be found in New York galleries. A good way to get a feel for the contemporary art scene is to visit the Museu de Arte Moderna in Flamengo before going to the galleries.

Prices are not low, although you pay far less in Brazil than in New York for work of equivalent quality. Prices generally range from $60 and up for unknown artists, and $250 and up for the more established and better known. At auctions, you will have to compete with Brazilian buyers who have plenty of money to bid up the prices.

Galleries usually are open late—till 10 p.m. Full listings of exhibits can be found in the Caderno section of Saturday's *Jornal do Brasil*.

Most of the galleries will be found in Copacabana and Ipanema. Exhibits change every three or four weeks.

Shopping Centers

Rio Sul, Av. Lauro Miller, 16, Botafogo, was the first big shopping center in Rio, and with Barra, ranks as one of the main complexes. There are branches of all the major stores including fashion, electric, and gift stores as well as a large supermarket. There are plenty of snack bars and restaurants—even one on the roof. Rio Sul is open Monday through Saturday, 10 till 10. There is free parking. Free buses run between the shopping center and most of the major hotels. Or you can take a cab—it's a short ride from all major hotels.

Cassino Atlântico, beneath the Rio Palace Hotel, in Copacabana (Av. Atlântico, 4240) is one of Rio's best-designed centers in terms of aesthetics. There are three levels. It's the best place to go for art and antique shops. On Saturdays from noon till 7 p.m., there are specials on certain antique objects. At 4 p.m., there's live classical music to listen to while you hunt for antiques.

At *Barra Shopping* (Av. das Americas, 4666, Barra da Tijuca), the biggest shopping center in the city, you'll find hundreds of shops and department stores in one place. The top stores in Brazil (Mesbla, Sears, C & A, Lojas Americanas, H. Stern, Cine, Babs) are here as well as the top brand names. There are three cinemas, an ice rink, and arcade games, as well as numerous snack bars, including a McDonald's. *Pe do Atleta* sells a huge array of sporting goods, from bikinis to tennis equipment, soccer balls, and sportswear. It's also a good place to pick up gifts for kids. Shoes are a great buy, with Adidas and Ocean Pacific sneakers in stock. In the southern lobby, there's a newsstand that stocks every U.S. magazine. *Elle et Lui* and *Pandemonium,* both good boutiques for women's clothing, can be found here. There is also an *H. Stern* outlet on the upper level. At *Rio Antigo,* have a snack of ice cream or pizza on a patio decorated in 1850s style. Barra Shopping Center is open Monday through Saturday, 10 till 10. Bus service is available between Barra and all parts of town. There's also a free shuttle bus that starts in Leme at 9:15, 10:45, 3:15, and 4:15, and stops at the major hotels along the ocean street.

Next to Barra is *Carrefour,* Rio's best supermarket, part of the largest supermarket chain in Brazil. It's open Monday through Saturday from 8 A.M. till 10 P.M.

At the *Rio Design Center,* Av. Ataulfo de Paiva, 270, in Leblon, you'll find dozens of stores that specialize in home goods: ceramics, furniture, tiles, paintings, wicker goods, and more. There are also exhibits, and on the lower floor, the *Nobili restaurant* is open from 11 A.M. to midnight. *Gea Revestimentos* is an interesting store that sells inlaid wood. On the first floor, *Arte Pura* is another store that's fun to browse through. At *Votre Galerie,* on the second level, you will find original art. There's also a gallery called *Casa Rustica* on the third floor that sells antiques and primitive art. Parking is free with a purchase or a meal.

The *Gávea* shopping center, at Rua Marquês de São Vicente, 52, Gávea, has 230 stores on four levels. Many of these are small, privately owned stores that sell all types of products for the home. There are some top furniture designers here, and some of the best art galleries. Gávea has three theaters and a cinema. It's open from Monday through Saturday. Paid parking.

Antiques

Most so-called antique shops in Rio are more closely akin to junk shops that display a jumble of household goods, some old, some just quaint, but they do have nice things and are fun to browse in.

Snob
Rua Barata Ribeiro, 244-A
Copacabana

Try Snob for fine copper plant holders and striking crystal decanters. There are fine brass wall plates too. String instruments are for sale, lovingly restored. Prices start at a dollar or two.

Canturias Antiquidades
Rua Inhanga, 7B
Copacabana

There's a good assortment of fine quality items to poke through at Canturias.

Old Style
Rua Francisco Sa, 51
Copacabana

At Old Style you'll find a true mixed bag. You can find lamp bases, soup tureens, vases, wall plates, old swords, etc.

Hippie Fairs

The Hippie Fair, or Feirarte I, is an outdoor flea market held in the Praça General Osório on Sunday from 9 A.M. till 6 P.M. Over a hundred booths sell handicraft items ranging from handbags, jewelry, tie-dyed shirts, paintings, and wood carvings to musical instruments. Goods are displayed on the ground, and the atmosphere is highly informal. This is not just a market but an event, so bring your camera.

There's another Hippie Fair, Feirarte II, that operates on Friday in the Praça 15 de Novembro from 9 A.M. to 5 P.M. There's a variety of goods from hammocks to handmade clothes and stalls that sell Bahian food.

Or stop in at the Hippie Center, Rua Visconde de Pirajá at Rua Garcia d'Avila, for recordings, posters, and sandals.

For Children

Children flying kites are one of the most common sights on Rio beaches. The most popular kite is the colorful papagallo (bird), spelled *papagaio* and pronounced papa-gayo. The kites are made of brightly colored cloth, and come in two sizes. The best place to buy them is from the beach vendors or at a folklore shop. Also sold at the beach are parachutes and styrofoam airplanes. All are excellent gifts for the children, large or small, who await you at home.

Carrossel Brinquedos
Rua Garcia d'Avila, 69
Ipanema
Circus Brinquedos
Rio Sul Shopping Center

These are two outlets for Brazilian-made toys that are worth visiting. Both have large selections, with the most interesting being toys for the beach that are different and not overly expensive.

Bookshops

Periodicals such as the *International Herald-Tribune* and *Reader's Digest* can be found at a number of places. More widely sold at kiosks around town are the Latin American edition of *Time* and the English language daily, the *Brazil Herald,* that comes with the *Daily Post.*

Entrelivros and Eldorado are chains with branches all over Rio. You can buy the *Herald-Tribune* here, as well as

North American books and magazines. The Entrelivros at Av. Copacabana and Rua Francisco Sa is particularly well stocked.

Behind the Copacabana Palace Hotel is Livraria Nova Galeria de Arte, Av. Copacabana, 291, which has a good selection too.

Finally, there's the newsstand at Praça General Osório, where you can buy English language dailies as well.

Music

Rio's music scene is still dominated by samba. Recordings of top stars in Brazil are sold in department stores and folklore shops. Folklore has a large selection. One of the most popular names is Silvio Caldas.

Liquor

Liquor stores as well as some supermarkets sell Brazilian wines and liqueurs. Aguardente de cana is one of the most famous; it's a potent sugar-cane extract used in batidas and caipirinhas. Aguardente is also called pinga and cachaça, and sells for $1 and up.

A good white wine is Precioso suave. Almadén and Granja União Merlot are good red wines. Crème de Café, a fine domestic coffee liqueur, is around $5 a bottle.

Two liquor stores downtown are Gryphus, on Rua Gonçalves Dias, and a shop in the main branch of the Colombo tea shop. There is also a liquor store for departing passengers in the Galeão International Airport.

Airport Shops

Galeão International has the usual duty-free liquor, tobacco, and coffee available. You can also purchase souvenirs made by Amazon Indians at Artindia Funai, and gemstones at the H. Stern outlets, open twenty-four hours.

Excursions

Trip possibilities out of Rio are numerous. The northern coast is a great attraction, and so are the mountains.

Niterói

Niterói, across the bay from Rio and reached by the Rio-Niterói bridge or by boat or ferry, was the capital of the state of Rio de Janeiro and was founded in 1573. The bridge offers spectacular views of the bay, of departing Rio, and of oncoming Niterói—the trip across the bridge is worthwhile by itself.

Niterói, with nearly 400,000 people, is the second city in the state of Rio de Janeiro. Previous to the merger of the states of Rio and Guanabara, Niterói stood alone, but is now almost a sister city. Niterói is interesting for two outstanding reasons, its beaches and its history. Its beaches on the bay are as polluted as those in Rio, but pretty. Icaraí, São Francisco, and Jurujuba are worth seeing for their beauty and their views of Rio. Farther away from the city core are beaches like Piratininga and Itacoatiara (both about twelve miles away) that are cleaner and just as beautiful.

The historical side of Niterói is quite interesting. The city is lined with churches dating back to the sixteenth century and outlined by forts. Past the beach at Jurujuba is Fortaleza de Santa Cruz, which dates back to 1565, when it was built to guard the bay. It was built by Villegagnon, who colonized Rio for the French, and is considered architecturally very important. Still used by the military, the fort is highly recommended.

Other forts are Imbuí on the point of Imbuí, which offers spectacular views of Barão do Rio Branco, built in 1633, and Gragoatá and Nossa Senhora da Boa Viagem.

The city's churches also highlight the past. São Francisco Xavier church, constructed in 1572 between the beaches of São Francisco and Charitas, is worth seeing. The church Nossa Senhora da Boa Viagem, right next to the fort, is beautiful. It is located on an island three kilometers off the mainland, but is connected by a causeway.

The city has a few museums, with the most interesting the Museu de Arquelogia de Itaipu at the ruins of the eighteenth-century Santa Teresa Convent.

A city of Niterói's size has a number of hotels. Novotel is probably the best and is located on Rua Cel. Tamarindo, 150, Praia de Gragoatá (phone 719-315). The Niterói Palace is located at Rua Andrade Neves, 134, Centro (phone 719-2155).

Búzios (North of Rio)

In the district of Cabo Frio, and about two and a half hours from Rio, Armação de Búzios, or Búzios, is a small vacation village on the coast. It was discovered only about twenty-five years ago, and has slowly transformed from a fishing village into an elite and exciting vacation town. Made popular by Brigitte Bardot, Búzios became the affluent outlet for the overcrowded Cabo Frio nearby. But with word trickling out, Búzios, too, is becoming more crowded.

Búzios was originally founded by Portuguese settlers protecting the land from pirates. The town, throughout the centuries, lived by leasing its beaches to fishermen. Fishing was the mainstay until tourism arrived.

What makes Búzios so attractive is its quaintness and serenity. Although popular, it is not yet overcrowded and retains a rustic nature. The wealthy who primarily occupied it kept their homes hidden and molded them to the setting; there is nothing towering or sparkling with glass. It has a lure to it that is almost like Newport, but on a much smaller and less ostentatious scale. The roads are unpaved, diminishing the number of cars and their speed. There are twenty-seven sandy coves, the water is clear, and there are seventeen beaches.

Azeda dos Búzios, Ferradura, Foca, Praia do Formo, and Brava are more private beaches, with Ferradurinha a hidden cover beach. More popular beaches are Ossos and João Fernandes.

Downtown there are many stores and boutiques. Búzios also has a lot of artist and artisan residents, who sell their work around town.

To get to Búzios from Rio, take a bus to Cabo Frio, the larger beach town nearby, and another bus to Búzios. Costair Airlines will fly you to Cabo Frio on Friday and Saturday, and you can bus it or take a taxi. Call 253-3001 (Rio).

There is a modern highway from Rio if you want to rent a car. Cross the Niterói bridge and follow signs to São Gonçalo and Rio Bonito, passing Campos and Manilha to BR-101. Take BR-101 to the outskirts of Cabo Frio, then pick up RJ-106, which will take you to Búzios.

Hotels in Búzios are called *pousadas* (inns) and have no addresses. It is necessary to book in advance.

Auberge de l'Hermitage is a four-star hotel, which is more a resort. On Manguinhos beach, L'Hermitage has sixteen apartments, and its own restaurant (one of the best). The hotel also is equipped with air conditioning, TV and video room, tennis courts, volleyball courts, sauna, conference facilities, and game room. In Rio call 222-8282, 222-8385, or 224-6757.

Cabanas de Búzios has thirty cabins close to Manguinhos Beach. The cabins have living rooms, double bedrooms, a bathroom, and a small bar with refrigerator, and can sleep two to four. There are two swimming pools, tennis, and a restaurant. In Rio call 294-7345.

Casas Brancas is located atop a hill overlooking the village. The pousada has eleven rooms, a pool, air conditioning, TV and video room, and a bar. Call 274-2030.

Gravatas is probably the largest pousada in Búzios with 62 rooms. It is situated on Geriba Beach and has air conditioning, TV room, bar, game room, sauna, and a restaurant that serves lunch, which is included in the daily rate. In Rio call 232-1601, 242-3204.

Mandragora is well equipped with tennis courts, squash courts, air conditioning, minibar in each room, bar, TV room, and restaurant. Its fourteen rooms are a short distance from the center of town. In Búzios call 224-2348.

Martim Pescador is atop a hill and offers a great view. This homey pousada has ten fully air-conditioned rooms, a bar, and a private restaurant. In Búzios call 224-2317.

Pousada nas Rocas (Inn on the Rocks) is a popular resort situated on a small island, Ilha Rosa, 700 meters from the coast. With sixty bungalow rooms, each with TV, minibar, and refrigerator, Rocas also has air conditioning, a video and game room, three bars, a pool, tennis courts, a jogging track, a helipad, its own airstrip, and the facilities for most watersports, including its own schooner and windsurfing. There is live music and a golf course is on the drawing board. In Rio call 253-0001, in Búzios 245-2303.

Restaurants: *Le Streghe*, Av. Ribeira Dantas; *Zill & Le Petit Truc; Cabana; L'Assisate; Fernando's Point; Oasis; Satiricon; Casa Velha*. All types of food can be found in Búzios.

Costa Verde (South of Rio)

Costa Verde (Green Coast) follows the Rio–Santos Highway. It is the coast that lines the area where the states of Rio de Janeiro and São Paulo meet (280 kilometers from Rio). As its name implies, the area is lush and dense with greenery and rolling hills. The verdant landscape is a beautiful counterpoint to the ocean. The area is quiet, calm, and very colonial in architecture.

Along the way are such places as the *Itatiaia National Park*, 174 kilometers from Rio, a preserved forest with many waterfalls. *Angra dos Reis* looks over the Ilha Grande Bay and has many beaches, islands, and marinas. Its colonial buildings are still intact. It is the site of Brazil's first atomic power station and has growing industries, but they are a small intrusion on the beauty. Look for *Frade Portogalo Hotel*, a fully equipped and luxurious resort, and *Hotel do Frade*, also luxurious.

Where the states of Rio de Janeiro and São Paulo meet is the historical town of *Parati* (280 kilometers from Rio). Founded in 1650, Parati was the major thoroughfare for gold coming from Minas Gerais headed for Portugal. With the completion of the Rio–São Paulo road, Parati lost its importance and literally faded from memory. Because of that isolation, Parati now, after its rediscovery in the twentieth century, is totally untouched and preserved, almost an antique from the colonial era. Parati is a national monument, and is considered by UNESCO to be one of the most important examples of colonial architecture in the world.

Parati means "Home of the Gods" in the Indian language of the Tupi-Guarani, and the town was the setting of John Doorman's film, *The Emerald Forest*.

Three of Parati's best pousadas are *Pousada Dom João*, with a pub, tea house, home cooking, and an eighteenth-century mansion; *Mercado de Pouso*, 230-0943; and *Frade Pousada Parati*, 267-7375.

There are no cars allowed in Parati.

Petrópolis

About one and a half hours from Rio in the mountains, the city of Petrópolis was the summer home of Dom Pedro I and II. Founded in 1829 by Dom Pedro I, the town is still, as it was then, a village of aristocrats.

During the yellow fever epidemic in Rio, Dom Pedro spent more time here, and the town became the primary escape for the wealthy and the elite. Its importance grew even more as it became a stop on the Rio–Minas Gerais Road.

Petrópolis was named after Emperor Pedro II, who spent all of his summers there with his family and entourage. The land was originally owned by the aristocratic families of the area.

The city now has 150,000 people and is no longer a community of nobles, but its mountainous beauty still exists and so do some of the relics of the age of Dom Pedro.

The summer palace of Dom Pedro II is now the Imperial Museum, which contains a gold crown, with over 500 diamonds and pearls, and the telephone given him by Alexander Graham Bell. The museum is open daily from noon till 5:30 (closed Monday), and one should visit the throne room containing Pedro II's gold crown and his gold-embroidered robe. The museum is located at Av. 7 de Setembro, set back from a garden which today is really a park.

The *Grand Quitandinha,* a haunt of kings and queens and once a classical and grand resort, still functions, but in a more pedestrian way. Its architecture, though, is intact and reveals some of its lordly past. Today a condo, it was in its day a famous hotel and casino catering to the jet-setters of the 40s and 50s. Its Norman architecture is still worth a visit.

Other sites include the cathedral where the tombs of the emperor and empress are located, Santos Dumont's house, and the Crystal Palace.

At an elevation of 2,800 feet, the drive is magnificent. Petrópolis is reached from Rio by following Av. Brasil past the airport to Rodovia Washington Luis.

In and around Petrópolis are small factories making cotton-knit items. Rua Tereza is lined with endless shops offering these items at supposed bargain prices. You can find the same items in Rio, but why not pick some up at the source, a trophy of your visit to Petrópolis.

Another mountain town and a retreat for Empress Teresa is Teresópolis, named for her. Now with a population of 80,000, Teresópolis is a small city with many vacation homes belonging to wealthy cariocas.

Serra dos Orgãos National Park, near Teresópolis, is recommended for its greenery, and in town one should see Colina do Mirantes Hill and the Imbui and the Amores waterfalls and lakes.

Nightlife

Nightlife in Rio is of course diverse and active. Bars, clubs, and restaurants stay open late, because cariocas love to party. There is an enormous variety of things to do at night, ranging from the opera to soccer matches, or frenzied visits to any of Rio's sinful establishments: piano bars, discotheques, strip joints, even an English pub decorated with pictures of the queen. There are also English-language cinemas and samba and macumba demonstrations. Cultural events, such as the theater, ballet, and fine classical concerts, are also readily available.

The best listings for all nightly events will be found in the daily newspaper *Jornal do Brasil* in the Caderno B section. Listings are in Portuguese but are easy to follow. You can also check the *Daily Post*, the English-language daily.

Teatro Municipal

Rio has its own first-rate ballet and opera companies and a number of orchestras, the finest being the Brazilian Symphony Orchestra (OSB) and the Orchestra of the Teatro Municipal. It is also a prime stop on the world tour circuit, attracting top names in all the above mentioned arts. The standard stop is the Teatro Municipal, a huge 2,000-seat theater located near the Praça Mahatma Gandhi at Av. Rio Branco and Praça Floriano downtown. You'll find the prices pleasantly moderate in view of the quality of the performances. The theater was modeled after the Paris opera house. I've enjoyed fine productions of *Otello* and *Rigoletto* at bargain prices. The Cafe do Teatro restaurant is here as well.

Check these theaters for classical music:

Sala Cecilia Meirelles
Largo da Lapa, 47
Downtown
Phone 232-9714

Teatro João Caetano
Praça Tiradentes
Downtown
Phone 221-0305

and for ballet and dance:

Teatro Nelson Rodrigues
Av. Chile, 230
Downtown
Phone 212-5695

Nacional
Hotel Nacional
São Conrado
Phone 322-1000

The Cinema

Brazil is one of the world's major movie markets and foreign movies are very popular, especially in Rio and São Paulo. Portuguese subtitles are added to foreign-language films in lieu of dubbing, so European and American releases can be seen with the original soundtracks. Check the *Jornal do Brasil* for listings. Dudley Moore in Portuguese is still Dudley Moore. Many of the good movie houses are located in Cinelandia, the downtown section around the Praça Mahatma Gandhi. In Copacabana, check along the Av. Copacabana and on Rua Visconde de Pirajá in Ipanema.

The Theater

For English-language drama, try the Escola Americana in Gavea, where admission is only about $4 for excellent performances. Tickets may be picked up at the American consulate (downtown) or at the British School. Curtain is at 8:30, and listings can be found in the *Jornal do Brasil* (phone 322-0825).

Samba

The beat of the samba is the beat of Rio. Samba music is heard everywhere—on car radios, in shops and restaurants, in boxes carried to the beach and in nightclubs.

People smile when they hear it, their step quickens and even elderly cariocas can be seen snapping their fingers as they hear a big samba beat. Part of a Rio experience is to "experience" samba. If you are here for Carnaval you'll hear enough samba in five days to last a lifetime. But the beat is alive year round and you'll want to watch the "pros," watch the cariocas, and watch your own feet. We guarantee you won't sit still for long. It's definitely contagious.

Samba Schools

To compensate yourself for missing Carnaval in Rio, be sure to visit a samba school, where you'll see the real thing, if only in rehearsal. Each school (actually a social club) creates floats, hand sews elaborate costumes, and prepares original songs and dance numbers around a set theme, in hopes of winning a Carnaval prize. Rehearsal schedules are printed in the *Jornal*. These are virtually year-round events.

A Samba Nightclub

Clube do Samba
Estrada da Barra da
Tijucá, 65
Barra
Phone 399-0892
11 P.M.–4 A.M.
Friday, Saturday

The Clube do Samba, organized by some of Rio's top names in samba, is the best place to see authentic samba performances. There's one large room with a stage and a live orchestra. Sandwiches, light meals, and drinks are available; tables are reserved. There's a bar in a small garden where you can go to cool off. A full program is offered Wednesday through Saturday, with big name stars on the weekends. There's a 1 A.M. show that lasts one and a half hours. The name of the performer for each night will be listed on the marquis. Check the newspaper for performers and times too. Cover is under $5.

Samba Dance Halls

Club Renascença
Maxwell Sports Club
Rua Maxwell, 174
Villa Isabel

Club Renascença is earthy, loud, and fun, and is frequented by Rio's working class. The pace is frenetic, particularly on weekends, when there's even dancing on tables. Dress is informal. A cab is needed to get there, but the ride is worth it.

Gafieira Estudantina
Praça Tiradentes, 79
Downtown
Phone 232-1149
10 P.M.–4A.M.
Friday, Saturday

Gafieira Estudantina is another great place for samba. Located on the second floor of an old building, there's a bandstand and lots of musicians. Dancing is on bare floors. Check newspapers or call for performers.

Elite
Rua Frei Caneca, 4
Praça da República
Downtown
Phonc 232-3217
11 P.M.–4 A.M.
Saturday, Sunday

Similar to Estudantina, but slightly tacky, is Elite. Head up a steep flight of stairs to the music, twenty musicians strong.

NOTE: The neighborhoods surrounding Elite and Estudantina are not safe for walking. Make sure you take a cab to the entrance and have them call one for you when you leave.

Nightclubs

The nightclub scene in Rio starts to move at 11 P.M. Dress is informal. In clubs with shows, cover charges are steep, and there's often a two-drink minimum as well. Drinks generally run about $1.50; $4 to $5 for imported liquors.

As in most Brazilian cities, the clubs in Rio are geared toward couples. Single men, if well-dressed, might be admitted, but unfortunately, unescorted women are often turned away by doormen. You can try showing your passport.

Show Clubs

These clubs present lavishly costumed and plumed dancing girls and singers, in Las Vegas-style shows.

Canecão
Rua Wenceslau Bras, 215
Botafogo
Phone 295-3044
8:30 P.M.–4A.M.
Reservations advised

Canecão is considered to be Rio's top nightclub. A Radio City Music Hall show done in Carioca-style, it holds two thousand people and presents really superior shows. There are two alternating orchestras, one Latin, and one U.S. pop. Shows change three or four times a year. The club is located near the Rio Sul shopping center beyond the tunnel.

Clubs with Live Music

Made in Brazil
Av. Armando Lombardi, 1000
Barra da Tijucá
Phone 399-2971
10 P.M.–5 A.M.
Friday, Saturday

Stop by Made in Brazil for the best stage music: live salsa, samba, bossa nova, rock, jazz, and reggae. It's a large and somewhat noisy club of several rooms located in a private house about ten minutes beyond the Sheraton in Barra. Food is served, but it's best to stick to drinks. Head downstairs for open-air seating beside the pool. Inside you'll find a stone fireplace and wooden chairs placed around tables.

People
Av. Bartolomeu Mitre,
370
Leblon
Phone 239-0198,
294-0547
7 P.M.–4 A.M.

The music starts at 9 P.M. and the bar is packed with young people. There is Brazilian music, jazz, and pop. Always crowded, there are lots of singles here, and single men and women are allowed to enter. There is no dancing. The club is dark and attractive, with an antique decor and musical instruments set into the walls. There's a cover for seating at the bar or a table; the show starts at 10:30.

Ilha dos Pescadores
Barra da Tijucá
11 P.M.–4 A.M.

There's a midnight samba show at Pescadores, which is located on a small island in Barra. The restaurant is reached by crossing a bridge from the parking lot; you'll be guided by a sign made of flashing lights in the shape of a fish. There is a samba show as well as a show featuring dancing mulatas.

Mistura Fina Studio
Estrada da Barra da
Tijucá, 1636
Barra
Phone 399-3460
Rua Garcia d'Avila, 15
Ipanema

Mistura Fina Studio is one of the most popular places to find live music: jazz, rock, and disco. There are two locations, Ipanema and Barra, although the one in a private house in Barra is better. It's comfortable, and the music is good. There are shows on the weekend. Single women are allowed here.

Circo Voador
Largo da Lapa
Lapa (Downtown)
Phone 265-2559
10 P.M.–3 A.M.
Friday, Saturday

The Circo Voador, or flying circus, features a circus-like arena with a dance floor that presents samba shows that alternate with singers. There are a few large bleachers and bandstands inside, although most people stand.

Popular and cheap, the circus is frequented mainly by the younger set.

Cafe Un Deux Trois
Av. Bartolomeu Mitre, 123
Leblon
Phone 239-5789
10 P.M.–4 A.M.
Seven days

Un Deux Trois features excellent local bands, playing nightly from 7 P.M. The show features Silvio Caldas, a Brazilian singer famous for his quiet romantic music and his sambas. There's a cover for the 10:30 show, which has music to dance to and the show at midnight as well. The club is dark and intimate with booths and tables available. Downstairs, there is a restaurant of the same name, offering international cuisine, from pato laranja to saumon bonne femme.

Shows for Tourists

These shows are colorful and flashy, with lavish costumes and many dancers. Shows generally run a year at a time and are packed—usually a tour bus or two are parked in front. If this is your cup of tea, enjoy!

Scala Rio
Av. Afranio de Melo Franco, 296
Leblon
Phone 239-4448
11 P.M. Monday, Thursday, Sunday
Midnight Friday, Saturday

Huge and well known, Scala was built with the idea of creating "the Moulin Rouge of Rio" by its owner, Chico Recarey. The club is immense, (it seats 1,500 people) with a large stage and dance floor and chandeliers hang ten feet above your head. Shows mix African music with bossa nova and samba. Besides the show, there is dancing and an a la carte menu offering anything from an entree to a drink. There's a separate bar on the second floor. The interior is comfortable, with plenty of air conditioning, and offers a great view.

Plataforma
Rua Adalberto Ferreira, 32
Leblon
Phone 274-4022
11 P.M.

The show at Plataforma traces the history of blacks from slavery to the present, using lavish costumes and a colorful display of folklore and rituals brought over from Africa. The story of Black Orpheus is re-enacted, using Carnival scenes as a backdrop. The show also includes a traditional Samba school parade. Shows at 11:30 and 1:30.

Oba Oba
Rua Humaita, 110
Botafogo
Phone 286-9848
11 P.M.

A dinner showplace, Oba Oba features stylish and tastefully done strip shows as well as traditional samba shows. There are long tables with chairs or booths; but the best places for watching the show are up a few steps and away from the stage. On the walls are pictures of showgirls. The club is in a private house, flamboyantly marked with a big lighted sign. M.C. Oswaldo Sargentelli is a houshold name in Rio. This show is not for children, as it is suggestive.

Hotel Nacional
Av. Niemeyer, 769
São Conrado
9 P.M.–4 A.M.

This club features some of Rio's top artists. Similar to but smaller than Scala and Plataforma, the quality is on par with them.

Discotheques

Rio's discotheques play everything from samba to acid rock to Frank Sinatra. Clubs generally open late and close very late. Dress is informal, and singles are welcome at some clubs.

Carinhoso
Rua Visconde de Pirajá, 22
Ipanema
Phone 287-3579
10 P.M.–5 A.M.

Carinhoso has a stage with two orchestras nightly in its bi-level interior. Lighting is intimate and lots of glass is used inside. You'll see the canopy entrance.

New Prive
Rua Jangadeiro, 28
(Praça Gen. Osório)
Ipanema
Phone 267-2544
10 P.M.–4 A.M.

New Prive is large and noisy, and a place to meet and mingle with other singles. There are two levels—downstairs for dancing, and upstairs for eating and drinking at tables. The music goes on till 4 A.M.

Studio C
Hotel Othon Palace
Rua Xavier da Silveira
Copacabana
Phone 236-0695
9:30 P.M.–4 A.M.
Seven days

This is one of the chic-est discos, with art deco decor, featuring black on white plaid satin upholstery. The music is loud, and continues into the early morning hours.

Regine's
Rua Gustavo Sampaio
Hotel Meridien
Leme

An elegant branch of the clubs created by Regine, the red-haired grande dame of disco, the club is frequented by jet-setters and often, tourists, although it's a private club. The interior is posh, with lots of mirrors, but the dress code is more relaxed than sister clubs internationally.

Help
Av. Atlântica, 3432
Copacabana
Phone 521-1296

Help, in Copacabana Beach, has an enormous dance floor with videos and elaborate lighting and sound effects. The club is capable of seating 2,000 people. It's on two levels, with seating all around the rim, and a view of the beach. The interior is done in black and yellow.

Hippopotamus
Rua Barão da Torre, 354
Ipanema
Phone 247-0351
11 P.M., seven days

This is an elegant club that offers French cuisine by the renowned Chef Claude Lepeyre. It's members only but guests at Rio's major hotels are frequently admitted. The restaurant upstairs has glass walls that look out on the garden. Try entrecote hippopotamus, steak au poivre vert or brochette de crevette. On the lower level are the disco and bar, this with leather seats and a glass ceiling.

Caligula
Rua Prudente de Morais, 129
Ipanema
Phone 287-1369

The disco is behind the piano bar and is entered through a swinging door. Roman decor is maintained inside, with columns and balconies. The crowd is mostly young.

Sarava
Hotel Sheraton
Gávea
Phone 274-1122
9 P.M.–2 A.M.

Sarava is one of the more popular discos. The music is live and hot, and the crowd very hip. Take the escalator down from the hotel lobby and turn left.

Zoom
Rua Rodolfo Dantas, 102
Copacabana
Phone 541-9196

Zoom is dominated by American music. There are two disc jockeys, who play it loud. The manager, Luis Koch, speaks perfect English. Although there's no cover, there's a minimum on Saturdays, when reservations are advised. For couples only. Open till 4 A.M.

Texas Club
Av. Atlântica, 974-A
Leme
Phone 275-0246
5 A.M.–3 A.M.

The Texas Club is decorated in true Texas style, with blowups of phoney $100 bills plastered above the bar, and a portrait of good old Sam Houston hanging on the wall. Country music blasts all around. It's half a block from the main Av. Princesa Isabel.

Noites Carioca
Av. Pasteur, 520
Botafogo
Phone 541-3737

This is a popular club for dancing, and the setting is unbeatable; it's halfway up Sugarloaf Mountain, and the view of Rio lit up at night is amazing. Take the cable car to get there, but arrive after 10 P.M., opening time, since the area is deserted until then.

Pub

Lord Jim
Rua Paul Redfern, 63
Ipanema
Phone 259-3047

Lord Jim, one of the most popular anomalies of Rio, is a real English pub, decorated with pictures of the queen, and abounding with emblems of jolly old England, for the homesick or merely curious. Draught beer is served in large mugs and there's a real English-style menu offering fish and chips, beef Wellington, steak and kidney pie, Irish stew, or pepper steak. Dining is upstairs.

Student Hangouts

Papillon Discotheque
Intercontinental Hotel
São Conrado
Phone 322-2200

Papillon is geared toward the young crowd, with most comers no older than 25. The disco is huge and ornate, with large booths and tables, and late hours—10 P.M. till 4 A.M. every day except Monday.

Amigo Fritz
Barão de Torre, 472
Ipanema
Phone 287-5848

The Mascagni opera no doubt inspired the name of this busy student hangout. There's a homey atmosphere here; seating is outside on a terrace, or in indoor booths. The menu offers sandwiches, a pork and sauerkraut platter, and a filet stroganoff.

Luna Bar
Ataulfo de Paiva
(Corner Gen. Venancio
Flores)
Leblon

At the Luna, there is a general sense of vigorous merrymaking. The crowd, mostly students, can be seen drinking and talking it up at the sidewalk tables. Beer, whiskey, and coffee are served.

New Jirau
Rua Siqueira Campos, 12-A
(between Av. Atlântica and Av. Copacabana)
Copacabana
Phone 255-5864
9 P.M.–4 A.M.

New Jirau attracts a young crowd. The atmosphere inside is warm and inviting, with black leather couches and mirrors above the dance floor.

Piano Bars

Biblo's Bar
Av. Epitácio Pessoa, 1484
Lagoa
Phone 521-2645
6 P.M.–4 A.M.

Biblo's is a small bar with live music and a friendly, intimate atmosphere. There are shows on Sunday, Monday, and Tuesday nights, featuring different artists. The interior is attractive, with lots of windows and greenery, and a view of Corcovado. It's next to the Restaurante Rive Gauche.

Chiko's Bar
Av. Epitácio Pessoa, 1560
Lagoa
Phone 267-0113
6 P.M.–4 A.M.

Chiko's bar, on the left bank of the Lagoa Rodrigo de Freitas, is open daily. Local artists perform on the piano and bass, along with singers Celeste and Fatima Regina. A guitarist often performs a repertoire of Brazilian songs on Monday and Tuesday nights. Inside, the bar is attractive, with lots of mirrors and bottles stacked up on the walls. The exterior is particularly striking, facing the lagoon, and beyond, the surrounding forest. Like Biblo's, Chiko's is next to a fine restaurant, Castel da Lagoa. Both are good meeting places patronized by local people.

Caligula
Rua Prudente de Morais
Praça General Osório
Ipanema
Phone 287-1369
7:30 P.M.–5 A.M.

The piano bar is annexed to the disco Caligula, and has a pianist, a guitarist, and a singer. The bar is quite comfortable: a private room of Roman design with pillars, a mirrored ceiling, and a white-and-red motif. Tables have cloths. The disco, which opens at 10, is loud and quite good.

Alo Alo
Rua Barão da Torre, 368
Ipanema
Phone 521-1460

This is Rio's only 5-to-5 bar, and it presents live music to dance to. Seating is comfortable, with red leather chairs set out on two levels. Interesting lighting effects are achieved with glass on the ceiling. Upstairs is the Sal & Pimenta restaurant.

Alvaro's Bar
Av. Ataulfo de Paiva, 500
Leblon
Phone 294-2148
8 P.M.–2A.M.
Seven days

Good for a late-night sandwich and/or chopp (stein) of beer. There is also decent pizza. A tavern atmosphere prevails, with heavy wooden tables and chairs.

Bip Bip
Rua Almirante
Gonçalves
(between Av.
Copacabana and
Av. Atlântica)
Copacabana

Decorated in an English motif, Bip Bip has a standard bar that opens out onto the street. It's good for a quick drink.

Asa Branca
Av. Mem da Sá, 17
Lapa
Phone 252-0966

Asa Branca, located in downtown Lapa, was inaugurated by the king of Spain, Don Juan Carlos I, in May 1983. There's live music downstairs; food is served upstairs in camarotes, private eating areas for groups of 8 or more. Escalopinho and badejo are both recommended.

Café Nice
Av. Rio Branco, 277
Sub-Solo 2
Downtown
Phone 240-0490

There's a cover for Café Nice, a restaurant with live and piped music, similar to Asa Branca. Crowded at night.

Hotel Bars

The Leme, Meridien, and Othon Palace Hotels have lounges with soft, romantic music and great views. There are generally no cover charges.

Bar Jakui
Hotel Intercontinental
São Conrado
Phone 322-2200
7 P.M.–2 A.M.

Bar Jakui, in the Hotel Intercontinental, is open till 3 A.M. on weekends. Listen to piano music with occasional brass accompaniment at the side of the pool.

121 Lounge
Sheraton Hotel
Av. Niemeyer, 121
Gavea
Phone 274-1122

121, in the lobby of the Sheraton, has live combos at night. It's attractive and comfortable, with huge brass columns, couches, and chairs.

Le Rond Point
Hotel Meridien
Av. Atlântica, 1020
Copacabana
Phone 275-9922

Rond Point, on the lower level of the Hotel Meridien, is a great meeting place with live piano music and shows. There are leather couches and a long, red leather bar. Piano music starts at 6 P.M. Shows on Thursday, Friday, and Saturday nights start at 10 P.M.

Leme Pub
Hotel Leme Palace
Av. Atlântica, 656
Leme
Phone 275-8080
6 P.M.–5 A.M.

Formerly a disco, Leme Pub now operates on a smaller scale. A pianist plays and entertains guests with his uninhibited patter. The bamboo interior is inviting. Piano music starts at 11 P.M.

Horse's Neck
Rio Palace Hotel
Av. Atlântica, 4270
Copacabana
Phone 521-3232

Here is an elegant club, and one of the best in town. From 7 P.M., the music of the Horse's Neck Quartet entertains guests.

Men Only

The libertine quality of Rio's nightlife is especially revealed by the number of strip joints. Prices are fair, if not always reasonable.

Assyrius
Av. Rio Branco, 277
Downtown
6 P.M.–5 A.M. (Closed Sunday)
Phone 220-1298

Large and almost elegant in furnishings, this club attracts many couples who come here for the erotic shows at midnight and 1:30 A.M., which include nude dancing and simulated sex. Nude go-go dancers encased in glass begin dancing at 7 P.M., and afterward join the male patrons at the bar. Women circulate and will join you if you wish. The Maitre speaks English as well as French and Spanish.

Erotika
Av. Prado Junior, 63
Copacabana
9:00 P.M.–4 A.M.
Closed Sundays
Phone 275-4899

Similar to Assyrius, Erotika is a cellar club where go-go girls begin at 10:30 P.M. Shows at 1 A.M. and 3 A.M. feature strippers, comics, and general eroticism. Girls circulate.

Bataclá
Av. Copacabana, 73
Copacabana
10 P.M.–4 A.M.
Phone 275-7248

Subterranean, Bataclá is designed to resemble a cave. Despite its wild, clashing colors, the club has a quieter atmosphere than most others of this type. Shows are at 12:30 and 2:30 A.M.

Munich
Rua Duvivier, 18B
Off Av. Atlântica
Copacabana
9 P.M.–4 A.M.

The nude dancers go-go all night, except during shows at 1 A.M. and 3 A.M. The shows feature strippers and occasional dancers. Small and informal, this club has a regular clientele that comes in for a few drinks and to watch the show.

New Scotch Bar
Av. Princesa Isabel, 7
Copacabana
4 P.M.–6 A.M.
Phone 275-5499

The New Scotch Bar has an attractive interior as well as dancing girls. There are striptease shows every half hour with more extensive shows at 11:30 P.M. and 1 A.M. Go-go girls too.

Bar Barela
Av. Princesa Isabel, 263
Copacabana
Phone 275-7349

Not far away is Bar Barela. Both of these are near the Hotel Plaza Copacabana.

Boite Las Vegas
Copacabana
10 P.M.–1 A.M.
Shows Mon., Sat.

Across from Bar Barela is Boite Las Vegas, with a large, lighted sign you can't miss.

Frank's Bar
Av. Princesa Isabel, 185
Copacabana
Phone 275-9398

Frank's Bar near Av. Copacabana, has Samba dancing and striptease on a small stage. It's easy to miss; look for cloaked figures on a wooden wall. Next to Frank's is Boite Miau, a whiskeria.

Within a one block area between Av. Copacabana and Av. Atlântica in Copacabana, are a number of bars to hop from and to, all devoted to the same theme. They are located between Rua Belfort Roxo and Ronaldo de Carvalho.

Pussy Cat Bar
Belfort Roxo, 88
Phone 275-8798

This is a disco bar, not bad looking, that is open from 9 P.M. The blinking sign will attract your eye.

Scherezade
Av. N.S. Copacabana, 187-A
Open 10 P.M.–4 A.M.
Phone 541-2248

A large, plush bar with a mirrored ceiling, this bar is packed with Brazilian women looking to pick up men.

Lido
Ronald Carvalho, 21
Copacabana
10 P.M.–4 A.M.
Phone 541-9248

A somewhat tacky skin joint with go-go girls, and more. Head upstairs to the second floor.

Golden Club
Rua Ronald de
Carvalho, 55
Copacabana
Phone 541-2748

Golden Club has a fancy bar, and mirrored ceiling. Seating is comfortable.

Night and Day
Av. Princesa Isabela

With go-go girls and erotic acts, this club has shows at 11:30 P.M. and 2:30 A.M.

Barman
Rua Belfort Roxo, 58
Copacabana
Phone 275-8599

In this area, the Barman Club is the best of the lot. It's large, with several rooms, and comfortable, with red leather bar and matching chairs. The atmosphere is relaxed and intimate, and there's no cover or minimum.

Gay Clubs

Gay men on the prowl should first head to the Galeria Alaska off Av. Atlântica in Copacabana. The arcade is packed at night with small eateries and clubs with a gay clientele.

Listed below are specific establishments frequented primarily by gays.

The Club
Travessa Cristiano
Lacorte, 54
7 P.M.–4 A.M.
Phone 521-4049

A cozy bar with no cover or minimum is The Club. There is a limited dinner menu, and the food is quite good. Action really begins at 10:30 or later, although the official opening time is 7 P.M. A pleasant atmosphere conducive to meeting new friends.

Sotão
Av. Copacabana, 1241
in the Galeria Alaska
Copacabana
10:30 P.M.–4 A.M. daily

A popular, dimly lit club and disco, Sotão has a bar and small dance floor. There's a two-drink minimum; no cover.

La Cueva
Rua Migel Lemos, 51
Copacabana
10 P.M.–5 A.M.
No minimum

Another club is La Cueva, with roughly the same type of comers.

Incontrus
Praça Serzedelo Correia,
15A
Copacabana
Phone 257-6498

A discotheque with flashing and psychedelic lights where men—usually young—dance together. At one end is the bar. It's in a plaza off Av. Copacabana and Atlântica, down a short flight of stairs.

Papagaio
Rua Borges de
Medeiros, 1426
Lagoa
Phone 274-7748

Fridays and Saturdays, this discotheque is for gay men. It's an enormous dance floor equipped with strobe lights, a DJ's cage, popcorn machines, and a sign that reads "Butterflies are Beautiful."

Gaivota
Rua Rodolfo Amoedo,
347
Barra
Phone 399-0550
Open 10 P.M.–4 A.M. Fri., Sat.
Sunday 4 P.M.–12 A.M.

In a private house, Gaivota has a large dance floor and pleasant interior, with white stucco walls.

Zig Zag
Av. Bartolomeu Mitre,
662
Leblon
Phone 511-1085
Open 10 P.M.–5 A.M.

A gay piano bar not far from People's, Zig Zag is a small place with a lounge upstairs.

Holy Gay
Rua do Passeio
Near Escola de Musica
Lapa

Holy Gay, in Lapa, is a large club with a gay show and a piano bar.

Rio's "Don't Miss" Events

Carnaval (Carnival)

Carnaval in Rio is internationally renowned and is probably peerless in its overwhelming effect upon a city. It is more attended to and important in Rio than Christmas and Easter. It is also the one image that people—whether informed or not—associate with Brazil and it identifies the country to people around the world. Carnaval is, to put it mildly, Rio's main event.

Carnaval is also a way for the poor to forget the overwhelming woes of life. Like futebol, Carnaval is a means to break out of your class and to go beyond the borders of both poverty and protocol. It is an egalitarian event and one beloved by all.

Ironically, Carnaval is not an organic element of Brazilian culture, and even less so of Rio's. Carnaval, (from Italian *carnevale*, "farewell to meat") is a pre-Lenten festival and lasts four days, ending on Ash Wednesday. Its roots are ancient and can be traced back to the celebrations of Osirus and Isis in Egypt and the festivals for Dionysus in Greece and Rome. The church order of the middle ages placed Carnaval before Ash Wednesday, hence making a clear distinction between riotous celebration and solemn homage. However, the major source for Brazil's Carnaval is the pre-Lenten festival in Portugal, which began in the Azores in the fifteenth and sixteenth centuries.

Carnaval, as with many other elements of Brazilian culture, was imported there via Salvador. The pre-Lenten celebration was initially known as Entrudo. Carnaval was created in 1884 as a substitute for Entrudo, which had become violent and out of control. Inherent in Entrudo was an elitism that had become unacceptable to the middle class and poor of Salvador. The rich held wild balls that were not open to the poor. Eventually the poor revolted and Entrudo turned into a mini-war. The press, the government, and the citizens of Salvador became tired of the fighting and in 1884 Carnaval was invented as a democratic and more peaceful alternative to Entrudo.

Rio inherited Entrudo from Salvador. Similar problems plagued Rio, and at one point the police banned all street activities and forced things inside; hence the origin of balls in Rio. The necessity of the balls, which excluded the poor, eventually forced the poor to develop an alternative way of celebrating—hence the street festivals. Cordões (groups of revellers) and the Zé Pereira were the leading groups of street organizers. The Cordões did folk interpretations of the past year's events. Soon afterward the middle class introduced more cohesive processions, which included floats and confetti. The first Carnaval Club, Congresso de Sumidades Carnavalescas was formed.

Zé Pereira eventually faded as Carnaval started to take on its more recent form. Groups like Cordão da Bola Preta, who still traditionally open Carnaval today, Tememtes do Diabo, Femiamos, and Democraticos started to emerge. At the end of the nineteenth century there was still no indigenous music for Carnaval; it was made up of polkas, square dances, mazurkas, waltzes, and the can-can. It was at the beginning of the twentieth century that Carnaval had its first song written: "Abre Alas," composed by Chiquinha Gonzaga for Cordão Rosas de Ouro. The first samba song was recorded in 1917, and in the thirties Carnaval developed its distinctive beat, the samba.

The Carnaval of today, its present form, is only about fifty years old. The celebration begins on Friday night with the mayor of Rio handing the keys of the city over to Rei (King) Momo. Fancy costume balls begin everywhere, with the first one at the Yacht Club. (Actually there is a ball Thursday night, sponsored by the soccer team Flamengo, but the Yacht Club ball is officially first.) Balls are also held on Sugarloaf, the club Monte Líbano, Canecão nightclub, and most five-star hotels. The better ones are at the Gloria, the Copacabana Palace, the Meridien, and the Rio Palace. The Baille da Cidade, City Ball, is held at Scala and gay balls are held at the disco Help and on Copacabana Beach. Awards are presented to those with the best costumes.

Saturday is a street carnival with bandas (bands), small groups with rhythm sections and scanty costumes and the more free-floating citywide festival. The Cordões are the ancestors of the component of Carnaval, which is basically a citywide party on the streets. Hook up with a banda to participate. They can be found in Copacabana, Ipanema, and Leblon. (There is no selection for a banda; just join.) The largest ones are Saturday in Av. Rio Branco.

Sunday night and Monday night are the famous samba school parades which are the highlights of the celebration. Samba became the reigning music for Carnaval when it was searching for its own music. Samba schools are social clubs primarily in the city's poorest areas.

The parade is so long and the route so crowded that an arena was built for Carnaval. Built by famous architect Oscar Niemeyer, the Sambodromo, on Apotheosis Square, has bleachers for 30,000 paying general admission, seating for 40,000 on reserved tickets, 3,500 tables on the street with bar service, and 100 boxes, with a capacity for 5,000, that come with dinner, bar service, and color TV for close-ups. But it is more fun to line the main route for the samba parade as it wends along Av. Marques de Sapucai to Av. Presidente Vargas, and Rua Frei Caneca.

The samba schools actually start preparing for Carnaval as early as the preceding August, when each school picks a theme, which must be strictly Brazilian. By November the schools are organized enough to allow visitors. The school decides upon its main dancers, they choreograph the dance, write the songs and make the costumes.

The actual parade (Desfile de Escolas de Samba) is a competition between the samba schools. Judges use such criteria as the percussion, harmony, samba, story-line, costumes, and the total effect. The judges also take into account the schools' effect upon the crowd and their punctuality.

A school can have as many as 5,000 members parading, and they are broken up into wings called "alos." The "samba machine" controls the procession and school and keeps time for the percussion and dancers. The introduction of the samba school is by "Abre-Alas," the spreading of the wings. The school is made up of the beteria, the percussion players; passistas, the best dancers; the porta-bandeira, mestre-sala, the dance master and flag bearer, who anchor the school; and finally the school director. Two other necessary and important components of the school are its allegoric floats, which are used in many ways, from holding some musicians to introducing the school, and the requisite "Baianas" section, which is in homage to Brazil's roots in Bahia and the African culture which is so dominant there and in the country. The winners parade the following weekend.

The Carnaval of today differs from that of the past by its rigid, competitive structure. The past was not without competition, but it was more spontaneous and disorganized. The three main parts of today's Carnaval are the initial balls, the street festivals and the Samba parade. Carnaval is a celebration to lose yourself in, shake your body like a milkshake and have fun.

Carnavals to come:

1988	Feb. 14	1994	Feb. 13
1989	Feb. 4	1995	Feb. 26
1990	Feb. 25	1996	Feb. 18
1991	Feb. 10	1997	Feb. 9
1992	March 1	1998	Feb. 22
1993	Feb. 21	1999	Feb. 14
		2000	March 5

Samba Schools

Samba, the driving force behind Carnaval, is the performing art of the poor. The schools are social clubs for the communities, places that showcase dancing talent, and, at times, stepping stones to greater fame.

Some samba schools have risen above the status of mere hangouts; they are stratified and competitive, but they still function as community centers.

Every samba is made up of music and dancing, and follows a story line. At this time, samba schools are almost wholly devoted to Carnaval, with most of the year spent in preparation for the festival.

It is possible to visit a school. Check Caderno B, the entertainment section of the *Jornal do Brasil* for listings. Most of the schools are in the Zona Norte and the favelas. There is an exception: Clube do Samba, Estrada da Barra da Tijuca, 65, phone 399-0899, which was formed by many samba stars and is more oriented to tourists (mentioned previously). Rehearsals are at 10 P.M., Wednesday through Sunday.

Primeira Mangueira
Estacāo Primeira de
Mangueira
Rua Visconde de
Niteroi, 1072
Mangueira
Phone 234-4129

Founded in 1928, Mangueira won the first unofficial contest four years later. It is the most popular school.

Portela
Rua Clara Nunes, 81
Madureira
Phone 390-0471

Founded in 1923, Portela has won the samba parade more than any other school.

Academicos dos
Salgueiro
Rua Silva Teles, 104
Tijuca
Phone 288-7822

The most innovative of the top four, Salgueiro was founded in 1953.

Império Serrano **Av. Min. Edgar Romero,** **114** **Madureira** **Phone 390-7285**	Another biggie, Serrano was begun in 1947.

Beija Flor **Rua Praçinha Walace** **Paes Leme, 1652** **Nilopolis** **Phone 791-3195**	Beija Flor has won the contest three times in a row.

A good place to see samba is *Vila Isabel,* close to Maracanã. There is a samba school there, also, called Vila Isabel, which is quite well known.

Macumba

Macumba is, like most everything in the New World, a hand-me-down from another continent and culture. Brought over initially to Bahia (where it is called Candomblé), Macumba is inherited from southwest Nigeria, where it was practiced by the Yoruba people and called Orixia.

Originally the faith of imported slaves, Macumba has now been thoroughly integrated into Brazilian society on all levels, with a cross current occurring between Christianity and the Indian faiths. At this point, more than 10,000,000 Brazilians practice it.

Macumba is a naturalistic faith, underlined by the belief in many gods and spirits, each of whom have power over a particular phenomenon. There are ten gods, ordered by power and status.

Macumba's survival in Brazil is a history of adaptation. Suppressed by slave owners and the Catholic Church, Macumba was pushed underground. Ceremonies were then held on beaches and in forests. To subvert the censorship of repression, Macumba leaders gave Christian names to their gods. The chief god Oxala became linked with Jesus. The goddess Iemanjá became connected to the Virgin Mary and their evil god Exu with Lucifer.

The overriding belief of Macumba is that the gods affect all parts of life and must be praised and prayed to. The rituals encourage the benevolent and constructive gods and repress and thwart the evil ones.

Each house of worship, called a terreiro, has cavalos, who are the mediums between the gods and the faithful. In the ceremony the cavalo calls on the gods and eventually becomes possessed by one, speaking in garbled tongues. The members of the terreiro line up to speak with the god as interpreted by the cavalo. There follows a cleansing ritual and the circulation of herbal medicines. The entire ceremony is counterpointed by singing and dancing and can last for hours.

Outside each terreiro is a small house, surrounded by candles, that keeps the evil god Exu imprisoned. Inside the terreiro, which is a large, dimly lit space, is an altar that holds a crucifix and statues of the Macumba gods, flowers, a glass of water, and a conch. Each terreiro has a headmaster.

Some terreiros are open to the public, but it is necessary to remain quiet and respectful; for it is a religious service, not a spectacle. Remember not to cross your legs—for it is believed to hinder the entry of the god into the terreiro— and no photos are permitted.

The concierge of your hotel can arrange a visit.

Here are some terrerios:

Pai Jeronimo, Rua Barão do Ubá, 423, Praça da Bandeira, Zona Norte.

Tenda Espírita Mirim, Av. Marechal, Rondon, 597, São Francisco Xavier, phone 261-3150.

Palácio de Iansã, Estrada Santa Efigenia, 152, Taquara, Jacarepagua, phone 372-2176.

Macumba charms are very popular. They are sold at: *Casa Expedito,* Prado Junior 160, *Copacabana* at Av. Copacabana, and Rua Ministro Viveiros de Castro; *Barraco de Dovo,* Rua Ministro Viveiros de Castro and Belfort Roxo.

Salvador

Seed of the Nation

he irony of any nation that has one city or one area that becomes almost mythical—New York, Paris, London—is that that place becomes almost a country of its own. Rio is so unbounding in reputation, so implacable a magnet for people, that it has become a culture of its own.

Salvador, Brazil's second most visited city and capital of the state of Bahia, more accurately reflects Brazil than does Rio. The seed of the nation and its first capital, the city's history is reflected in its architecture, landmarks, and rhythm. Like the rest of the New World, its makeup is not homogeneous but is an odd mixture. Bahia is an alluring amalgam of influences and backgrounds; it is a firm concoction of Indian, Portuguese, and African cultures. Initially they worked against each other, but Salvador's uniqueness is its working blend of the three.

The city, built on two levels overlooking stunning Todos os Santos (All Saints) Bay, is blessed with fabulous beaches, crystal blue water, and weather that allows year round swimming. In my opinion, All Saints Bay surpasses Rio's and Hong Kong's bay in sheer beauty.

In the lower city, *Cidade Baixa,* the port area is alive with open-air markets, sidewalk musicians, and elegant yachts. The upper city, *Cidade Alta,* is a thriving area with deluxe hotels, fabulous dining choices, and modern apartment buildings.

The two levels are linked by a century-old elevator originally built to tote whale oil.

Religious fervor and historical traditions are part and parcel of Salvador. Legend has it that there is a different church for every day of the year. It's only a slight exaggeration.

Many Bahians practice a form of voodoo called Candomblé and you will want to visit a ceremony during your stay here. You will also want to purchase handicrafts sold at lively flea markets and savor typical Brazilian food which originated in Bahia with the African slaves. Seafood and chicken dishes prepared with unusual spices and oils are not to be missed. Salvador, a rare hybrid, is a special place.

History

The indigenous Indians first came into contact with Europe in 1500, when Portuguese explorer Pedro Cabral landed in Porto Seguro, about 425 miles south of Salvador. Soon after, the import of slaves began.

Salvador was founded in 1549. It soon became the capital of the country—it stayed so until 1763—and originally had a population of 1,200. In 1624 the Dutch attempted to occupy the city, but were repelled. Between 1627 and 1649, the Dutch repeatedly tried to capture the city and were consistently unsuccessful.

Thereafter the Portuguese were firmly in control. With the international threat repulsed, the struggle for power eventually turned inward. The Bahian people battled against the Portuguese, and in 1822 became independent.

Brazil is the largest Catholic state in the world, and it is clear in Salvador. The city is riddled with churches—165 in the city and 365 in the state—and is infused with a great religious spirit. There is a constant chain of festivals, with each day having its own color and saint that is worshiped. The entrance to Salvador is Baia de Todos os Santos (Bay of All Saints).

African Culture

The strong African influence is probably most apparent in the practice of Candomblé (Macumba in Rio). Originally from southwest Nigeria and practiced by the Yoruba people, Candomblé was brought over with the slaves. Called Orixia in Africa, the religion is based on the worship of ten gods, each representing some phenomenon, who are ordered by status and power. The faithful are also broken into levels, with the headmasters or priests, Pai de Santo or Mãe de Santo, at the top.

The liturgy is very strict and private. The goal is for a person to become linked and possessed with a specific god. An Initiator serves as medium between the congregant and the god. If communication is successful, a continuing series of rituals takes place. Foremost, the god teaches and advises the person through the Initiator's gestures, signs, symbols, and voice, usually speaking in tongues. Finally, a blessing is made by the headmaster of the certain house. Sacrifices are part of the religious process.

The name *Candomblé,* which applies to the sanctuary, is Brazilian and one of the many side effects of the religion's transference to Brazil. Its survival here is marked by many adaptations. Opposition was first encountered from slave owners, forcing it underground. But the most powerful censorship came from the Catholic church. To circumvent its suppression, the Africans gave a Christian name to each one of their gods. Oxala, Orixia's head god, was counterparted with Christ; Yemanjá, goddess of creation, became linked to Mary; Exu, the evil god and messenger god, was identified as Lucifer; and so on.

Originally practiced solely by African descendants, the religion became more and more integrated into Bahian society. It has been injected into mainstream Christian faith. A devoted Christian will turn to Candomblé for advice and a Candomblé follower will do the same for

Christianity. The two theologies have mixed in a subtle way; they are distinguishable from each other of course, but are not rejected by the other now and they do cross over in interesting ways. At this time, the religion is practiced by some ten million people.

Capoeira, another legacy from Africa, mainly Angola, has also lastingly penetrated Brazilian culture. A form of self-defense blended with dance, capoeira is performed mainly through leg movements. It is now very popular in the country.

Bahian Folklore

Handicraft, folk art, expresses much of Bahian culture. Through pieces of work—both utilitarian and artistic—parts of the mystical side of the culture are revealed. Utilized by all sectors of Bahian society, the pieces reflect each artist's affiliations and beliefs. Whereas a black artist will create handicrafts of Candomblé figures, another artist will sculpt Christian deities. Most works are in leather, wood, clay, metal, or fiber and the articles are usually such things as pots, spoons, handbags, and sandals.

Orientation

Arriving at Dois de Julho airport, one gets immediately oriented to two things: the weather and the water. There is a fine warm sun all year round. (Brazil's summer is December to March, with the rainy season May to September.)

There is an obligatory but smooth immigration check. The airport has a State Tourist Office (Bahiatursa) that will provide hotel and other information and will make hotel reservations for you. In the airport there are also car rentals, travel agencies, and a Club Med reservations center. As you leave the airport, the billboard reminds you to "Smile—you are in Bahia."

The airport is about twenty miles from the inner city. Buses to the city are reasonable; taxi prices vary with the location desired.

The ride to the city is south along the central road, *Av. Getulio Vargas,* which parallels the Atlantic. Just beyond the airport is Itapoã, followed by Piatã, Corsário, Boca do Rio, Armacão, and Jardim de Alá. These areas are all a bit far from the inner city to find a hotel. Inland from Boca do Rio is the Convention Center and Iguatemi shopping center is inland from Armacão.

As the city gets closer, more signs of industry are evident; Salvador is sustained by tourism, agriculture, tobacco, mining, and cattle. Many good hotels worth considering are on the Atlantic and will soon become visible. Pituba Plaza will be the first to appear and will soon be followed by the Meridien on Rio Vermelho beach and the Hotel Othon and Hotel Salvador Praia on Ondina beach.

Av. Getulio Vargas turns into *Av. 7 de Setembro* at the curve of the Atlantic and the bay. The turn will be highlighted by the lighthouse on the tip, which is called *Farol da Barra* and which also has a fort, Forte de Santo Antônio da Barra. Farol da Barra is a central marking point for the city.

The visible body of water is All Saints Bay, Todos os Santos Bay, and soon the forts of Santa Maria and São Diogo appear. The Salvador Yacht Club (Iate Clube da Bahia) is right after the Farol da Barra. The Costa Pinto Museum is the next marking point as you near the city, and off in the distance, to the right, is the large soccer stadium.

Right outside the city, Av. 7 de Setembro becomes *Av. do Contorno.* The Museum of Modern Art is probably the last prominent landmark before entering the center of the city.

Downtown is fronted by the bay. The city is very steep and has two levels, connected by the Lacerda Elevator and steps. The lower level, Cidade Baixa, contains the ports and several open-air markets and is the more prominent commercial sector of the city; it is also referred to as Comercio. There are many splendid churches on the Lower Level.

The Upper Level, Cidade Alta, also known as Centro, begins the sprawl of Salvador, working backward to the Atlantic. The old mansions and baroque churches mix with the more modern structures of twentieth-century Salvador. Winding and narrow streets trace the city and are lined with shops, boutiques, and museums. All government buildings are in the Upper City.

The city is large and is home to over 1.4 million people. Over one million tourists visit Salvador each year.

Hotels

Because of Salvador's coastline location, all hotels are in a general circumference of the ocean, some of course closer than others. Although none pose a great trek to the beach, hotels farther away, and less dependent on the water, will usually have some feature that will provide an alternative.

There are actually 120 hotels scattered around the metropolitan area of Salvador. Staying in the midst of the inner city, one is less dependent on the hotel itself; guests are closer to the life of the city and have the feel of a neighborhood.

Hotels here can rival Rio, not necessarily in variety, but surely in taste and luxury. Most of the deluxe properties are located on the Atlantic side of the city. In most cases they are worlds unto themselves, abundant with services.

All hotels are rated by the government tourist office and are generally lower in price than comparative American lodgings. On average, a deluxe room will range between $75 and $100 for a double. But there is also a wide variety of moderately priced places, with a mean of around $50.

All hotels include a Brazilian breakfast, served in buffet style with eggs, cheese, fruit, cereal, coffee, and juice. All accept credit cards—American Express, Diners, MasterCard, and Visa, but it is best to pay in cruzados.

Hotel Meridien 5*
Rua Fonte do Boi, 216
Rio Vermelho

Phone 071-248-8011
Telex 711-1029

The Hotel Meridien is a towering modern structure offering five-star accommodations. Conveniently located between the airport and midtown, the hotel offers a luxurious feel. Most rooms have a view of the ocean, and there are pools, tennis courts, a sauna, a disco, an elegant French restaurant, and a fine coffee shop. The top floor, the twenty-third, houses meeting facilities for business travelers, secretarial services, blackboards, projectors, Xerox machines, and typewriters. There are TV, laundry, room service, elevators, stocked refrigerators in the rooms, and a garage. Expensive.

Hotel Quatro Rodas 5*
Rua da Passargada
50 yards from Itapoa Beach

Phone 071-249-9611
Telex 071-2449-ORHN-BR

Enclosed in its own little park, Hotel Quatro Rodas is eight stories high and has 195 rooms. Although forty minutes from the city's center, the hotel offers its own petite lake and expansive swimming pool. Surrounded by flat land, views are equally as spectacular as places closer to the ocean. There is an outdoor restaurant, a nine-hole golf course, tennis courts, both outdoor and indoor, sauna, steambath, and massage service. Rooms and motif are definitely Spanish Colonial style. Expensive.

Bahia Othon Palace 5*
Av. Pres. Vargas, 2456
Ondina Section

Phone 071-247-1044
Telex 071-1217

Looking out over the Atlantic Ocean, this hotel is its own little resort. It literally hugs the water, and there is also a large pool with a deck and bar adjacent. On the grounds there is a shopping arcade and an art gallery. There are three restaurants, meeting facilities for up to 800, and independent apartments available in the front of the hotel. The hotel also offers a disco called Hippopotamus and has laundry service, color TV, and parking. Expensive.

Salvador Praia Hotel 5*
Av. Pres. Vargas, 2338
Ondina Section
Phone 245-5033
Telex 071-1430

Next door to the Othon is another hotel on the beach with 139 rooms and 24 suites. There are two pools—children and adult—and a beauty parlor and a barber shop on the premises. The hotel offers air conditioning, color TV, laundry, garage, safe deposits, and videocassette rentals. The hotel has two restaurants—one, the Porto Seguro, is listed as one of our recommendations. There is also the excellent Champagne nightclub, recommended in our nightlife section. Expensive.

Hotel da Bahia
Tropical 5*
Praça Dois de Julho, 2
Downtown, Campo
Grande Section
Phone 071-237-3699
Telex 071-1136

Newly renovated, Hotel da Bahia Tropical is owned by Varig Airlines and is part of the Tropical chain. Perfectly located, the sleek white building is in the heart of Carnival area. There are eight floors with 292 rooms; there's an art gallery on the second floor. There are two restaurants, 24-hour room service, color TV, and elevators. The pool sits in a little enclave in front of the building near the beach. Other highlights include impeccable service and courtesy. Expensive.

Luxor Convento do
Carmo 5*
Largo do Carmo, 1
Downtown
Phone 071-242-3111
Telex 071-1513

Located in the heart of downtown, the hotel is a sixteenth-century monastery of colonial architecture. Flat and long, the converted monastery has a classical feel to it. There are seventy rooms, a round swimming pool in the courtyard, a restaurant and a coffee shop, color TV, air conditioning, 24-hour room service, and a bar. The hotel is part of the fine Luxor chain and offers its guests a trip back to the sixteenth century. The large Spanish suites facing the Atlantic are delightful and in great demand. Expensive.

Enseada das Lages
Av. Oceânica, 511
Rio Vermelho
Phone 237-1027
No Telex

This almost secluded hotel has a private colonial touch to it and is a Jet Set mecca. Thatched roofs and wooden beams are the lure, along with a private beach, a pool, and a restaurant. There are only eight rooms in this private home, so write ahead for reservations. Expensive.

Praiamar Hotel 4*
Av. 7 de Setembro, 3577
Porto da Barra
Phone 247-7011
Telex 071-1871

Managed by the Swiss, this hotel, directly on the waterfront, has a European ambience. It offers a pool, a snack bar, two restaurants, a beauty parlor, secretary service, and babysitting service. There is also a private garage, car service, 24-hour laundry service, and nice views of the bay. Moderate.

Pituba Plaza Hotel 4*
Av. Manoel Dias da
Silva, 2495
Pituba Beach Section
Phone 248-1022
Telex 071-2881

A five-story box, opened in 1985, the hotel is deluxe, with an open modern lobby with a mini-atrium. All rooms are off the lobby and have color TV, air conditioning, and minibar. Pituba Beach is directly across. The hotel is twenty minutes from downtown, and that's the only drawback. There are two restaurants, laundry service, and apartments available. Moderate.

Hotel do Farol 4*
Av. Pres. Vargas, 68
Barra
Phone 247-7611
Telex 071-1542
This hotel, next to Barra shopping center, at the curve between the Atlantic and the bay, has a pool and a colonial American interior, sixty-four rooms on eight floors, and a coffee shop. Great location, reasonable prices. Moderate.

Grande Hotel da
Barra 4*
Av. 7 de Setembro, 3564
Porto da Barra
Phone 247-6011
Telex 071-2300
In the heart of the Barra district with shopping and swimming nearby, the hotel has 117 rooms spread over five floors. The main building is flanked by two smaller ones. The hotel features a large kidney-shaped pool. Moderate.

Bahia Flat Salvador
Av. Pres. Vargas, 235
Farol da Barra
Phone 071-247-4233
No Telex
Not Rated
This is an all-suite hotel, with options ranging from studios to four bedrooms. It is surrounded by palm trees with a tropical look. The hotel has a bar, restaurant, sauna, and pool. The rooms are equipped with refrigerators, ovens, TV, and air conditioning. Excellent choice for families. Inexpensive.

Ondina Praia Hotel 3*
Av. Pres. Vargas, 2275
Ondina Beach
Phone 247-1033
Telex 071-1025
Across the street from the Othon Palace, the Ondina Praia is another grand structure. Cloaked in modern furnishings, the hotel has air conditioning, color TV, a pool, a bar, a coffee shop, a garage, and meeting facilities. There are 100 rooms spread over ten floors. Inexpensive.

Hotel Bahia do Sol 3*
Av. 7 de Setembro, 2009
Victoria Section
Phone 247-7211
Telex 071-1849

In this skinny white modern building, there are eighty-four rooms on nine floors. There is room service, American-style coffee shop, and bar. No pool. Cheap.

Hotel Vila Velha 3*
Av. 7 de Setembro,
1971 Victoria Section
Phone 247-8722
Telex 071-1500

Located on a busy avenue next door to the Bahia Sol Hotel, this seven-story building resembles an apartment building. This ninety-eight room hotel has modern facilities and a pleasant decor. Inexpensive.

Marazul Hotel 4*
Av. 7 de Setembro, 3937
Barra
Phone 237-2110
Telex 071-2296

The 124 rooms of this hotel overlook the bay. There is an oval pool on the first floor and the hotel has a restaurant and a coffee shop. Moderate.

Restaurants

Eating in Salvador can be a festival. Some cultures are less dietetically inclined and are uninterested in food as part of their character. Bahia, and Brazil in general, is persuasively a food culture.

Bahia established Brazil's only unique and native cuisine. Like the city, there are layers of influence; the food is rich, unpredictable, and hot.

The common denominators of all dishes are the African ingredients of palm oil and pepper. From the Indians came the common use of manioc flour, with dishes like corn cereal and sweet potatoes. The Portuguese infused the growing diet with meat and chicken, sweets, and the use of olive oil as opposed to palm oil.

Here are sample dishes:

Vatapá is made of palm oil, coconut milk, peanuts, cashews, garlic, pepper, shrimp, and herring, and has a soft bread center.

Caruru is a pasta dish made with okra, peanuts, cashews, dried shrimp, onion, salt, and palm oil.

Moqueca is a fish stew whose main ingredient is oysters, crab, lobster, shrimp, or octopus. It also contains palm oil, coconut milk, tomato, onion, coriander, lime, and salt.

Sarapatel is made with pork giblets, mint, garlic, black pepper, bay leaf, salt, pork lard, blood, and peppers.

Xinxim de Galinha is a mixture of palm oil and manioc flour and is made with onions and dried shrimp.

Acarajé is a bean dish with salt, onions, palm oil, peppers, and shrimp.

Salvador is overwhelmed with fruit juices and alcoholic drinks. The most popular is the batida. Small but potent, it is a mixture of fresh fruit, Brazilian rum (cachaça), sugar, and ice—originally the Indians made batida with manioc liquor. The drink is adaptable and subject to supply; it is widely experimented with and comes in many forms. (One such variation uses oryx milk.) It is also inexpensive.

Caipirinha is a blend of limes, sugar, and cachaça. Vodka (caipiroska) can be substituted for the cachaça.

There are many good Brazilian beers. *Cerveja* is beer from a bottle and *chope* is beer from the tap.

Salvador has many restaurants; all are not listed. Although one may specialize in a specific type of food—Italian, French, etc.—its general orientation will be Bahian.

Restaurants are inexpensive when put on an American scale. Unlike New York and Rio, restaurants here close earlier—about 10:30 or 11—and open, on an average, at about 7 P.M.

Bahian

Bargaço
Jardim Armacão
Boco do Rio
Phone 231-5141
Noon–4, 7–midnight
Expensive

Typically Bahian, Bargaço is a good place to try the local food; the restaurant claims to be where the locals eat (*onde os baianos comen*). It is open-sided and has a slanted wooden roof. Flags of all nations line the restaurant and a picture of Pelé is prominent as you enter. Try the ensopado, moqueca, or the soft-shell crabs. The owner, Leonel, is the Bahian representative chef on certain sailings of the QE II.

Solar do Unhão
Av. do Contorno
Lower City
Phone 245-5551
Noon–3, 7–midnight
Expensive

Three hundred years old, Solar do Unhão is on a cobblestoned road in a mansion that used to house Pedro Unhão Castello Branco, a judge. Specifically located in the servants' quarters, the restaurant has an interesting history. At one time it was a factory; there are railroad tracks running through it. Solar do Unhão is very popular with the city's residents; it has a certain allure that makes it just a bit more heated and exciting than other places. Waitresses are in typical Bahian outfits and waiters wear red vests. There are three menus, and a folklore show is presented late in the evening.

Senac
Largo do Pelourinho
Phone 242-5503
11:30–3:30, 6:30–10:30
Moderate

In a building that houses a cinema and a theater, Senac, which offers a forty-dish, twenty-dessert buffet, is a good place to try Bahian food. It's in the heart of the colonial district, Pelourinho Square, and is surrounded by

lovely houses. Try the moqueca, xinxim, vatapá, and
caruru. There is a bar that opens at five.

Churrascaria

Baby Beef
Av. Antônio Carlos
Magalhaes
Phone 244-0811
11 A.M.–1 A.M.
Sunday 11–midnight
Moderate

Baby Beef's menu (in English,
Spanish, and Portuguese) features an array of meats: chicken,
steak, turkey, pork, and fish. The
meat is cooked at the table, in
proper churrascaria style, and
two superlative dishes are the
contra filet and the filet mignon. Near the Iguatemi shopping center, this restaurant is packed on Sunday.

Continental

Tiffany's
Rua Barão de Sergy, 37
Barra
Phone 247-4025
6–midnight
Moderate

Conveniently located, Tiffany's
has a re-created Hollywood atmosphere, with green and white
furnishings, and a stereo bar.
Try the T-bone steak, the roque-
fort burger, the steak au poivre,
or the chateaubriand.

French

Le Saint Honoré
Hotel Meridien
Rio Vermelho
Phone 248-8011
Expensive

Le Saint Honoré is the flagship
restaurant of the Meridien chain
worldwide and it would be a
first-class French restaurant no
matter where it were located. It
has a panoramic view (it's on the
twenty-third floor) and a peace-
ful, candle-lit atmosphere. The salads are excellent, as are
the cheeses and desserts. Try the canard tangerine, the
lobster, the shrimp cocktail, and the steak au poivre.

Italian

Casa d'Italia
Av. 7 de Setembro, 1238
Vitória
Phone 245-8564
11:30–2, 7–10
Closed Tuesday
Moderate

A typical Italian restaurant that features gnocchi and canelloni, Casa d'Italia is small and comfortable.

Chinese

Yan Ping
Rua Marques de Leao, 40
Barra
Phone 245-0015
6–11
Moderate

Yan Ping is decorated with red lanterns and masks, and has several rooms. Ask for Cigana, the charming waitress, and try the frango frito with bones, the chop suey de legumes, or peixe agri doce (sweet and sour fish). There is a sister restaurant twenty minutes away, in Pituba.

Japanese

Gan
Praça Alexandra Fernandes, 29
Fazenda Garcia
Phone 245-2206
6:30–12:30
Closed Monday
Moderate

Gan has a small bar, small tables, and a simple menu. The restaurant has typical Japanese fare, usually cooked at your table. Try the milho (corn), pele de frango (chicken), contra filet (steak), fígado (liver), and lombo (pork).

Salvador by Day

Salvador and its environs have no shortage of things to do and see. From museums to markets, the city is well endowed with activities.

The axis of the city's tourism, the center of information and knowledge, is the *Bahiatursa*. Its main office is Rua da Graça, 411, near the Mercado Modelo, and there are offices in the airport and bus terminals. With all services free, the office not only gives literature, maps, guides, and calendars of events, but also disseminates helpful, maybe invaluable, information and advice.

Carnaval

Carnaval is the most famous and most extensive activity; it overshadows, by sheer force, everything else. It lasts five days and starts the Friday before Ash Wednesday, when King Momo receives the key to the city from the mayor.

Salvador had its first Carnaval in 1884. Its quirky history is that it was originally intended to be an alternative to a more frenzied, fierce festival called *Entrudo*. The problem was that Entrudo was elitist; the rich held lavish masquerades, excluding the poor. Their reaction, over time, was to crash the parties in resentment. The rich and the poor then mutually showed their teeth.

In the ensuing tension, many of the uninvolved began to complain. The press and the administration were displeased. The more democratic Carnaval then evolved to quietly replace Entrudo.

Yet Entrudo was what the wealthy of Salvador had inherited from the Portuguese. Originally conceived in a distant and murky form during the Roman period, it was a festival paying homage to Dionysus (Bacchus) and was elaborated upon by Julius Caesar.

With Christianity's growing domination, the church declared that the festival could only take place before Ash Wednesday. (Irreverence was thus excused before Ash Wednesday but not after.) The Italians adopted the word Carnevale—a farewell to meat—for the period preceding Easter. Eventually the festival spread to Portugal and on its arrival in Brazil was called Entrudo.

It was around the second half of the eighteenth century that complaints about Entrudo surfaced. Yet its real exile is directly connected to Salvador's growing prosperity. More money spread to more hands, and local merchants realized that Carnaval was profitable. Entrudo became an anachronism.

Public parties began to replace private ones. Theaters, clubs, stores, the government, and the police began to sponsor and host parties and fashion competitions. Special costume groups formed and the city began to parade and show all the styles and designs.

But Carnaval is still a battleground for power. Although it was the middle class that sealed Entrudo's coffin, they also created another schism. They formed a club called Clube Carnavalesco Cruz Vermelha. They dressed up a car for the parade, creating a crude float. It soon reigned as the main attraction of the Carnaval.

Simultaneously, the ex-aristocrats formed a club of their own. They began to host public balls and to vie for status with the Cruz Vermelha. They each wanted to be recognized as the cornerstone of the festival—to dictate its flavor. It was also a fight between old and new; symbolically, Cruz Vermelha had broken the tradition of Entrudo.

By the turn of the century the Carnaval had swelled in numbers and popularity. Essentially, it was a festival of white people and European culture, but blacks began to participate. They injected the only solemnity into the chaos. They paraded in a consecrated way, marching strictly and pacifically.

Now, of course, there are numerous clubs, groups, parties, cars, floats, and sponsors. Yet the Carnaval still remains a subtle struggle for power and favoritism. Although no longer restricted, Carnaval still has a hard edge of competition to it.

Although the Carnaval in Salvador is less chaotic than Rio's and less expensive, it is still a time of legal and desired insanity. People get swept up with the crowd, and get sucked into a spirit of adrenaline. It is a time for foreigners to uninhibitedly lose themselves and have fun.

Walking Tour

A Stroll through Historical Salvador

To savor the beat that is Salvador you'll definitely want to explore its historic downtown area. Here the city's two levels are connected by a series of steep slanting streets called *ladeiras,* by funicular railroad, and by public lifts. The lower part is a bustling port, with outdoor markets, street vendors, impromptu street dancers and musicians, and contemporary buildings. It is called *Baixa* (lower) or *Comércio.* The upper level, rather more subdued, rises some 220 feet above the port and houses the oldest churches and buildings in Salvador, many of which date from the seventeenth and eighteenth centuries. This upper part, known as *Alta* or *Centro,* has been declared a National Monument and extensive restoration has been undertaken. You'll want to start your stroll in this area, where the ornate spires and towers of scores of churches dominate the skyline. A popular Brazilian folksong pays tribute to Bahia's religious furor and describes the city's 365 churches—one for every day of the year. Actually the city has only 166 churches (plus an unknown number of Candomblé terreiros) and many of the most illustrious ones are in or near the *Praça de Sé,* also known as Terreiro de Jesus, the city's major bus terminus and the starting point of our stroll. In this busy square (which at one time was three square blocks long) stand three churches. The largest and most important of the three is the *Cathedral* (Catedral Basílica). Hours are 8 to 11, 2 to 6 and it is closed Monday. Construction started in 1657 by the Jesuit order, who modeled it after a church in Portugal. The marble façade was brought from Lios, Portugal, as were the interior stone walls. The high altar is gold leaf and the murals were done by one of the brothers. A "don't miss" here is the center ceiling, decorated with paintings of the four evangelists and the crest of the Jesuit order. When the order was expelled from Brazil in 1759, the local archdiocese took over administration of the Cathedral.

As you leave the Cathedral, turn left around the square. By the way, the Terreiro is the site of the local *Hippie Market,* the generic term for an outdoor flea market. Held every Sunday, it's a great spot to buy primitive art, handicrafts, and leather products. Prices are generally lower than in shops, bargaining is a must, and since the artists are young and struggling you may someday be the proud owner of a famous masterpiece. The church on the corner is the seventeenth-century *Church of the Venerable Third Order of the Dominicans,* followed by the eighteenth-century *Church of San Pedro of the Clerics,* both worth a peek. Far more interesting are the *Church and Convent of São Francisco* and the *Church of the Third Order of São Francisco* located side by side on Anchieta Square, an extension of Terreiro de Jesus and one block away.

The smaller Church of the Third Order of São Francisco was in existence when the Franciscan order came to Brazil to stay. Its façade of square gray stones is in Spanish baroque style and it was completed in 1703 (open daily 8 to 11:30, 2 to 5; Saturday 8:30 to 11:30 only). A century later in 1708 the Franciscans undertook the construction of the church that is Brazil's richest, the stunning São Francisco, known as the gold church. While the outer façade was completed in 1720, the carved gold interior took many more years to complete. The entrance is marked by panels of Portuguese blue and white glazed tiles which describe the birth of St. Francis. The interior gold carving depicts grapevines with birds and boys gathering the grapes. The marble basins were a gift from the Portuguese king. The adjoining monastery has a beautiful tiled courtyard. Men can tour the courtyard with a Franciscan guide; however, women can view it only from the doorway.

Stroll back through Praça Anchieta to Santo Domingo Church and then right onto *Rua Alfredo de Brito.* A short stroll away is *Ladeira de Pelourinho* (Pillory Square), where slaves were tortured in colonial times. Pelourinho is now a wonderful neighborhood of steep cobblestoned streets, gaily colored colonial houses with their balconies intact (these were the favorite viewing points for ladies to observe the pillorying at a discreet distance), and some fine seventeenth- and eighteenth-century buildings now used by the local government.

Stop in at the Museu da Cidade (City Museum), which traces the history of the Afro-Bahian people and contains a fine Candomblé exhibit as well (8 to noon, 2 to 6; closed Sunday). Worth a visit too is the nearby *Church of Our Lady of the Rosary for Blacks*. This colorful church, built by and for the slaves, has a strong Indian flavor and even today has a totally black sisterhood. In Pillory (Pelourinho) Square, stop for lunch or a drink at *Senac*, a self-service restaurant featuring Bahian specialties and also a good handicraft shop.

Feel like walking farther? Head up the steep steps of *Ladeira do Carmo* to the *Church and Convent of Carmo*. The lovely Carmelite church, founded in 1585, now houses a religious museum with both Christian saints and Candomblé gods represented. There is a fine view of the city and harbor at this point. In the *Carmo Square* there are lots of shops selling lace, embroidery, silver, and antiques. If you prefer, return to Praça da Sé, where you can either hop the Gonçalves Funicular to Lower City or stroll through Terreiro Square three blocks away, passing the old Town Council Hall, the Archbishop's Palace, and the Palace of the Governor General (now City Hall). In *Praça Municipal*, hop the Lacerda Lift (try to be in front) for the Lower City. This part of Baixa is full of bustle and activity. The colorful open-air markets are scenes of frenetic bargaining and counterbargaining. The swirl of color (on the women and their wares) and the exotic tastes and smells are hypnotic and great photos are taken here—watch out for pickpockets, however. The streets surrounding the market and port are filled with large Bahian women in multicolored skirts selling a brown fried fritter made of ground beans and stuffed with ground shrimp. Try one with hot sauce. If you are lucky you may see an impromptu capoeira dance. Capoeira is a ritual footfight developed because the slaves were forbidden to fight by their Portuguese masters. At this point, you might decide to head for one of the city's beautiful beaches or back to your hotel for a cooling swim.

Forts

Salvador's historical bodyguard has been its forts; they have preserved and sustained the city. In 1549, Salvador's birth year, the governor general was ordered to fortify the city. He had built a strong, yet futile, wooden fence, whose circumference formed the first marking of the city. But its presence instilled no security; people still fled to the woods when an attack was expected. So, Manoel Teles Barreto, captain and governor, built Santo Antônio da Barra and Monte Serrat, two large, sturdy structures. For two centuries these strategic forts were enlarged and they became the initial buttress of the city.

In time more forts were built. They became obsolete in the nineteenth century and eventually turned into museums.

São Marcelo, or N.S. Populo, fort has become the best-known and most visited. Perched on a sandbank three hundred meters from the dock, the fort faces the Mercado Modelo. Construction began on it in 1650 and was completed in 1725. It is a solid circular structure, with walls of stone more than a meter in thickness. Until the middle of the eighteenth century, the fort had eighteen cannons of brass and iron.

The central tower, where the cannons were located, later contained a clock for the city. A cannon was fired a certain number of times for certain purposes: wake-up, evening, and bedtime. Cannons were also fired to warn residents of fire and to celebrate holidays.

The chapel on the right was used as a prison throughout the fort's history. Many famous political prisoners were held captive in the chapel, with the most famous probably being the two nationalist revolutionaries, Bento Gonçalves and Antônio de Souza Lima.

In 1885 the fort became a naval school; in 1937 the government took over the property and it eventually became the headquarters for the sea scouts.

The only way to get there is by boat, which can be chartered at the Mercado Modelo. The entrance of the fort is marked by the emblem of Brazil during the imperial era.

Monte Serrat, located on a hill, offers a beautiful view of the city. One of the two original forts, it was occupied by the Dutch twice. Between 1583 and 1587 the fort went through various name changes: São Felipe, Fortaleza, and Castelo de Itapagipe.

Shaped like an irregular hexagon, the fort is located at Boa Viagem, on a hill on the west side of Itapagipe Peninsula.

Santo Antônio da Barra doubles today as a hydrography (nautical) museum and a lighthouse. The fort was constructed between 1591 and 1602 of rock and limestone; it was built with six outstanding angles and four entryways. During the Dutch invasion, it formed cross-fire with Monte Serrat. It is located east of the entrance to the Barra.

São Lourenço, on Itaparica Island, was built by the Dutch under the supervision of Von Schkoppe. Destroyed by the Dutch as they moved north to Recife, it was rebuilt by Don Lourenço.

Ponta do Padrão is reached by a tunnel that surfaces at the fort's staircase. It is located in Farol da Barra.

Morro de São Paulo, built in 1630 to defend against French pirates invading the Bay of All Saints, is most famous for having been the launching point for the native Brazilian army going off to fight the Portuguese for independence. The fort is also a lighthouse.

There are many more forts interspersed around the city and its environs. Santa Maria and Barbalho exist today as Navy bases. N.S. do Monte Corino is occupied by the military police, St. Peter's by the army. There are also the forts of Lagartixa and São Diogo to visit.

Lacerda Elevator

The Lacerda Elevator, the link between the two levels of the city, is worth visiting for the ride, architecture, and symbolism. First used in 1930 to transport whale oil, the lift enabled the city to function more efficiently. The elevator was a product of the city's growth and urbanization; it also served as a necessary unifier. It connected the government, which was on the Upper Level, to the market on the Lower Level. The elevator has a vertical distance of 215 feet and a ride costs five cents.Look out on the harbor and down on the Mercado Modelo.

Churches

Salvador was nurtured on churches. The sheer number of them, 166, reveals the religious fortitude here. They, even more than the forts, trace and link Salvador's early history.

The churches also illuminate the many architectural styles experimented with and developed. One can observe the influences of the renaissance, baroque, rococo and neo-classic periods.

Located in the historic center of the city—where many other beautiful churches are located—is the *Basílica Cathedral*. Inspired by the priest Simão de Vasconcelos, who wanted the church to equal the massive churches of Portugal, the basílica took nearly fifteen years to build—from 1657 to 1672. Considered the most important monument of religious art in the state, the church has a renaissance design with marble both inside and out.

The facing stones of the cathedral are made of marble imported from Lios, Portugal. The interior is like a large gallery or hall with lateral chapels and two intersecting chapels in the hinted-at form of a cross. The total cathedral is considered the best example of mannerist carving of the seventeenth century in Brazil and Portugal. The paintings on the walls were done by Brother Domingos Rodrigues.

The designs in the cathedral begin to hint at the novel Portuguese baroque influence. It is seen in the twisted columns. The ceiling is decorated with the four evangelists. A huge central medal contains the visage of Jesus. The images of São Francisco Xavier and Saint Inacio de Loyola are some of the most beautiful paintings in the country.

The richest, most lavish church in Salvador is São Francisco, the Church of Gold. Minutely detailed, everything is in gold and the church almost sparkles; it is resplendent with carvings and sculptures infinite in lines and figures. The carvings have as a general motif grapevines, boys and birds picking fruit, and branches of acanthus.

The church began as a Franciscan convent in 1587. In 1708 the chapel was transformed into its present state.

The tiles at the entryway are from Portugal, and they narrate the story of São Francisco's birth. The tale is that he, like Christ, was born in a stable. The second set of tiles depicts São Francisco abandoning his material wealth and praying at São Damião Church.

A sculpture of São Pedro de Alcântara, done by Manoel Inacio da Costa, was done at the end of the eighteenth century and is considered a masterpiece. The altar is one of the most beautiful in the country and the church contains many pieces of sacred art.

The façade of the church is mannerist, but the interior is Baroque and Rococo in style. The church is the most beautiful in Brazil.

The best-known church in Salvador is on the Lower Level. The *Basílica do Bonfim* sits on a "sacred hill" and is revered throughout the city. Its façade is typically Rococo but its interior is Neoclassical, especially the ceiling painting, which was done by Antonio Joaquim Franco Velasco in 1819.

Part of the church's status derives from its being the site of many miracles. The "miracle room" is the specific site of the extraordinary happenings, and it is lined with the belongings of the people said to have experienced them.

The church's popularity stems from its being the base for the January festival of washing. The festival begins at the church of Conceição da Praia, with the city's residents, all in white, carrying flowers and pots of water. Reaching the Bonfim, the people begin washing the church in a ritual of renewal and vitality.

Conceição da Praia is enveloped in myth and history. Dating from the conception of Salvador, the church was originally a straw tent. Located close to the port on top of a mountain, its present structure, begun in 1739, rose from stones imported from Portugal.

Built by numbered stones sent over from Portugal, the process eventually became too complex. Originally constructed through a tight communication between a tile manufacturer in Lisbon and a quarry foreman in Salvador, their computations were left undeciphered when the quarryman died. His son attempted to overcome the problem, but was unsuccessful. Finally, the correct sequence was found by the original man's grandson, and he finished the construction.

The myth surrounding the church and its construction says that in order for the stones to make it to Salvador's shores, the sailors shipping them had to visit the realm of Iemanjá, Queen of the Sea.

The ceiling of the church is illusionist in style. The tiles are magnificent and there is a fantastic image of Nossa Senhora da Conceição.

The church is also the starting point for three festivals: Festa of N.S. da Conceição on December 8; the procession of Noss Senhor dos Navegantes on January 1; and the festival of washing.

The church of Nossa Senhora da Graça is saturated in folklore and was the first church in Salvador. Catarina Álvares, daughter of an Indian chief, dreamt that she saw a beautiful woman—"Madre de Deus"—drown in a shipwreck in Salvador's harbor. Indeed, there did turn out to be a shipwreck. Her father asked the rescue crews if they had seen anyone resembling the image his daughter had dreamt of. No one said they had.

Eventually a statue was retrieved from the wreckage and was recognized by Catarina as the woman she saw in her dreams.

Zealously motivated, she had Salvador's first church built in Our Lady's name. Incorporated in *São Bento* monastery, the church has paintings depicting the sinking and the adventures of Catarina's father, Diogo Álvares.

The mystery of *Ordem Terceira de São Francisco* is that its sculpted stonework was covered over by paint for five centuries. It was rediscovered in 1932 and has fourteen paintings of the Stations of the Cross.

Other churches worth seeing are *Pilar* in the lower city and some churches in the nearby suburbs, mainly: *Boqueirão* in Antonio *Além do Carmo* and *Órfão de São Joaquim* in Calçada.

Pelourinho Square

Pelourinho Square (Torture Square) and its immediately surrounding streets form a small enclave of untouched colonial mansions and houses. The square is indicative not only of Brazilian colonial architecture, which is unique because of its tangled blueprint of three cultures, but of seventeenth- and eighteenth-century justice. The stocks in the square were the devices used to kill political prisoners and dissident slaves. Stop at the church of Nossa Senhora do Rosario dos Pretos (Our Lady of the Rosary of the Blacks).

Candomblé

The liturgy of Candomblé is broken into three parts. In the morning a sacrifice is made. This part is strictly private. In the afternoon there is communal prayer and drumming in order to get the attention of the gods. At night, the ritual turns frenzied with dancing and singing as members become possessed by a certain god.

The afternoon service is open to the public. No pictures can be taken—this is enforced. Although a spectacle, it is not a show. One is allowed to observe but not trivialize. It is also forbidden to wear shorts or bermudas. Advance permission from a Pai de Santo must be received; either a clerk at your hotel or the Bahiatursa can make the arrangements.

Capoeira

Capoeira has been transformed through the years from an underground method of street fighting to a ritualized, systematized, and accepted contact sport. With dance-like moves, almost choreographed, and much sound, capoeira can be observed and attempted.

To see it in a more genuine and uninhibited atmosphere, walk through the poorer sections of the city or go to the Mercado Modelo on a Saturday morning. To try it, go to one of the many schools.

Some academies are:

Acaí, Macapá, 474, Ondina.

Aluvião Regional, Jardim João XXIII, Brotas.

Associação de Capoeira Três Amigos, Apolinario Santana, 154, Engenho Velho da Federação.

Centro Esportivo de Capoeira, Dr. Miguel I, 44, Fazenda Garcia.

Beaches

Salvador, being both tropical and on the coast, is, of course, a place to swim and tan. There are more than thirty miles of beaches, with the majority being on the Atlantic. At night, the ocean can get rough; the bay stays calm.

The nearest beach is *Porto da Barra*. It is near the Santa Maria and São Diogo fortresses and is packed on weekends.

The beach at the *Farol da Barra* is rocky and not recommended for swimming; the sea is also turbulent at this point. Marked by the lighthouse and the Santo Antônio fort, it may be, nonetheless, interesting to stop at.

Ondina is considered one of the city's prettiest beaches. The water is extremely transparent and has formed a curious pool above the reefs.

Rio Vermelho is connected by three beaches: Mariquita, Santana, and Paciência. The festival of Iemanjá is held here, but swimming is not recommended.

Amaralina is both a beach and a market, with a cluster of vendors along the shore selling handicrafts. The beach is very long and great for surfers; the best swimming is in front of the Vitória Club.

Pituba is a small rocky beach without much vegetation. It is convenient for those staying nearby and tends to be a local beach anyhow.

There are many others.

The Zoo

There is a zoo at Av. Oceânica, close to Rio Vermelho. It is open from 8 till 5; there is an entrance fee.

Museums

In all, twenty-seven museums document and preserve Salvador's rich cultural history. Many of these are located in old houses or churches. Since Brazil represents a unique blending of European, African, and Indian cultures, an interesting entanglement ensues and is on display. Admissions are a bargain, generally under $1.

Museu de Arte Sacra (Museum of Sacred Art), located in the Church of Santa Teresa, houses the largest religious collection of its sort in South America. Many of the over 400 sculptures and images in clay, soapstone, ivory, and wood are from the Old World, but some are local. Of particular note is an image of gilded wood by the great

Brazilian sculptor, Aleijadinjho, the silver altar in the chapel, and a bust of Santa Lúzia dating from 1630. The museum's construction dates from the eighteenth century. Rua do Sodré, 25, phone 243-6310. Open Tuesday through Saturday, 10 A.M.–11:30 A.M., 2 P.M.–5:30 P.M.

Museu Carlos Costa Pinto contains one of the finest collections of furniture, silver, jewels, and other objects of art of Bahia. The items come from the extensive collection of businessman Carlos Costa Pinto. The museum first opened in 1969. Av. 7 de Setembro, 2490, phone 247-6081. Open 3 P.M.–7 P.M., except Tuesdays.

Museu de Arte da Bahia is highlighted by the paintings of the Scenes of Passion by José Joaquim de Rocha, considered the patriarch of the Bahian school of painting. The collection, however, is made up of paintings, ceramics, jewelry, furniture, and decorative tiles. Av. Joana Angélica, 198, (at Solar Goes Calmon) Nazaré, phone 243-2892. Open 9 A.M.–noon, 2 P.M.–5:30 P.M.; Saturdays and Sundays 3 P.M.–5:30 P.M.

Museu do Carmo, housed in the church and convent of Carmo, has a collection largely displaying art and artifacts from Brazil's colonial period: the seventeenth, eighteenth, and nineteenth centuries. Images, including carvings by Francisco Manuel das Chagas and a large collection of oratórios, furniture, crowns, and vestments make up the collection. Ladeiro do Carmo, phone 242-0182. Open 8 A.M.–noon, 2 P.M.–6 P.M. daily.

Of special interest historically, but somewhat inaccessible by public transportation, is the *Museu Wanderley Pinho.* This museum is situated inside the Freguesia sugar mill, which dates back to 1522. Historian Wanderley de Araujo Pinho restored the museum in 1971, and it is the only one in Brazil that records the rural life of the sixteenth century. Located on BR-324, ten miles from Centro. Open 9 A.M.–noon, 2 P.M.–5 P.M.

If you enjoy sacred art, another collection worth visiting is that of the *Museu Abelardo Rodrigues,* containing a rich amalgam of 762 pieces of sacred art, and recently installed in Salvador's beautiful Ferrão Mansion. Rua Gregoria de Matos, 45, Solar do Ferrão, phone 241-3791. Open daily, 10 A.M.–noon, 2 P.M.–5 P.M.

Yet another collection may be found in the *Santa Casa de Misericórdia,* located next to the Santa Casa Church and containing religious paintings and portraits by Bahia painters. Rua da Misericórdia, 6, phone 243-4310. Open Monday through Friday, 2 P.M.–5 P.M.

Museu de Arte Antiga e Arte Popular (Museum of Ancient and Popular Art) has a collection of ancient art, most noteworthy the restored chapel of the former diocese. Mons. Flaviano, 2, Politeama, phone 245-7522. Open Monday through Friday, 8 A.M.–noon, 2 P.M.–5 P.M.; Saturday 8 A.M.–noon.

Highlighting the particular and unique Bahian heritage is the *Afro-Brasileiro Museum,* located in the former medical school. This museum compares African and Bahian orixas (deities), celebrations, murals, and carvings. Free Tuesday. 9 A.M.–11:30, 2 P.M.–5:30 P.M. Closed Monday.

For a facsimile of the tourists' favorite, the wax museum, try *Museu da Cidade,* where life-size dolls represent ladies, slave housemaids, "missies," and figures of Candomblé. Lgo. do Pelourinho, 3 (center of old upper city). Open Monday through Saturday, 11 A.M.–5 P.M. Free admission.

Nightlife

Salvador's nightlife is most exciting with the rituals of Candomblé, Capoeira, and Carnaval. Carnaval in Salvador is particularly lively. The pre-Carnaval festive season is very long, with the first festas commencing at the end of November. Theater and cinema are also available, and the city offers a variety of nightclubs.

What makes Salvador's nightlife interesting, aside from its unique events, is the general atmosphere. Things have an exotic, almost sultry, touch. Discos are western but have a samba base and theater is unusual because it is unwestern.

Candomblé

The third portion of the Candomblé ritual occurs at night and can be seen by tourists on Sundays and religious holidays. There are countless terreiros (areas of Candomblé ceremonies) in Salvador. The principle terreiros are:

Axé Opô Afonjá (Estrada de São Gonçalo do Retiro, Retiro)

Bate-Folha-Mata Escura (Retiro)

Bogum (Lad. do Bogum, Federacão)

Camilo (Rua Vila America, 25, Rio Vermelho de Baixo)

Casa Branca (Av. Vasco da Gama, 436, Vasco da Gama)

Cico de Confa Olorum (Rua Silvestre Faira, 53, Vasco da Gama)

Menininha do Gantois (Alto do Gantois, 23, Federacão)

Ile Ola Denan (Rua la Barrelia, 36, Monte Serrat)

Mãe Josefina (Rua Antônio Viana, 65, Cosme de Farias)

Neive Branca (Rua Campinas de Brotas, 100, Brotas)

Nile Axé Ba Ogum (Rua Sergio de Carvalho, 39, Vasco da Gama)

Olga de Alaketo (Rua Luis Anselmo, 67, Matatu)

Orile Eda Efan Ju (Rua do Oriente, 125, São Caetano)

Pai Celestino (Rua Conselheiro Zacarias, 61, casa 11, fundos, Uruguai)

Pai Cícero (Trav. Carneiro, 100, Caminho de Areia)

Pilão de Prata (Rua Tomas Gonzaga, 198, Boca do Rio)

Santo Antônio (Rua Durval Aguiar, 80, Matatu de Brotas)

Terreiro de Ajaguna (Rua Melo Morais Filho, 487, Retiro)

Terreiro de Oxossi (Rua Tomas Gonzaga, 530, Pernambues)

Terreiro de Oxum (Rua Sergio Carvalho, 19, Vasco da Gama)

For dates, times, and other details regarding ceremonies, contact your hotel concierge or the tourist office (Bahiatursa). Remember that visitors should maintain respect and above all, silence, throughout any ceremony they attend. It is forbidden to enter a terreiro in shorts or bermudas. Photographing, filming, and recording are also prohibited. Do not cross your legs, please.

Capoeira

A bout of capoeira, the popular Brazilian hybrid of self-defense and dance, is best seen in the poorer neighborhoods on weekends. It is also possible to see exhibitions in academies. Check with your concierge.

Theater

At Campo Grande (magnificently lit at night) is the Castro Alves theatre, where concerts are given daily (Pca. 2 de Julho, phone 245-9384). Others include:

Teatro da Gamboa (Rua da Gamboa, 3, Aflitos)

Teatro Vila Velha (Passejo Publico, phone 245-7324).

Teatro Senac (Lgo. do Pelourinho, 13, phone 242-5503).

Teatro Instituto Cultural Brasil—Alemanha (Av. 7 de Setembro, 1809, phone 247-6647).

Teatro Santo Antônio, Escola de Teatro da Universidade Federal da Bahia (Rua Araújo Pinho, 292, Canela, phone 247-8162).

Teatro Arena Gregorio de Matos (Pca. Castro Alves, phone 243-0352).

Nightclubs

The "electricity" that beckons in Brazil at night can be felt in its nightclubs. Salvador has quite a few, including some that offer shows to cater to specialized tastes.

Champagne
Salvador Praia Hotel
Av. Pres. Vargas, 2338
Ondina
10 P.M.–4 A.M.
Closed Sunday

Champagne is found at the rear of the hotel Salvador Praia in the Ondina Section. The club operates as a discotheque Monday through Thursday, but has live music on Friday and Saturday nights. Its large main room, lined with red carpet and with glass ceiling overhead, offers a beautiful view of the ocean. Seating is around large, round tables. Usually frequented by the younger set, the club is crowded more often than not.

Le Zodiaque
Hotel Meridien
Rua Fonte do Boi, 216
Rio Vermelho
Phone 248-8011, ext. 574
11 P.M.–4 A.M.
Closed Sunday

If you prefer something more sensational, you may want to try Le Zodiaque (formerly Regine's), located on the lower level of the Hotel Meridien. This club features leather couchettes grouped around a wall of cascading water. Le Zodiaque is a discotheque only, but at the bar next door, you can sample some live music.

Hippopotamus
Bahia Othon Palace
Hotel
Av. Pres. Vargas, 2456
Phone 247-1044
11 P.M.–4 A.M.
Closed Monday

Hippopotamus is another place to dance. This club offers a true discotheque atmosphere—late-night dancing under a mirrored ceiling. It is very popular. Head on beyond the pool.

Bual 'Amour
Av. Otavio Mangabeira
Praia do Corsário
Phone 231-9775
9 P.M.–4 A.M.
Closed Monday

An alternative to the choice between disco and live music is Bual 'Amour, which of all the clubs in Salvador is the only one to combine nostalgia tunes with the very latest in rock music. Located inside a white house in the Praia dos Corsarios section, the club is only a twenty-minute cab ride from downtown. Within, couches, leather chairs around tables, and recessed lights create an atmosphere of piquant glamor. All credit cards are accepted, and the owner, Wilton, is available to attend to individual needs and requests.

Adega dos Orixás
Hotel Quatro Rodas
Olinda
Phone 249-9611

For a quiet evening out, you might try Adegas dos Orixás in the Hotel Quatro Rodas. This spot offers wine and cheese on weekends in a subdued but pleasant setting.

Other Choices

For a typical show after dinner, try *Tenda dos Milagres,* Amaralina (at 11 P.M.), or *Bonzo Bar* (Praça José de Alencar, 6, Pelourinho), which is popular with tourists. Gay shows may be seen at *Safari* (Ladeira de Santa Tereza, 8, Centro) and *Holmes* (Rua Gamboa de Cima, 24, phone 245-2493). Striptease is offered at *Number One* (Rua Carlos Gomes, 89, Centro).

Shopping

Shopping in this city works on two levels (literally also, with the city's division). There is the international shopping, similar to that done in large western cities. It moves at a quieter pace, there is less tension between customer and seller, and it is more precise; stores are defined by their objects and prices are defined.

Localized shopping is almost the complete opposite. It is frenetic, there is always a dialogue of bargaining, and it is random. Many vendors will congregate in one area and the shopper peruses the whole spectrum.

A Bahian mall, the *Mercado Modelo* (Model Market) is a large building with hundreds of artisans and craftsmen selling their goods. Located in the former Customs House in the lower city, the market has an infinite amount of goods: leatherworks, ceramics, lace, silverwork, ropes, beads, instruments, religious artifacts, pottery, paintings, mystical objects, and figa (the most typical, a good-luck charm shaped like a fist), to name just a few. The goods are made out of many things, from clay to wood.

The market is also a center for dancing and indigenous shows—capoeira can be seen here—and has many restaurants. There are two on the top floor and they have large balconies that provide a great view of the harbor. The restaurants on the ground floor are cheaper. It is open Monday through Saturday 8 A.M. till 6 P.M. ; Sunday 8 till twelve.

Iguatemi is the largest shopping center in the city and is near the airport. There is an *H. Stern* jewelry shop there, plus many other shops, cinemas, restaurants, and fast-food places. Shopping here is more westernized.

Five kilometers from Mercado Modelo, along the sea, is *Feira de São Joaquim,* an old western frontier-like, smelly market. Paved with mud, literally, the place is a circus of boats, trucks, horses, and people. But it is authentic. It is very cheap and there is really good African-style pottery and basketwork available here. Closed Sundays.

Instituto Mauá, Av. 7 de Setembro, 261, at the Barra, also sells handicrafts, but with fixed prices.

Centro Artesanal do Maciel, Largo do Pelourinho, 12, is good for handicrafts. It is open from 11 till 8 but closed Sundays.

H. Stern, the international jeweler, has four locations in the city—the airport, Iguatemi shopping center, and the hotels Meridien and Othon.

Woven Tapestries

Thanks to malaria, Salvador's tapestry art industry was created when Bolivian-born Patrick Kennedy arrived from the jungles of Brazil, where he was mining for gold. The son of an Irish doctor and an Inca-descendant mother, Kennedy, who had been taught weaving as a child, developed his skill in tapestry weaving while recovering from malaria in Salvador. Kennedy still lives there and operates a huge art gallery off the beach at Praia Jardim dos Namorados, where you can visit his gallery, show room, and his private apartment on the upper floors. The motifs and colors are gorgeous—costumes of Bahians, street scenes, local flowers, birds, fishing boats, palm trees, and the sea. Definitely worth a visit. Prices are high but so is the quality. They will ship your purchase or you can take it with you.

Excursions

Recôncavo

As in any other modern city, Salvador's suburbs have taken on more importance. They are a result of technology, mobility, and growth; most of the industry has settled there.

Ten miles from Salvador is the Industrial Center of Aratu. It spans the area adjacent to the Bay of Aratu and houses more than a hundred separate businesses. It can be reached by highway BR-324.

The Camaçari Petrochemical Complex was originally built in 1974. It has grown, since, to occupy a much larger area. These two industrial sites are parts of the expansive 200-kilometer radius defined by the Bay of All Saints and called *Recôncavo*. It stretches from the Farol da Bahia, in Salvador, to Ponta dos Graçes, in the south, and includes more than thirty islands and twenty-two municipalities.

Historically defined by its industrial makeup, Recôncavo was one of the chief centers of early sugar and tobacco manufacturing and exportation in the sixteenth century.

Recôncavo, though, is more like a sibling to the city than a child. It has been affected by the same sociology—the odd cultural mix—and has its own historical communities, with their own story, culture, and attractions.

Cachoeira, eighty-five miles from Salvador, is the most important town in the Recôncavo. The city was twice the capital of Bahia, once in 1624–25 during the Dutch invasion and again in 1822–23. It played a strategic role in Brazil's struggle for independence. In 1822, when temporarily capital, it sheltered the people fleeing from the Portuguese General Madeira de Melo. At that time, 141 newspapers circulated, while the city buzzed with politics and revolt.

Famous for being the birthplace of Ana Neri, known as Mother of Brazil for her nursing efforts during the Paraguayan War (1865–70), the small city has many colonial houses and has been declared a national landmark. Deteriorated sugar mills surround the city and fine houses and buildings stuff the inside. Some worth seeing are Bairro do Caquende, Casa da Câmara e Cadela, Santa Casa Misericórdia, Ponto Rodoferroviaria Dom Pedro II, and the Monastery of the Carmelites' Third Order.

Churches worth seeing are Igreja e Convento da Ordem do Carmo, Convento de Santo Antônio do Paraguacu, and Matriz de Santiago. The best-known, though, is called Nossa Senhora da Ajuda. The church of Ordem Terceira do Carmo has beautiful carvings, maybe the finest in Brazil. The church of Nossa Senhora do Rosario, built between the seventeenth and eighteenth centuries, has the largest panel of glazed tiles in the country.

There are several museums—one of colonial art, another of furniture, and finally the house of Ana Neri and the works of German-Bahian artists, Karl and Ilse Hansen.

Itaparica

Itaparica is the largest island in All Saints bay. It is thirty-five square kilometers large and can be reached by ferry from the Mercado Modelo (it is possible to rent a private boat at the Mercado) or car ferry, leaving every half hour, from São Joaquim. There is another ferry from Praia da Conceicão, near the Lacerda Elevator, that leaves every hour. It takes thirty to forty-five minutes and the ferry ride can be wonderful. There is also a bridge, the Funnel Bridge at BR-101.

The island has three major towns—Villa Itaparica, Mar Grande, and Cacha-Prego—and many beaches, and is good to explore by foot. It is long and narrow and parallels Salvador for eighteen miles of beach.

The island is crowded from December to February, but the rest of the year it is quiet, peaceful, and remote, working at a slow pace. Itaparica's local residents are mainly farmers and fishermen.

Mar Grande is the center of tourism, and two of the island's four first-class hotels are there. The town is dominated by seventeenth-century churches. *Penha,* near the village, is a cove that houses the homes of the Bahian rich.

Villa Itaparica has narrow streets, quiet plazas, and a small harbor, and is the location of the sixteenth-century São Lourenco Chapel, one of Brazil's oldest.

Cacha-Prego is the most active, and is the center for local business and labor; fishing and boat-building are situated here.

Conta-costa, the opposite side of the island, is almost completely isolated.

São Lourenço church was built in the seventeenth century and is worth seeing. Highlighting the change of architecture from a rural design to a more urban style, the church is made of stones and tiles and has a huge tower with a pyramid on top. The church has important images of São Lourenco, Senhor dos Mártires, and Senhor da Cruz.

There is a minibus system between Villa Itaparica and Mar Grande. The island can also serve as a springboard to the small colonial part of Jaquaribe and to the market of Nazaré.

There is a *Club Mediterraneé* on the island. They have two-story air conditioned bungalows facing the bay, and offer a pool, sailing, windsurfing, tennis (17 courts), squash, soccer, yoga, sauna, archery, volleyball, basketball, a fitness room, Ping-Pong, and horseback and bicycle riding. Built on eighty-six lush acres facing the Atlantic, the white beaches and warm reef-protected waters of this resort make it the perfect get-away vacation spot.

The resort provides baby-sitting services; there are two restaurants, a boutique, a disco, a cabaret, and a library. The telephone is 241-0354, Telex 071-1804.

Other hotels to be considered are *Galeão Sacramento* and *Casarão da Ilha* in Mar Grande, and the *Grande Hotel* in Villa Itaparica.

Feira de Santana

Feira de Santana, seventy miles from Salvador, on coastal BR-109 and inland BR-116, is a great cattle city and has a leather market. Bus from Salvador takes about two hours.

Santo Amaro da Purificação

Santo Amaro da Purificação, seventy-three kilometers from Salvador, is an old sugar center and is noted for its churches, the municipal palace built in 1769, a fine main square, and mansions. Nearby are the falls of Vitória and many good beaches.

Porto Seguro

Porto Seguro, about 450 miles from Salvador, is the founding spot of Brazil. It is where the Portuguese explorer, Cabral, landed in 1500, and where Brazil was first created. There are fifty-two buildings preserved by the Historical Heritage Foundation. The monument of discovery is a piece of marble brought over by Cabral.

Only the ruins of Brazil's first church, Gloria, remain. But the church of Nossa Senhora da Penha still stands. Built in 1535 and remodeled in 1773, the church has the oldest Brazilian image of São Francisco de Assis. It was brought over in 1503.

Another church worth visiting is Nossa Senhora do Rosário dos Jesuitas, built between 1549 and 1551.

Santo Cruz Cabralia

In Santo Cruz Cabralia, fifteen miles away, is Coroa Vermelha beach (Red Crown), where the first mass was celebrated in Brazil.

Ilhéus

Ilhéus, 235 miles from Salvador, lies between the ocean and a river tributary and is partly an island reached only by bridge. The city produces sixty-five percent of all Brazilian cacao. It is famous for being the setting of Jorge Armando's novel *Gabriela, Clove and Cinnamon*. The city has fantastic beaches; the Museum of Sacred Art and a number of churches, mainly São Jorge from 1556, also are there. There are many French-style houses, although some are being ripped down in favor of more modern architecture.

Valença

Valença, 170 miles from Salvador, is cut in half by the River Una. It is a small but bustling river city that has a constant stream of boats and rafts. With small, narrow streets, the city has two churches rising above it. Nossa Senhora do Amparo is recommended. The River Una enters a mangrove swamp and leads to the island of Tinharé, which has many isolated beaches.

The immense southern coastline (*Litoral Sul*) of Bahia is over hundreds of miles of towns, beaches, and cities. Highway BR-101, along the coast, is the main artery for the whole stretch.

The Maritin Club

The Maritin Club, thirty miles from the airport and 220 square meters large, is part of a chain of German hotels. Formerly owned by Klaus Brothers and Manfredo Peters, the resort was founded by Otni, a tour operator, and Steingenberger hotels of Germany.

Similar to Club Med, the resort has apartments, horseback riding, bicycle riding, fishing, tennis, a gym, and other sports activities. Boat tours are offered, as well as tours of the city and country, and nature walks. There is a disco, a theater, and private beaches.

Three meals are included in the general price. (Rua Areal de Cima, 17, phone 241-1184, Telex 071-1302 CERQ.)

Salvador Potpourri

Art Galleries

There are three excellent art galleries, at Av. Presidente Vargas in the Hotel Salvador Praia in Ondina.

Boutique

My favorite boutique is the Boutique Bagus, located at Rua da Passárgada, Hotel Quatro Rodas, phone 249-9611. Definitely worth the visit.

Bus Station

The main bus depot is at Av. Antônio Carlos Magalhães, phone 231-0952.

Department Stores

Mesbla and Casa Sloper—There are several shops throughout the city, mostly downtown.

English Tourist Information

If you need advice, dial 131 and an English-speaking person will offer you free tourist information. You can get in touch with the Brazilian airlines in Salvador at:

> VARIG/CRUZEIRO
> Rua Carlos Gomes, 6
> Phone 243-1344

Racetrack

The local hipódromo, the Jockey Club de Salvador, is at Lauro de Freitas.

Manaus

The Jungle's Door

till looking for something different? Something unique and breathtaking? A real adventure? Then pack your bag and hop on the next plane to Manaus, capital of Brazil's largest state, Amazonas, and the perfect base for exploring both the Amazon jungle, all 580,000 square miles of it, and the Amazon River, the world's largest.

You'll enjoy visiting the city itself, for in many ways Manaus is separated from both Brazil's past and its present. Founded in the first half of the seventeenth century, it slumbered till the nineteenth century, when it became the center of the region's natural rubber industry. A city grew out of the jungle but it remained sequestered from the rest of Brazil. During the subsequent building boom, a magnificent opera house was constructed. Teatro Amazonas, in which Caruso sang, still stands today, a testament to those heady days.

Now Manaus, a city of 620,000, is the core of life in this unexplored region. It is to Manaus' floating docks that natives bring their fish, their produce, and their handicrafts. A visit to the Municipal Market, patterned after Paris' Les Halles, is an experience not to be missed. You will probably buy some of the handicrafts, for they are unique and will be constant reminders of your visit here.

You can explore the jungle for a day or two or even longer and your options range from a roughing-it trip where your bed is a hammock on deck to a luxurious cruise with gourmet food. Most of you will opt for something in between. Covering one half of Brazil's territory, the jungle is home to 1,800 species of colorful birds, over 250 kinds of mammals, and the longest, widest snakes you've ever seen. Through this vast unexplored region runs the mighty Amazon River in whose murky brown waters live 1,500 species of fish, including the toothy piranha. The river and its tributaries (including the Rio Negro, on which Manaus is located) serve as the major source of transportation for the area and its lifeline. As you explore the area you will notice that the rivers are as crowded as highways.

Don't miss this experience and don't leave your camera behind.

Portuguese interest in exploring and risking the dangers of the Amazon and the jungle was spurred by fear of its being colonized by someone else — the French, the Dutch, or the English. A military expedition was launched in 1639 and made its way up the Amazon to its fork with the Rio Negro (Black River). Initially called Lugar da Barra, the minuscule town languished with a population consisting mainly of Indians, interspersed with Portuguese soldiers, missionaries, slaves, and intrepid merchants. A census taken in 1778 records 34 white men and 220 Indians.

Named after the Indian tribe that originally inhabited the city, Manaus started to grow as the nineteenth century was coming to an end. Charles Goodyear's invention of the process of vulcanization in 1848 and Dunlop's invention of the tire in 1888 generated the western need for rubber. Tire companies penetrated the jungle, stripping it for rubber and simultaneously building up Manaus.

With western money flowing in, the city's indigenous people prospered, and the city became a magnet for entrepreneurs from around the world. The population swelled with western businessmen and corporations, and they began to build up the city in their image; the structures, landmarks, and architecture were of classical Europe.

Under the governorship of Eduardo Ribeiro, who came to power in 1892, western money began to sponsor such projects as the Opera House, Teatro Amazonas (where

Caruso sang), designed and planned by the Lisbon Engineering School and modeled after L'Opera in Paris; the Customs House, built in Italian Renaissance style with bricks imported from Britain; the Municipal Market, an art-nouveau styled structure, copied from Les Halles in Paris; the Rio Negro Palace; and the floating docks, the largest in the world, built by English engineers.

The city, for the next twenty years, was frenetic with construction and movement. With the influx of so much wealth, Manaus became an exotic stomping ground for the opulent of America and Europe. Electricity was installed, (Manaus was the second city in Brazil to receive it) and telephones wired.

Manaus existed almost in a shell. Its origins did not resemble those of any other city in Brazil and its growth was unquestionably unique and dissimilar. There was no historic continuity. Not only was the city isolated geographically—the river being its only means of communication, exportation, and movement—its specific demography and chronology are unrelated to the rest of the country in most ways.

Like any overheated capitalist venture, it quickly evaporated. In 1910 rubber began to be harvested from plantations in Ceylon, Java, and Sumatra. Soon afterward, the manufacturing of synthetic rubber began, and Manaus fell from its short-lived prominence.

For nearly forty years, Manaus lay quiet, abandoned and almost a ghost town. Sparked by foreign money and invigorated by foreigners, the city became stripped of its life with their departure. Like San Francisco immediately after the Gold Rush, the city lay exposed but silent.

However, a modern foundation had been laid that eventually was reinvigorated during World War II. With the Japanese occupation of Malaysia, Manaus again became a center of rubber production. This time, though, its manipulators and suppliers were Brazilians. The wartime boom continued right into 1967, when Manaus, consistent with its international and monetary roots, became a Free Zone.

The establishment of the Free Zone—foreign merchandise is completely exempt from taxes—stimulated urban development, tourism, and business. The city's infrastructure was greatly enhanced (two highways, one paved southwest to Porto Velho and one unpaved north to Boa Vista, now connect Manaus, for the first time, to central Brazil, Venezuela, and Guayana). The city also improved its sewage and water systems, expanded with the creation of new neighborhoods, increased its tourist facilities (hotels and restaurants), and broadened its university.

The city's indigenous industry—other than rubber—began to grow. The Free Zone is under the supervision of the Superintendency of the Manaus Free Zone—Organ of Regional Development, a branch of the Department of the Interior (SUFRAMA). SUFRAMA has subsidized the beginning of more than 200 companies, while building an industrial district ten kilometers from the city where space is sold. SUFRAMA also owns nearly 600 hectares of land that is sold to farmers and cattle raisers (the farmland lies adjacent to BR-174, the highway to Boa Vista). All companies and farmers are exempt from taxes; thus Manaus is a free-floating and untaxed fulcrum for international, as well as domestic, business, similar to the Royal Dutch Antilles.

The Amazon forest—the largest in the world—covers nearly 2.5 million square miles, two fifths of South America. The river itself—the second largest in the world—is networked by about 1,100 tributaries. The river equals one fifth of the world's fresh water, and ten of the largest twenty rivers in the world are in the region, funneling in and out of the Amazon.

There are nearly 250 varieties of animals in the forest and nearly 1,800 species of birds. Ironically, though, the forest is so dense, so thick, and so unlighted, that, at a glance, the flora is unimpressive and scant. Yet, at the forest's high points, there is an abundance of plant life. The trees, in their dominance, supply the earth with fifty percent of its replenished oxygen. (Trees can reach as high as 150 feet.)

The river is full of life, from fish (including the infamous piranha) to reptiles and plant life. The jungle is home to man's greatest nemesis, the snake, which is represented admirably here by the endless anaconda, which can be as long as thirty-three feet.

Manaus, then, is court to this. The Amazon forest is one of the few parts of the earth not totally chartered and mapped yet. It breathes its own unfettered air, and is minimally adulterated by civilization. With more and more of the earth becoming concrete, the Amazon is not only special to Brazil, but to the world. Manaus is the jungle's door.

Orientation

Manaus is three and a half hours by plane from Rio and two and a half from Brasília. Flying direct from Miami, the flight is overnight and flights leave Miami once a week. Being so far west of the coast, Manaus is an hour behind the rest of Brazil; don't forget to set your watch back.

Eduardo Gomes International Airport is eleven miles outside the city and six miles from the Hotel Tropical, the largest of Manaus' hotels. The airport has banks, a duty-free shop, and a Hertz car-rental outlet.

Customs for overseas travelers is perfunctory, but in this free port and free trade zone, all foreign property must be declared upon entry. There are federal revenue officers at the three possible entryways to Manaus: the airport, the river, and the highway. You must declare foreign goods because the untaxed limit on foreign purchases in the city is $1,200. Over that, taxes ensue, so goods bought outside of the city should not be counted in your declaration. (Brazilian-made goods are not taken into consideration.) Although this is official government policy, most personal goods are not checked. The regulations are designed more for Brazilians who come here to shop.

There are both buses and taxis from the airport into the city. Taxis are under $10, while buses are 30 cents (they do not, however, have space for luggage). The Tropical, twenty miles from downtown, provides its own bus service for a slight charge.

Ships arrive at the floating docks, which are right on Rio Negro, in the heart of downtown.

Manaus is spread over hills and is surrounded by trees. The area is divided into four major sections. Downtown in the primary section, the main streets are Av. Eduardo Ribeiro, which stretches from the docks to the Opera House, and Av. Getulio Vargas, which parallels Eduardo Ribeiro. The second section of Manaus is its Industrial Zone and Free Trade Zone, about six miles outside the city on highway BR-174. Third, the meeting of the Amazon (called Solimões by the Indians) and the Rio Negro is a major tourist site and is about eleven miles from downtown. Last, the Tropical Hotel is a city unto itself, with a shopping center, a zoo, expansive grounds, and a beach. The hotel is about twenty miles from downtown.

As you come in from the airport, the first landmark passed in the city is the Opera House, which is slightly off Av. Epaminondas, on Av. Eduardo Ribeiro. Soon after, you are right in the center of the city, on the Rio Negro.

Modern skyscrapers now mingle with Manaus' classical past. All hotels, except the Hotel Tropical, are downtown near the floating docks and the Customs House. They all surround the cathedral, the centerpiece of the city, and are near the Municipal Market, which lies on the river. The Amazonas State Tourism Authority is located at Av. Tarumã, 379. The bus station is located downtown at Rua Recife, 2800.

The city is only sixty-eight feet above sea level and is extremely hot. Summer is July through October and the weather can be stifling, with little rain. Winter is November through June, with rains very heavy at times.

The main beaches of Manaus are on the Rio Negro, located in Ponta Negra near the Tropical Hotel. All along the river there are many white sand beaches. Do not swim randomly, though; the rivers can be dangerous.

Hotels

The government rates all hotels with a reliable star system. With the exception of the Hotel Tropical, all of the hotels in Manaus are located within the city limits. One of these, Novotel, is located in the Industrial Zone. Breakfast will be included in the rate.

If money is not an object, we highly recommend the Hotel Tropical because it is a unique experience. The Novotel is an international property with fine, high-quality facilities, but it is six miles from downtown.

Hotel Tropical 5*
Estrada da Ponta Negra
Phone 238-5757
Telex (092) 2173

The Hotel Tropical is a true picture-postcard hotel: a huge, red-roofed, J-shape complex built on the Rio Negro amidst the jade-green forest. Cranes and tropical birds that wander freely, gardens, and a small zoo with a resident jaguar re-create a tropical paradise. The outdoor pool has a small waterfall and a Jacuzzi, and music is piped in. There are three floors and 358 rooms, all with television, air conditioning, refrigerator, and music. Each bathroom is equipped with two sinks, as well as a telephone; all rooms have balconies. Dark wood floors and handcarved furniture make up the interior. Rooms are lit by hanging lanterns. The hotel complex has an outdoor shopping center, a restaurant, bars and cocktail lounges, a discotheque, a beauty parlor, tennis courts, a travel agency, and an airlines ticket office. Twenty minutes from Manaus, the hotel provides its own transportation to town. A hotel somewhat like Paradores of Spain, Hotel Tropical has a ninety percent occupancy rate. Travelers should write for reservations. Expensive.

Hotel Amazonas 4*
Praça Adalberto Vale
Phone 234-7679
Telex (092) 2277

The oldest hotel in Manaus is the Hotel Amazonas, centrally located downtown overlooking the port and the market. Nine floors contain 180 rooms, each with private bath, air conditioning, color television, bar, and refrigerator. The hotel has a restaurant, a coffee shop, and a bar (Mandy's Bar); there is also a pool complete with men's and women's saunas. In the lobby there is a fine travel agency, Selvatur, that runs trips into the jungle. Moderate.

Lord Hotel 3*
Rua Marcilio Dias, 217
Phone 234-9741
Telex (092) 2278

The Lord Hotel, in the city's shopping area, has ninety-five rooms, on six floors. Rooms are equipped with private bath, air conditioning, color TV, and refrigerator. It's located in a blue building that is under renovation. The lobby is small; a travel agency is located there, and a few steps down is the Tropicus Restaurant, recommended. Moderate.

Imperial Hotel 4*
Av. Getulio Vargas, 227
Phone 234-4065
Telex (092) 2231

Another hotel in downtown Manaus is the Imperial Hotel, with one hundred rooms. Rooms have TV and video system, refrigerator, and central air conditioning. There's a pool on the main level and a 24-hour coffee shop; in the lobby, a travel agency and a beauty parlor. The hotel also offers car rental and a private garage. Moderate.

Ana Cassia Palace 3*
Rua dos Andradas, 14
Phone 232-6201
Telex (092) 2713

Ana Cassia Palace Hotel, downtown, has eighty-nine rooms, on eight floors with air conditioning, refrigerator, color television, and music in all rooms. The hotel is in a white building with a large, red-carpeted lobby. The restaurant on the seventh floor affords a good view of the bustling city. Moderate.

Novotel 4*
Av. Mandi, 4
Distrito Industrial
Phone 237-1211
Telex (092) 2429

Fifteen minutes from the center of town in the industrial section is Novotel. There are three floors and 113 rooms with private bath, air conditioning, color TV, direct-dial phones, and video cassette. There are large outdoor pool, tennis courts, and lots of open space inside and out. Dark-brown wood and tile floors are the motif inside. The attractive, split-level lobby has many shops. Many luxuries and an appealing decor make location this hotel's only drawback. It is part of the French hotel chain and is very popular with businessmen and conventions. Expensive.

Lider Hotel 3*
Av. 7 de Setembro, 827
Phone 234-1966
Telex (092) 2781

Lider Hotel has six floors, sixty rooms. Rooms have air conditioning, refrigerator, and color TV. There is no pool. Off to the right is the lobby, which contains a blaring television and, farther off, a large goldfish tank. The fifth floor harbors a bar and restaurant. Inexpensive.

Hotel Internacional 3*
Rua Dr. Moreira, 168
Phone 234-1315
No Telex

This hotel is located downtown like the others and has four floors, twenty-nine rooms with color TV, air conditioning, and refrigerator. No pool. Seating is in the rear of the lobby. Next door you will find the Restaurant Forasteiro, usually crowded with locals. Inexpensive.

Hotel Central 2*
Rua Dr. Moreira, 202
Phone 234-2197
Telex (092) 2765

Stepping down a bit, Hotel Central is on the same street and has two floors, fifty rooms with air conditioning, and color TV, and 24-hour room service. There is a small lobby. Inexpensive.

Rei Salomão Hotel 2*
Rua Dr. Moreira, 119
Phone 234-7374

A simple, four-story hotel with twenty-eight rooms, also nearby, is Rei Salomão Hotel. A small, narrow entranceway gives way to the front desk. Rooms have air conditioning, telephone, music, and TV. The fifth floor is a restaurant. Inexpensive.

Restaurants

The regional foods and dishes of Manaus reflect its special character as a jungle city. Its staple foods have been the same for centuries, and were adopted from the Indians who originally lived and coped with the environment of the tropical rain forest, which is unsuitable for the cultivation of crops. In the absence of agriculture, fish and a dry flour called *farinha*, which is extracted from a manioc root species, became the staple foods of the Amazon. The result is a variety of fish dishes that are often flavored with *tucupi*, a hot sauce made from a manioc root species (in its raw form tucupi is poisonous, and is used by inhabitants of the interior to kill ants by throwing it on the anthills).

Typical Amazonian fare will include a number of fish species new to the traveler: the giant *piracuru*, served grilled, fried, or boiled; *tambaqui*, best barbecued in cutlets; and *tucunaré*, boiled in a delicious local stew called caldeirada, which is served in a dish along with farinha and a sauce made from a local pepper called *murupi*. Other local varieties of fish are *cará-açu*, *paçu*, *river sardine*, and *jaraqui*, all these served grilled or fried. Fish is often served peixe moqueado — grilled with scales on and served with chopped onions and tomato farinha and murupi sauce. Another local specialty is *pato no tucupi* (duck in tucupi sauce), frequently served on festive occasions. *Tacacá*, prepared from tucupi which is spiced with onions, jambu leaves, and dry shrimp, and made into a thick soup to be served in *cuias* (small bowls made from the inedible fruit of a native tree), is an authentic representation of local taste.

Fruits and vegetables come in varieties as exotic as the fish of the region. Vegetables tend to be rare and expensive due to the lack of consistent agriculture here, but a delicious vegetable to try fried is *macacheira*, a manioc species. Local fruits, which are delicious, include *graviola* (bull's heart fruit) and *cupuaçu*, from which dessert dishes and drinks are also made. More common tropical fruits are available throughout most of the year: red papayas, pineapples, guavas, cashews (the fruit as well as the nuts), and watermelons. The most unusual fruits (and nuts) are those that come from palm trees: pupunha, which is cooked and eaten with coffee, and tucumã. Apart from this exotic food, Manaus has no shortage of international food.

The restaurants of Manaus provide plenty of opportunities to sample local cuisine and offer excellent places to indulge in international dining as well. Restaurants are not open late and are not fancy like the ones in Rio. But prices are lower and the food, especially the local food, is certainly good.

Continental

Tarumã
Tropical Hotel
Estrada da Ponta Negra
Phone 238-5757
7 P.M.–midnight
Moderate

Tarumã, located in the Tropical Hotel, is a real treat. A romantic atmosphere, with grand piano and strings playing on the upper staircase, and great food, local as well as continental, make this the best restaurant in town. A superb dish is filet de tucanare nantua (sautéed river fish with mushrooms, chopped shrimp, and mashed potatoes). Pato assado ao molho de castanhas (duck in a tangy sauce) is another good one, and daily specials are also offered. For dessert, choose from crêpe Suzette, cherries jubilee, and mousse au chocolate. Coffee comes with cookies and sweet cream, and there is a dessert cart too. High beamed ceilings, wall tapestries, and Spanish colonial lanterns create an old-world setting. The restaurant is air-conditioned; service is smooth and polished.

Restaurante Timoneiro
Rua Paraiba, 7
Parque, 10
Phone 236-1679
6 P.M.–midnight
(dinner only)
(lunch weekends only)
Moderate

For typical Amazonas food, try Restaurante Timoneiro. The menu includes many different types of fish and shrimp, cooked in a variety of ways that are not restricted to regional cuisine. Inside, straw ceiling and lamps, hanging baskets, hammocks, and animal skins create a flamboyantly exotic atmosphere. The restaurant is five minutes by cab from the downtown area, ten minutes from the Tropical Hotel.

Churrascarias

Roda Viva Churrascaria
Av. Ajuricaba, 1005-A
Phone 232-2687
11–3, 6–midnight
Moderate

A churrascaria with open-air dining is Roda Viva Churrascaria, which is entered by passing a small zoo in the garden. A small jaguar, a monkey, parrots, and other types of birds are on view. For a reasonable price, you'll have all you can eat, including steak, pork, or chicken. The meat is cut at your table. Wines and appetizers are on display. Although it isn't fancy, (plastic covers are spread over the white tablecloths), the food here is good and the setting pleasant. There are huge trees in the rear.

Churrasco
Tropical Hotel
Estrada da Ponta Negra
7 p.m.–midnight
Moderate

Weather permitting, you can dine under the stars at Churrasco, in the Tropical Hotel. It's alongside the hotel pool, and music plays continuously. Dinner is a bargain for all you can eat; dishes range from chicken, sausage, and steaks to salads. Dress is informal. On a warm, clear night, you can spend a truly enjoyable evening.

Regional

La Barca
Rua Recife
Phone 236-8544
Noon–3, 7–midnight
All day Sunday
Moderate

An excellent choice, La Barca offers regional dining with music and a live singer at night. The restaurant resembles a ship from without. Inside, a rounded ceiling with fans and long rows of tables leading up to an attractive bar give an impression of space and elegance. More tables are placed on the patio outside. The typical Amazonas specialty, *pato ao tucupi,* is well worth a try here, as is *caldeirada de camarão* (Amazonas fish stew with a shrimp variation, served in a soup bowl). Moqueca de peixe is another good bet. This is the most expensive restaurant in Manaus.

Restaurante Palhoca
Estrada da Ponta Negra
Phone 238-3831
4–midnight
Moderate

Restaurant Palhoca is a huge house, completely made of straw, where regional dishes, especially fish, are specialties. On a stage that is constructed of straw, dancing takes place to live music (daily except Sundays). Open air on both sides and a ceiling fan keep the place cool inside. Here the fish is shown to you before cooking. A wide selection of seafood specialties includes moqueca de tucuaré. Lights adorned with fish scales give the place an authentic local touch. Mrs. Dionea, who owns the restaurant with her husband Moisés, speaks some English.

Restaurante Panorama
Boulevard Rio Negro, 199
Educandos
Phone 232-9030
11–3, 6–midnight
Moderate

For regional seafood and fruit specialties and a view overlooking the Rio Negro, try Restaurante Panorama. There is an enormous variety of fish dishes to choose from. One of the less odd, but certainly good, is filet de peixe á milanesa. Outdoor dining is enhanced by proximity to the river.

Restaurante Panorama
Rua Recife, 900
Adrianópolis
Phone 232-3177
11–3, 6–midnight
Moderate

Another restaurant of the same name is located in the wealthy suburb of Adrianópolis near the Artesanato Market. Here open-air tables overlook noisy street traffic instead of the calm of the river, but the menu selection is as large.

Italian

Fiorentina
Praça Roosevelt, 44
Phone 232-1295
11–2:30, 6–11
Moderate

Fiorentina is my favorite Italian restaurant in Manaus, offering pizzas in three sizes and a great variety of pasta dishes. The restaurant is decorated with an oven motif and is quite spacious inside. Of the several rooms, the one on the terrace is open-sided and is recommended, along with that on the upper floor, which overlooks the street. Tile floors, covered tables, and travel posters of Italy make it cheerful inside.

Fiorella
Rua Pará, 640
11:30–2:30, 9–midnight
Saturday, Sunday
11:30–4
Moderate

Fiorella is a pizza bar that offers an astounding variety of pizzas, meat and fish dishes, fruits, desserts, and drinks of every kind. There are several rooms, decorated with heraldic Italian swords and armor, around an outdoor garden; tables are available outside or on the terrace. The entrance, protected by a long canopy, cannot be missed. A great place to pass the time.

Pizzeria Buonasera
Rua Bernardo Ramos, 167
Phone 232-5763
7–midnight
Saturday, Sunday till 2 A.M.
Closed Monday
Moderate

A novel international dining experience will be had at Pizzeria Buonasera. This restaurant is located in an old house on a street where lights from colonial times have been preserved. Inside are several rooms with wood floors and an attractive look is achieved by wine bottles placed in niches and scenes and maps of Italy painted on walls. The food is good and includes lasagna and other pasta dishes as well as pizzas.

Chinese

Restaurante China
Av. Getulio Vargas, 1127
Phone 232-7196
Noon–2:30, 7–11
Closed Tuesday
Moderate

The best Chinese food in town in at Restaurante China, in a two-story private house with about ten tables. The menu is in English. Sliced, boned chicken sautéed with mushrooms and sliced beef sautéed with onions and/or pepper are both recommended.

Mandarim
Av. Eduardo Ribeiro, 650
Phone 234-9834
11–2, 6–11
Moderate

Another Chinese restaurant downtown is Mandarim, which serves common Chinese dishes. Not as good as Restaurante China.

Japanese

Miako
San Luis, 230
Adrianópolis
Phone 234-4837
11:30–2:30, 6–midnight
Sunday 11:30–3, 6–1 A.M.
Moderate

For Japanese food, try Miako, where wooden tables are set out for open-air dining and the specialty is Lagosta ao Molho de Camarão (lobster with shrimp sauce). Both Chinese and Japanese food are served.

Coffee Shops

Tucano
Tropical Hotel
Estrada da Ponta Negra
Noon–3, 6–midnight
Moderate

Tucano, the coffee shop on the second floor of the Tropical Hotel, offers a buffet as well as á la carte selections. This is a good place to try grilled loin of pirarucu, fried fish fillet, or grilled frango (chicken), but hamburgers and steaks are also available. The buffet includes dessert. Breakfast is also served here. With several rooms, smooth, tiled floors, and white tablecloths, the place is more like a hotel restaurant than a coffee shop. Hanging metal lights keep the interior well lit, and there are photos of the Amazon on the walls.

Tropicus Restaurant
Hotel Lord
Rua Marcilio Dias, 217
Phone 234-9741
Moderate

This attractive air-conditioned coffee shop, located in the Hotel Lord, offers a large selection of fish, meat, and drinks. A canopied bar and wood panels decorated with Amazonas themes make this a pleasant place to sit.

Hotel Amazonas
Praça Adalberto Vale
Phone 234-7679
Moderate

With outdoor tables and a varied menu, the coffee shop in this hotel provides a great stop when downtown or shopping. Hamburgers, sandwiches, and hot plates of meat and fish are available. Leather two-seaters and booths make a comfortable interior, while outside dining is made particularly agreeable by proximity to the hotel pool, which is off to the side, and by a view of the street scene. Beyond the coffee shop is Mandy's Bar, a popular nightspot.

Sightseeing

Manaus is unique due to its proximity to the jungle, unspoiled and so dense that much of it is accessible only by water. Numerous tours can be taken by boat to various water sites and natural reserves within the jungle. Longer excursions for fishing, hiking, or exploring can also be arranged. Inside the city limits, certain sights should not be missed, like the cathedral, the waterfront with its floating docks, and Manaus' famous nineteenth century opera house, imported stone by stone from Europe.

Walking Tour

To see Manaus close up and in its entirety, we suggest a walk around the city, which will cover the more minute and specific details, and will take about two and a half hours. Detailed descriptions of each sight follow the walking tour.

Start at the *Municipal Market,* on Rua Marquês de São Cruz, one of Manaus' many European hallmarks and modeled after Les Halles in Paris. Behind the building the boats on the river are visible and the market is teeming with people. Its smelly, working atmosphere is interesting to observe and, of course, purchasing food is the priority.

From there walk left to the *Customs House* which was built in Italian renaissance style, with bricks imported from Britain.

Continue along the same route to the *floating docks,* the famous and singular all-purpose docks that can't flood. Made of concrete and mounted on iron girders, the docks always stay above the water.

Turn right along Rua Marechal Deodoro to Av. Sete de Setembro and left to the *cathedral,* the central marking point for the city. This area of downtown has Manaus' hotels.

Head right on Av. Eduardo Ribeiro, the main thoroughfare of the city, to the *Opera House* on São Sebastian Square. Along the way is the *Public Library* on Rua Henrique Martins and the *Court of Justice* on Rua J. Clemente.

The famous theater was host to Caruso and is the specialty of the city's imported classical past. Considered one of the most beautiful structures in the world, Teatro Amazonas is in neoclassical style, with a huge metallic dome, covered with tiles, and pillars.

The motif both on the outside of the theater and the inside is the meeting of the two rivers, highlighted by the

Monument to the Opening of the Ports, which was erected in 1900 of bronze, marble and granite. Below are four ships representing four continents—Europe, Africa, Asia, and the Americas. The theater was restored in 1929, 1962, and 1974 at the cost of $3,000,000. The curtains inside take up where the monument leaves off and show the meeting of the waters, the Amazon and the Rio Negro. The mechanism that opens and closes the curtain animates the theme. The chandelier may be lowered and raised. The floor is inlaid with 12,000 pieces of imported and Brazilian wood. Doorways were imported from Italy and the artwork is mainly from Brazilian artists.

Municipal Market

Seeing the Municipal Market, where produce from the interior is brought by boat to be sold or traded, will give you a real taste of life in this area of the country. The market is located on the riverfront and is one of Manaus' European legacies. Opened in 1906, the sprawling cast-iron complex that shelters the stalls is modeled after the art nouveau-style of Les Halles of Paris, and all the materials used to make it were imported from Europe.

The market is divided into three sections, where cereal and rice, handicrafts, and fish and meats are sold respectively. Fruits are displayed in the rear. The dock area is the real hub of activity, where throngs of people press together, buying and selling rice, beans, and other food products. Behind them are the boats, lined up so closely together that their masts seem to form a picket fence. A constant stream of men moves back and forth, loading and unloading huge sacks of wheat, rice, and manioc flour. The Indian cast of the features of these men, who come from the interior, is noticeable. Many of them sleep on hammocks strung up on the decks of the boats. A visit to the market, with its smells and primitive atmosphere, will give you a real feel for the life of the interior and should not be missed. The Municipal Market is open from 5 A.M. to 6 P.M.

Floating Docks

The floating docks are located on the Rio Negro opposite the cathedral. A special type of construction was devised for them to avoid the flooding that would occur if they were not afloat. Concrete piers, mounted on iron girders, are held up by buoys at water level. This arrangement allows the docks to lower or rise with the water level, so that ships of all sizes may anchor there year round. A chart on the dock shows the river's high points, which occurred in 1976 and 1922, with 1953 as the record. The minimum depth of the river is approximately one hundred feet. It rises another forty to forty-five feet and is at its highest in June. Nearby is the Customs House (Alfândega), a large, imposing brown building that was shipped in blocks from England.

The river-bank area is the mooring point for regional boats that come to unload products from the outlying areas as well as those that transport people from place to place; they are the buses of the region.

Teatro Amazonas/Opera House

The square at São Sebastian church, a paved area of black and white stones set in a wavy design that symbolizes the meeting of the black waters of the Rio Negro with the waters of the Amazon, forms the stage from which the Teatro Amazonas is approached. In the center of the square is the Monument to the Opening of the Ports, erected in 1900 to commemorate the opening of the ports of the Amazon to all nations. Of bronze, marble, and granite, the monument was sculpted by Domenico de Angelis and shows the Amazon personified as a goddess of Greek mythology. Below her are four ships, representing the four continents — Europe, Africa, Asia, and the Americas.

The opera house, a magnificent example of neoclassical architecture, is considered one of the most beautiful theaters in the world. A huge metallic dome, covered with tiles, rises above the body of the building, which is rectangular. The façade, a series of pillars beneath a semicircular roof, creates with the dome and the main structure a harmonious balance of forms typical of classical architecture.

Built during the governorship of the famous Eduardo Gonçalves Ribeiro, who initiated most of the public works that transformed Manaus from a village into a city, the opera house was seventeen years in construction. It was restored in 1929, 1962, and again, significantly, in 1974, at a cost of approximately $3,000,000. Exterior construction was by the Engineering School of Lisbon, while the decor within was done by Crispim do Amaral, scenographer of the Comédie Française. Do Amaral was assisted in his work by the Italian painter Domenica de Angelis, who was responsible for most of the artwork found within.

In the auditorium, four tiers containing eight hundred seats look across at a stage that can be raised or lowered. The new seats, installed in 1974, are of red felt. A few of the original seats, which were backless, are on display. On the stage curtain is painted a scene showing the meeting of the waters of the Amazon and the Rio Negro. The mechanism that controls the opening of the curtain is designed to animate this scene with a rippling motion. The bronze chandelier may be raised and lowered like the stage. The ceiling panels show allegories to music, tragedy, and drama, inspired by characters from the operas of Carlos Gomes. The doors were imported from Verona.

Upstairs is the reception room. Visitors must remove their shoes to walk on the floor, which is inlaid with 12,000 pieces of imported and Brazilian wood. Doorways of Italian marble are topped by busts of famous Brazilian artist. Sixteen columns, imported from England, are of cast iron covered with plaster. The ceiling panel, "Glorification of the Arts in Amazon," gives way to a panel showing a scene from José de Alencar's "O Guarany," Peri rescuing Ceci from the fire, on the wall that opens to the auditorium. Crystal mirrors, im-

ported from France, are set in the walls. When the chandeliers are lit, these mirrors have the magical effect of reflecting
a series of images that seems to go on indefinitely. From this
room, one may proceed to a balcony that overlooks the city.
Not to be missed!

Cecomiz

Cecomiz was erected in the middle of the industrial area to
take advantage of Manaus' duty-free zone. The industrial
zone is not just a commercial center; the Pope celebrated
mass here during his last visit to Brazil. From June 15 to
July 15, there is dancing every night in the Praça Bola da
Suframa. Across the way you will find the Exposition Center, where products of Amazonas are made (these not for
sale). Cecomiz is open for shopping from 9 A.M. till 9 P.M.

Indian Museum

The Indian Museum, run by the Salesian mission, contains
rooms full of tools, artifacts, and decorative objects that
illustrate the life, death, and culture of local Indian tribes.
Most of these objects stem from the Tucano tribes, who
live in the outlying regions. They are thought to have lived
in Colombian territory prior to the age of discovery. On
the lower level of the museum, handicrafts made by Indians who have been trained by priests of the Salesian mission are displayed for sale. Upstairs, five rooms display
objects pertaining to various aspects of Indian life.

The first room shows objects connected with ritual. Especially notable are sacred masks made from the bark of the
tauari tree, each representing an animal. These are used in
the feast of the *Wax-ti*, or "jungle spirit." This room also
contains jewelry, headgear, and musical instruments, including a tambor, a large wooden instrument with drilled
holes that is played with a drumstick. The next room contains tools and utensils for cooking, carrying water, and
fermenting fruit. In the following room are arrows, spears,

and nets for fishing and hunting, as well as baskets and hammocks for sleeping. The fourth room has many decorative artifacts: animal skins, neck and head ornaments, and feather bracelets and crowns. The fifth room is devoted to funerary objects and attire. There is a sixth room promoting the efforts of the Salesian mission. Located at the corner of Duque de Caxias and Av. Sete de Setembro, the museum is open from 9 to 11 A.M. and 2 to 5 P.M. Monday through Saturday.

Zoo

The CIGS zoo is run by the military for the purpose of training soldiers in jungle warfare. Located on the Estrada da Ponta Negra, it is easily accessible by the public bus that stops in front of the Military College. The zoo is worth a visit since it contains animals captured during military training that might not be seen normally. Turtles, alligators, snakes, and a black panther are some of the animals that may be seen there. Open daily, 9 A.M. till 6 P.M.

Capela de Santo Antonio

One of Manaus' curiosities is the Capela de Santo Antonio, or the Capela do Pobre Diabo (Church of the Poor Devil), a narrow little church with a blue and white façade on the way to the industrial zone (on Rua Borba). The story behind it is that it was built by a sick man, who vowed to erect a church if he recovered. He did! Although it is rarely open, one can usually see candles lit in front when passing by.

Court of Justice

If you have time, visit the Court of Justice, built in the 1900s in neoclassical style. The building houses the Supreme Court and is located on Rua J. Clemente off Av. Eduardo Ribeiro.

Day Trips

A series of excursions are sponsored by the Tropical Hotel, including a Meeting of the Waters tour that stops at the Island of Terra Nova in the Amazon. Most of their tours are designed for private groups. A half-day cruise on the Rio Negro visits Salvador Lake and includes hiking, fishing, and swimming. A full-day fishing tour, a sunset cruise, a half-day trip to Love Waterfall, and an overnight cruise to Salvador Lake are also available. Other agencies around town (Selvatur in the Hotel Amazonas is a good one) offer similar trips.

Meeting of the Waters

The Meeting of the Waters tour takes you to the meeting point of the Negro and Amazon rivers, one of Manaus' most famous sites. The boat makes its way along the bank of the Rio Negro where the entire city is laid out, so that section after section comes into view as you make your way down river. The stilted houses of Educandos, a suburb of Manaus, will give way to the Municipal Market and the ferries docked next to it, passing on the way many regional boats that are going to or from the city to load or unload produce and discharge passengers. Next you'll pass the factories of the industrial zone, heralded by the appearance of Brahma beer factory, which uses Amazon water to make its beer. A few miles downstream is the meeting of the waters. The muddy brown waters of the Amazon flow alongside the black Rio Negro for miles without mixing, due to differences in temperature, density, and velocity. The meeting of the waters is a theme that has been utilized in the art of the region, particularly that of the opera house.

By noontime, the boat will have reached a thatched hut floating on the river, complete with a bar. A family-style lunch will be served there. From here, visitors embark for Salvador Lake, traveling along the igarape (flooded woodlands) in small motorized canoes. The lake is part of a natural reserve where tapirs, capybaras, jaguars, monkeys, turtles, snakes, and birds can be seen. There are alligators and piranhas in the lake. Swimming is allowed, since these animals ostensibly prefer fish to people. You may also fish, or hike along the two-mile forest trail to the Guedes River narrows. The trip lasts seven hours.

Jungle Trips also has a seven-hour Meeting of Waters tour. Its Tucano tour is a ten-hour trip through igarapes in covered, motorized canoes, with lunch provided. An alligator-flashing tour is available at night. Overnight excursions into the jungle can be made for two- or three-day periods. One of these, the Tapiri is so called because travelers sleep in hammocks in tapirs—open-walled thatched huts on stilts. One- to ten-day fishing trips and a V.I.P. overnight on a large yacht that floats up the Rio Negro are also offered.

Three-day excursions to Mamori Lake, fifty-five kilometers from Manaus on the Solimões River, are offered by Ata Turismo and Wagon Lits. By the way, the Amazon is often referred to by its local name, the Solimões River.

An alternative to the usual tour packages is the Amazon Lodge, a floating wooden shelter on Lake Juma, which accommodates eight to ten people for three-day periods. Another is a three- or six-day trip offered by Safari Ecológico to the lower Rio Negro and the Anavilhanas islands. These areas are relatively remote and visited much less often than most of the other sites. The Ecológico tours are designed to provide an indepth introduction to the Amazon, and are accompanied by a scientist from INPA (National Institute for Research on the Amazon) and a physician from the Manaus Tropical Disease Hospital, as well as an experienced guide.

A cruise along the Amazon between Belém and Manaus may be taken on a luxury catamaran run by Enasa. This trip takes five to six days.

Finally, a first-class getaway may be found at Pousada dos Gaunavenas, located on the island of Silves, some two hundred kilometers from Manaus. The hotel is built entirely of wood and has fourteen air-conditioned apartments. Transportation is by bus (three hours from Manaus) or by seaplane (one hour from Manaus).

An Amazonian Legend

The legends surrounding both the name and the history of the Amazon are numerous and rich. The original myth of female warriors comes from Greece, and involves women who were stunning, beautiful, agile equestrians. Their only connection with men was an annual two-month-long ritual of procreation. A year later, the boys were given back to their fathers and the girls were kept. Part of the myth also says that women cut off their right breasts to be able to control a bow more efficiently. The name *Amazon* in ancient Greek means "without a breast."

The Brazilian legend is similar but not identical. The first reported sighting of Amazons in Brazil was made in 1542 by the Spanish conquistador Francisco de Orellana and chronicled by the Dominican friar, Jaspar de Carvajal. Part of a 6,000 man expedition, they separated from the main body to search for food for their supplies were almost exhausted. A month later they stumbled on a huge river and soon thereafter upon a dark body of water crisscrossing the main river. This they called Rio Negro (Black River). Soon thereafter this group of 60 was confronted by a group of fiercely painted Indians led by a dozen "Amazons." Carvajal describes them as fearsome and relentless and he states that when most of these mighty female warriors were dead the men they led fled into the jungle.

Capturing one alive, Orellana learned that the women lived in isolated communities mingling with men from nearby villages only for the purpose of reproduction. Male children were sent to their fathers while females were kept in the Amazon villages. They had a queen, worshipped the sun, wore fine clothing and held a tight reign over the male tribes nearby.

This was the initial sighting of female warriors in Brazil and began the deeply layered myth of matriarchal societies living in remote parts of the Amazon jungle. Orellana, it has been deduced, had his encounter with the Amazons on the Nhamunda River, which is located just below Guyana and enters the Amazon much farther east of Manaus.

This legend has been embellished or discounted by Europeans ever since. However, in the Amazon River Basin, Indian tribes cling to the stories of powerful female warriors and all female communitites and tribes. From these legends superstitions have arisen about the mesmerizing, seductive effects and the preciousness and importance of the green stones (gems) worn by these fearless warriors. One such, states that on an island on the Lake of the Mirror of the Moon, Amazons still live, seeing men once a year. Each year they hand over the male children born of the previous year's mating. Each child wears a "muira-guita," a green stone from the lake which will bring them good luck.

Nightlife

Manaus in not well known for its nightlife, and there isn't a lot to do here at night. Most night spots are open only on weekends, and except for the Hotel Tropical, none of these is really first class. If you are in need of something to do at night, however, you might try one of the establishments listed here.

Tropical Show Club
Rua Borba, 937
Phone 232-3503
Friday, Saturday,
Sunday
8 P.M.–4 A.M.

Tropical Show Club offers dancing and a show for a small cover. There are two live bands, with a dance floor open on both sides. The show is adequate; the dancing is fine.

Clube do Samba
Cachoeirinha Section
Friday, Saturday,
Sunday
8 P.M.–2 A.M.

Clube do Samba is recommended for samba enthusiasts. The show takes place on a high stage; customers watch from the garden. During Carnaval, this club is open every night. Ten-minute ride by taxi from downtown.

Bar Igapó
Hotel Tropical
Seven days
5–midnight

Bar Igapó, a few steps away from the Tarumã Restaurant (see Restaurants) in the Hotel Tropical, is a first-class place for a quiet drink—high ceilings, dark and romantic. Serious drinkers hang around the bar, the others sit on couches around large tables.

Starship
Av. Castantino Nery
Downtown
Friday, Saturday,
Sunday
10 P.M.–4 A.M.

For a little more excitement, Starship is an interesting club with a discotheque (not live) and a screen for video movies. It's a small intimate place right downtown at the corner of Av. Leonardo Malcher. You'll see the blue awning opposite FIAT.

The In-Crowd Club
Rua Bolivar Vivaldo
Lima, 27
Phone 232-6793
Friday, Saturday,
Sunday
10 P.M.–4 A.M.

The In-Crowd Club, though not perhaps as elite as its name implies, seems to draw a lot of comers. Situated near Manaus' red-light district, it can be recognized by its black-and-white entrance. Down one flight in an apartment house, you'll find a long narrow space lined with couches and mirrors, the walls adorned with painted scenes. A few steps up is the dance floor, surrounded by mirrored walls.

Note: *This downtown area near the In-Crowd Club is Manaus "Red-Light" district.*

As Mil e uma Noites
Rua Marcilio Dias, 269
Downtown
Phone 234-1696
Seven days
5–midnight

Open seven days, As Mil e uma Noites has a show every half hour from 5 P.M. to midnight, nonstop thereafter. It's a large place, mainly a pick-up joint, with booths, a bandstand, and a virtually unused dance floor. The walls have been painted red and are lit by lanterns. Near the Lord Hotel, the club is easily recognizable from the outside by its large neon sign. Head up one flight of stairs to find it.

Cathedral
Rua Saldanha Marinhao
Downtown
Seven days
10 P.M.–3 A.M.

Similar to As Mil e uma Noites, Cathedral is also a pick-up joint, with striptease and go-go girls. It's downtown, open every day.

Jet Set
Rua 10 de Julho
Downtown

Another pick-up place is Jet Set, where chances are most of the women you see will be professionals. Located near the Opera House.

Faces in the Groove
Av. Djalma Batista
Weekends only

If none of these sound engaging, Faces in the Groove is another disco downtown that you might want to try.

Shopping

Shopping in Manaus' Municipal Market and Industrial Free Zone is colorful and rewarding. Local artisans produce interesting artifacts and handicrafts such as baskets and masks. In the Free Zone, no tax is levied on foreign items up to the price of $1,200 and there is no tax at all on Brazilian-made goods. Because of the heat, stores are closed between the hours of noon and 2 p.m. Here are the places you should try:

Central de Artesanato do Amazonas
Rua Recife, 1999

The Central de Artesanato do Amazonas houses twenty shops that sell handicrafts, fruit, and confections of the region. The center is open from 9 a.m.–8 p.m. daily; Sundays 3 to 6 p.m. Wander from shop to shop to get a feel for the varied local handicrafts. I purchased a hand-carved oar at the Branco E Silva Shop.

Casa da Arte Indígena

Of special interest is the Casa da Arte Indígena, across from the Amazonas Hotel, which is run by the National Foundation for Indians, and is one of the best places to buy artifacts made by Amazonian Indians. Throughout this downtown area, many shops and booths may be found near the Hotel Lord and on Rua Marcilio Dias in front of the Amazonas Hotel.

Hotel Tropical Shopping Arcade

There is also a shopping area in the Tropical Hotel. The group of stores here includes an *H. Stern* outlet for jewelry fashioned from Brazilian gemstones; *J. Mojican,* a boutique for clothing, leather goods, and bikinis; and *Carrossel,* which is a great toy store. Also, there is *Artesanato Brasi-*

leiro, an outstanding store for artifacts such as handcarved oars, masks, piranhas, and hanging baskets; *Elegance* sells fine imported textiles.

Industrial Zone Shopping

Cecomiz is the shopping mall in the Industrial Zone. A range of products from sound systems and video cassettes to toys and clothes are sold here duty-free, as well as food and handicrafts of the region. Opposite the exposition center, it's open daily from 9 A.M.–9 P.M. Closed Monday.

The Municipal Market

The Municipal Market, open 6 A.M.–5 P.M. daily, is a good place to sample fresh fruits, produce, and fish of the region. The market has a section for handicrafts as well.

Airport

Finally, there are shops in the airport where departing passengers may pick up anything they've forgotten. Of special interest are two H. Stern outlets, and an Artesanato shop, as well as places to buy T-shirts and candy.

Manaus Potpourri

Airlines

Varig/Cruzeiro is located on Av. Eduardo Ribeiro at the corner of Henrique Martins. Phone 234-1116.

Car Rentals

Hertz, at the airport and downtown. Your concierge can also arrange for a car. All you need is a passport, a driver's license, and a credit card.

Churches

Manaus has many Catholic churches. There are also Baptist and Pentecostal houses of worship, along with a synagogue. Check with your hotel clerk.

Consulates

U.S. Consulate: Rua Silva Ramos, 120, phone 234-4807; British Consulate, phone 232-1723.

Pharmacies

As is true all over Brazil, some drug stores are open twenty-four hours and are marked by the "Turno" sign. A red light indicates that the shop is open.

Post Office

The main Post Office of Manaus is at Rua Marchal Deodoro, and is open from 8 A.M. to 7 P.M., Saturday from 8 A.M. to 6 P.M.

Public Library

Rua Henrique Martins, Monday through Friday 7–9, Saturday 8–3. It's an imposing building with interesting architecture that houses a collection of Amazon history.

Transportation

Getting around town is possible by bus, but they have no air conditioning and are hard to figure out. Cabs are cheap and can be rented by the hour. The two types are *comun*, common cabs, and the *special* larger cabs with air conditioning.

Brasília

There Shall Be Born a Great Civilization

Brasília is the future today, almost. Totally planned and just over twenty-five years old, it is the capital; hence a city revolving around the government. What makes Brasília so fascinating is its modernity, its architecture, and its symmetry, everything being in place. But the wonder behind it is its rise out of nowhere—its elevation from a large patch of barren, deserted, and unproductive land.

Officially opened April 21, 1960, Brasília, city of hope, became the capital of Brazil. Its realization fulfilled a constitutional decree to position the capital in the interior of the country (the old capital was Rio). As its grand opening implied, the city was minutely planned, with every street, building, bench, park, church, house, and school the product of a master blueprint.

The city is the outcome of several men's visions. The original impetus came earlier in the century, grounded in the idea that power must be centralized (the same theory behind the creation of Washington, D.C.). Not until 1956 and the elevation to power of Juscelino Kubitschek, did the government consider moving the capital away from Rio a priority. Indeed, Kubitschek's overriding political vision was the city, and most of his energy was devoted to it.

Juscelino Kubitschek had a long history of official service, in both the military and civilian sides. He was governor of the state of Minas Gerais, which served as his springboard to the presidency. Although his election was marked by turmoil and graft, the army stepped in and Kubitschek took power. Almost immediately the rumble of Brasília was heard.

On the morning of April 18, 1956, Kubitschek sent a message from the town of Anápolis in the state of Goiás to the Congress in Rio. He urged the creation of Brasília in the state of Goiás, in the heart of the country. With his letter, Brasília was in essence guaranteed.

The site chosen was initially barren and deserted, with only a few intrepid farmers. That October trucks brought the first materials for the construction of the city. Just a few weeks later, power was supplied through a generator, a radio station was installed, connecting the infant Brasília with Rio, and the interim presidential house was built. Called Catetinho, the new, and transitional, house was named after the Catete, the presidential palace in Rio.

On November 9, 1956, the city was inaugurated and JK signed the first official document from the new capital. The next day a permanent generator was installed. By February 1957, three thousand workers had arrived and the city's growth continued at the furious pace set forth by JK. On May 3, 1957, the first Mass in Brasília was said by Dom Carlos Carmelo de Vasconcelos Mota, Cardinal Archbishop of São Paulo.

Following the initial groundwork, a nationwide contest was initiated to choose the designer of the city, a person to plan and structure every nook. There was a four-month period between the announcement and the deadline, and all entries would be judged by a team of Brazilian and foreign architects. Twenty-six urban planners and architects submitted their ideas.

The contest was won by well-known Brazilian architect Lucio Costa. His plan was selected because of its attention to simplicity and quality of life. Costa's design, a Pilot Plan, was based on the shape of an airplane, with central fuselage and flanking wings. The premise is efficiency, lack of congestion, order, and coherence.

Oscar Niemeyer, the architect of the U.N., was chosen to design all the buildings. His work here is both imaginative and bold, but not unwieldy. The two central government buildings, the House and the Senate, resemble the U.N., with all the buildings having a green hue.

With JK, Costa, and Niemeyer, Roberto Burle Marx became the last of the four men who controlled and put together Brasília. Marx was chosen as the landscaper. His mark is evident, and is integral to Costa's vision. The city has the largest park in Latin Amercia and the National Park, five minutes from the city, has natural springs and running pool water, with parts sectioned off as observation areas for flora and fauna. Brasília is referred to as a green city.

The city has now settled a bit. It was initially plagued by its lack of depth and variety, a problem arising from the fact that the city had no evolution, and was strictly utilitarian. For years, the bureaucrats and politicians forced to work and live here would race out of the city for Rio come Friday. That has slowed down a lot, but because of it the city's personality is dominated by its stationary workers, the people who work in construction and industry and are less wealthy than the politicians. These people, who mainly live in the satellite cities just outside Brasília, are predominantly from the northeast, the more impoverished part of Brazil, and they have dictated the nonpolitical life of the city and have given it some homegrown culture.

In an area of eight thousand square miles, the city is the most rapidly growing in the country, with a population increase of thirty percent a year. It is the city of the future, not only in its design and look, but because more than half its population is less than twenty years of age. It has the largest concentration of elementary and high schools in the country, with 250,000 of its just over a million residents in school.

The satellite cities, the home for most of Brasília's working class and the product of Brasília, are dotted around the radius of the capital. Some of the cities grew directly out of Brasília's growth, some just grew in importance. As mentioned, they are poorer and are dominated, now, by north-eastern culture. Some of the main cities are Planaltina, oldest of the bunch, and Taguatinga, the largest, with a population of more than 200,000.

Orientation

Built on flat land, Brasília is made up of its central nucleus and its outlying towns, satellite cities. Constructed in the shape of an airplane, the city is divided by two main high-ways, Eixo Monumental, the fuselage, and Eixo Rodovia-rio, the wings.

In the western tip, heading away from the city, are the largest structures in Brasília—Television Tower, the Juscelino Kubitschek Monument and, a bit farther out, the military complex. Beyond the western road is pure wilderness. Just below the right angle of Eixo Monumental and Eixo Rodo-viario, which is the site of the ultramodern bus station, is a parallel row of nineteen government buildings that leads up to the twin towers of the legislative branch of government. The twin towers, flanked by a large cup and a large saucer, begin the circle of Three Powers Square, made up of the legislative, judicial, and executive buildings.

Forming a large circle between Television Tower and the beginning of the government buildings, on both sides of the Eixos, are the sections designated for hotels, banks, business, and culture.

The eastern tip of the city, on Eixo Monumental, is the man-made lake, Paranoá Lake, which is fifty miles in perim-eter, three miles across, and eight feet deep. It is the only area allowed for private housing and is where most of the leisure activities take place—boating, yacht clubs, tennis, etc.

The embassies are all lined up on the southern bank of the lake. Across the lake on a peninsula called Lago Sul, there are the two shopping centers, Gilberto Salomão and

Gilbertinho. Good restaurants and most nightclubs are centered there.

The wings north and south on Eixo Rodoviario are the residential sections. Living, for the bureaucrats, is in superquadras, blocks of eleven six-story apartment buildings. Each quadra is totally self-contained, with autonomous commons, pool, primary school, and nursery. Each block is divided by feeder roads, where the local stores, cinemas, and restaurants are located. Each wing has its own public utilities office and fire station. Numbered according to their relation to Eixo Monumental, the 100s indicate its closeness and 400s its distance.

Compact and ordered, the city is easy to trace and follow. It is almost a grandiose compass, with its geographical demarcations easily readable. In its master plan there is a designated sector for everything: hotels, both north and south; living, both north and south; military, west; government, east; municipal government, near JK Tower; leisure, east by the lake; convention center and camping area, northeast; and college, north lake.

November to March is the rainy season. The weather otherwise is always sunny and warm, with breezes at night cool enough for a jacket.

Arrival

The airport is just as modern as the city. It is four miles from the city, just beyond Lago Sul, and has arrivals and departures on separate floors. There is a telephone service for calling hotels and making reservations; the tourist office there has a list of rated hotels. There is a government tourist office in the city as well.

Taxis are reasonable and it is a ten-minute trip to your hotel. There are buses, but there is no room for luggage.

Hotels

All hotels are rated by the same government star system throughout Brazil. Prices include breakfast. All hotel prices are reasonable, at about a third less than in Rio. All of our recommended hotels are within walking distance of each other, the only obstacle being the ten-lane Eixo Monumental Highway that divides the north and south hotel sectors. The majority of the hotels, and the best of them, will be found in the southern zone. In all, fourteen hotels are recommended here, of which nine are in the southern sector.

Hotel Nacional 5*
Setor Hoteleiro Sul
Phone 226-8180
Telex 061-1062

The Hotel Nacional, in the southern sector, is part of the Horsa chain of hotels based in Rio, which includes Nacional and Excelsior. There are ten floors and 350 rooms, and the hotel has a pool. Travel agencies and airlines offices located here include KLM, Varig, VASP, Swissair, Transbrasil, Air France, and Alitalia. A barbecue restaurant and the French restaurant called La Belle Epoque (see Restaurants) are located here as well. There is also an H. Stern jewelry shop. The hotel is less modern than others but best for businessmen. Moderate.

Carlton Hotel 5*
Setor Hoteleiro Sul
Quadro 5G, Bloco
Phone: 224-8819
Telex 061-1981

The Carlton is probably the best hotel in town. Opened in 1979, the hotel is fifteen stories high, with a sauna and a pool on an adjacent patio fronting the entrance. There are 201 rooms equipped with TV, air conditioning, and refrigerators. The mezzanine, fully carpeted, is furnished with leather couches. Head upstairs on the spiral staircase—there are four bars as well as a restaurant, La Fontaine. Moderate.

St. Paul Park Hotel 4*
Setor Hoteleiro Sul
Sul Quadro 2, Bloco B
Phone 226-1515
Telex 061-3721

Across from the Hotel Nacional in the southern sector, the St. Paul Park Hotel, opened in 1984, is the home of an excellent restaurant, Flowers, and Club Prive, the most popular disco in Brasília. There are fifteen floors and 364 rooms. A small heart-shaped pool is located on the roof. TV includes videocassette and American programing. The restaurant is located on the mezzanine. Corte, a private club, may be entered either as a guest or a tourist. It is the best club in town and always crowded. Moderate

San Marco Hotel 5*
Setor Hoteleiro Sul
Quadra 5, Bloco C
Phone 226-2211
Telex 061-3744

The San Marco, another in the southern sector, is an eight-story building with 235 rooms. The hotel is near the Television Tower, and its rooftop pool offers a great view of the city. There are a bar and a restaurant near the pool; another very good restaurant is located on the mezzanine, where there is also a beauty salon. TV in rooms includes American programing. Moderate.

Garvey Park Hotel 4*
Setor Hoteleiro Norte
Quadra 2, Bloco J
Phone 223-9800
Telex 061-2199

The Garvey Park Hotel, in the northern hotel sector, has twelve floors, 446 rooms. A pool, a sauna, three restaurants, and a piano bar are all located on one level, one flight up from the ground floor. There is a small shopping arcade. Inexpensive.

Aracoara Hotel 4*
Setor Hoteleiro Norte
Quadra 5, Bloco C
Phone 225-1650
Telex 061-1589

The Aracoara Hotel in the northern zone is an excellent hotel, though without a pool. Its 141 air-conditioned rooms have TV and radio. The first-floor restaurant serves both Brazilian and international dishes. The Scotch Bar has live musical entertainment. There are conference rooms and a beauty shop. Inexpensive.

Eron Brasília Hotel 4*
Eixo Monumental Setor Norte
Quadra 5, Bloco A
Phone 226-2125
Telex 061-1422

Eron Brasília is a tall glass building in the northern zone. The bar and Restaurante Panorâmico on the seventeenth floor have great views of the city. Pan Am, Lufthansa, and VASP have offices here. There is a beauty salon on the first floor. Access to a tennis and pool club, ten minutes away, is arranged through the hotel. Inexpensive.

Hotel das Nações 3*
Setor Hoteleiro Sul
Quadra 4, Bloco D
Phone 225-8050
Telex 061-1484

Hotel das Nações is located two blocks up from the St. Paul Park Hotel in the southern zone. There are eleven floors and 130 rooms; there is no pool. On the first floor are the restaurant Panelas do Brasil and a bar, Garrafas. Inexpensive.

Bristol Hotel 3*
Setor Hoteleiro Sul
Quadra 4, Bloco F
Phone 225-6170
Telex 061-3443

The Bristol Hotel, next to Hotel das Nações, is a thirteen-story glass and cement building with 143 rooms. The exterior is pleasing, and there is a small rooftop pool. The restaurant is on the first floor. Inexpensive.

Hotel das Américas 3*
Setor Hoteleiro Sul
Quadra 4, Bloco D
Phone 233-4490

Similar to Hotel das Nações, and of the same chain, Hotel das Américas is another in the southern sector. There are thirteen floors, and 144 rooms, with a restaurant and bar on the first floor. There is no pool. Inexpensive.

Alvorada Hotel 3*
Setor Hoteleiro Sul
Quadra 4, Bloco D
Phone 225-3050
Telex 061-1484

Also in this chain is the Alvorada Hotel, with eleven floors, 130 rooms, and a restaurant and bar on the first floor. All of these hotels are close to each other, with the Alvorada nearest to the Eixo Monumental highway. Inexpensive.

Torre Palace Hotel 4*
Eixo Monumental Norte
Quadra 4, Bloco A
Phone 226-3360
Telex 061-1905

The Torre Palace, in the northern sector in front of the Television Tower, is a thirteen-story hotel with 128 rooms, but no pool. The reception area downstairs, done in black and white tiles, is pretty. The restaurant on the roof offers twenty different Lebanese dishes. Inexpensive.

Hotel Phenicia 4*
Setor Hoteleiro Sul
Quadra 5, Bloco J
Phone 224-3125
Telex 061-2254

Phenicia Hotel has eight stories with a bar and restaurant on the ninth floor and a sauna two flights down. There are 130 rooms (no pool). The hotel boasts 24-hour room service, which is rare in Brazil. Inexpensive.

Hotel Casablanca 3*
Setor Hoteleiro Norte
Quadra 3, Lote A
Phone 226-0255

Hotel Casablanca, in the northern zone, is a small but somewhat attractive hotel with three floors and fifty-eight rooms. The building is flat and has long arches in its façade. The restaurant is simple and comfortable, and there is a 24-hour snack bar. No pool. Inexpensive.

Restaurants

Because of its brief history, Brasília has no traditional food that dates back for centuries. As an international city (all nations have embassies here), it has every type of food—both typical Brazilian and international cuisine. Whether you seek French, Italian, Chinese, Churrascaria, or Lebanese, you'll find it all here.

Continental

GAF
Centro Comercial
Gilberto Salomão
Phone 248-1754,
248-1103
Noon–2; 7–4 A.M.
Expensive

GAF, a French restaurant somewhat like Café des Artistes in New York, has live music every night. Two carpeted rooms are decorated with painted wood panels set into the walls. There's a bar on the side. Diners are seated in upholstered chairs with wicker backs. The menu, in French and Portuguese, offers a large variety of French dishes, including frog legs a la Provençale, and Brazilian dishes too, especially fish. GAF was awarded a star in the 1986 edition of Quatro Rodas. The owner, Levi Chuery (called Roberto) is a well-known man about town. He owns the local nightclub Chez Levi as well.

Florentino
Superquadra 402 Sul
S.C.L.S. Q 402
Phone 233-7577
Noon–2 A.M.
Expensive

Florentino is perhaps the best restaurant in the city. The interior is beautifully decorated, with an elegant bar area and red Scotch plaid walls. The menu places a heavy emphasis on fish, with different types served each day of the week. However, the French dishes are also good. Try *Chateaubriand Café de Paris*. For its good food, elegance, and sophisticiation, this restaurant is like its sister in Rio. Ask for a table on the patio, where you'll sit in wicker chairs.

Piantella
CLS Bloco A, Loja 34
Comercio Local Sul,
202
Phone 224-9408
Noon–3:30; 7–2 A.M.
Expensive

Piantella, formerly Tarantella, offers international dining with an emphasis on Italian. Although better under its previous ownership, this restaurant is still quite good. The downstairs room is small and simply furnished, with a bar on the side and wine bottles set into the walls. Wood paneling gives way to wall hangings on the upper walls. Tables and wooden chairs are arranged well. Head upstairs for a more luxurious setting with a view. This room overlooks the park of Super Quadra Sul. The decor, including the bar area, is much brighter, and seating is on uphostered chairs and couches. *Fettuccine Alfredo, lasagne, chateaubriand bearnaise, caneton à l'orange, lapin chasseur* are all recommended. There are many fish dishes, but shrimp and lobster, as throughout Brazil, are somewhat expensive.

Restaurante La Belle
Epoque
Hotel Nacional
11:30–4; 7–midnight
Moderate

Dine alongside the pool near the piano bar at Restaurante La Belle Epoque, in the Hotel Nacional. A number of international and Brazilian dishes are offered at a fixed price, including *camarões* (shrimp) *a baiana, steak au poivre, escalopinha ao marsala*. Try the Brazilian soup, *canja á Brasileira*. Carpeting and candlelit tables keep the place comfortable, not fancy.

Flowers Restaurant
St. Paul Park Hotel
Mezzanine
Noon–4; 7–midnight
Moderate

True to its name, Flowers Restaurant, on the mezzanine of the St. Paul Park Hotel, sports large, splashy murals of flowers on its walls. Bright red brick arches that frame the window tables make it even more colorful. The bilingual menu (Portuguese-English) offers a large variety of fish—*badejo a Flower* (grilled with spinach and mushrooms) is a good dish to try. *Medalhões de filé* and steak with orange sauce are also recommended. Seating is on chairs or couches around tables. In the center, the chef, wearing a white chef's hat, can be seen preparing the food. There is also a piano. A much fancier alternative to the Hotel Nacional.

Restaurante Executivo
San Marco Hotel
Mezzanine
6 P.M.–midnight

At Restaurante Executivo, in the San Marco Hotel, the emphasis is on privacy. Booths built into the walls are almost like private rooms. Inside, the place is charming and clean. Flowers have been placed on tables that are comfortable and well spaced. Music plays during dinner, and there is a bar cart. Meat and fish dishes are both excellent—try *peixe a ceviche, T-bone steak,* or *salmão de fumado* (smoked salmon). Shrimp and lobster are also available, though expensive. For dessert, try *banana flambé,* or *cereja* (cherry) *jubileu*.

Italian

La Fornarina
CLS 405, Bloco D, Loja 36
Phone 244-6333
Noon–3; 7–midnight
Expensive

Brasília's best Italian restaurant is La Fornarina, located in a private house with an upper level as well as a terrace for open-air dining. Its namesake, pictured on the menu, is a mysterious Italian lady who looks as though she might have been painted by Raphael. A large range of pasta dishes are available—*spaghetti alla carbonara, tagliatelle quattro formaggi*, with mussels, gorgonzola, parmesan—and the list goes on. Select also from their shrimp (gamberi) and fish dishes: *gamberi alla fornarina, pesce con gamberetti e funghi* (fish with shrimp and mushrooms).

La Giaconda
CLS 102, Bloco D, Loja 35
Phone 224-4989
11:30–midnight
Inexpensive

La Giaconda is a large Italian restaurant with two stories and an outside dining area that serves pizza and pasta. Forty kinds of pizza can be ordered to eat in or take out. Lasagna, spaghetti, gnocchi Bolognese, ravioli, and canneloni are served up to pasta lovers. Wooden tables and chairs with rattan backs in the three dining rooms make a setting that is comfortable, not fancy. Tables outside are open-air, with a covering above; this area has a separate entrance.

Churrascarias

Churrascaria Do Lago
Setor Turismo Norte
Phone 223-9266
Noon–midnight
Moderate

Churrascaria do Lago is located on Lago Paranoá near the presidential palace and was the first steak house in Brasília in 1961. On a clear night, you may dine outside in a quiet spot beside the artificial lake, overlooked by palm trees. Tables and chairs with umbrellas have been provided for this purpose. Indoor dining is in a large tiled room with wooden chairs. The restaurant can hold over 1,000 people and it is recommended that you have a drink first by the lake and then dine.

Restaurante Panorama
Television Tower
Noon–3; 7–midnight
Moderate

As its name suggests, a strong point of Restaurante Panorama is its view. Located on the first level of the Television Tower, the view is more important than the food. This churrascaria is a good place for lunch. On Friday and Saturday nights, there is live music here, with a separate cover.

Churrascaria Tabu
Hotel Nacional
Phone 226-8180
Noon–3 A.M.
Moderate

This churrascaria is open late nights and offers a great variety of beef, chicken, and pork dishes as well as pizzas of all types. Chicken dishes are relatively low-priced; the filet mignon and *maminha de alcatra* (round steak) are worth trying. Open-air dining is offered here, with some covering over the central tables. The waiters are dressed smartly in blue jackets, and the maître d' wears a black tuxedo.

Japanese

Restaurante Tokyo
Centro Comercial
Gilberto Salomão
Noon–3; 7–midnight
Closed Monday
Inexpensive

Restaurante Tokyo is a fancy Japanese restaurant where the food is cooked in the open. Typical Japanese amenities will be found here, like hot towels brought to cleanse the hands before eating and a *tatami* room where diners remove shoes and sit on the floor at low tables in the traditional manner. The restaurant recommends itself by its large Japanese clientele. A large menu offers shrimp and vegetable tempura, sukiyaki, sashimi, and *yakizakana*, a Brazilian-influenced dish also known as *peixe assado*. There is live music here.

Restaurante Nipon
CLS 403, Bloco A,
Loja 28
CLS 413, Bloco C,
Loja 36
Phone 224-0430
Noon–3; 7–11
Sunday Noon–3; 6–11
Closed Monday
Inexpensive

Restaurante Nipon is a small Japanese restaurant serving typical Japanese dishes; shrimp and vegetable tempura, sushi, sashimi, and sukiyaki. Its sparse, traditional Japanese interior is divided in half by hanging beads. Ten blocks away, in Bloco C, is another similar establishment.

Chinese

Restaurante China
CLS-RUV 103, Bloco
D, Loja 02
Phone 224-3339
11:30–3; 7–midnight
Sunday Noon–5;
7–midnight
Inexpensive

Larger and prettier than most Chinese restaurants, Restaurante China is entered by passing under a large green awning. The sign outside shows the restaurant's mascot, a peacock etched on green glass. Within, hanging lanterns, a wood-beamed ceiling, and red cloths make a pleasant impression. Recommended dishes are chop suey de legumes (vegetables) or de camarão (shrimp), won ton frito, and soups with carne de porco (pork). Phone orders accepted.

236 Brazil on Your Own

German

Bier-Fass
Centro Comercial
Gilberto Salomão
Phone 248-1513
4–after midnight
Inexpensive

Brasília's international cuisine offers German food along with the more usual French, Italian, and Oriental. A German restaurant that does not stick exclusively to German food is Bier-Fass. Housed in a large, brick building, it has a wood ceiling, and offers a pianist for entertainment. Meat and fish dishes and pizzas are available, but Eisben is especially recommended. Eisben comes in several varieties; try *Kesseler* (knockwurst) or *salsechão* (sausage). Mostly frequented by a young crowd.

Fritz
SLS 405
Noon–midnight

Across from La Fornarina is a German restaurant called Fritz. Many typical German dishes are served here: *Wurstsalat* (sausage vinaigrette), *Eisben, Wiener Schnitzel, Schweinskotelletes* (pork), or *Gulsachuppe* (a German soup). Bratwurst, knockwurst, frankfurters, and sauerbraten are all reasonably priced.

Seafood

Trapiche
SLS 104 Sul
Phone 225-8883
11–3; 6–midnight
Moderate

A good seafood restaurant is Trapiche, across the street from Restaurante China, and recognizable by the lobster on the side of the building and the blue awning in front. Enter through a small garden into an attractive, L-shaped room, with a piano bar. *Frutos do mar, filet de peixe com molho de camarão,* lobster thermidor, and shrimp any way you want (try baiana or Provençale). Also, frango (chicken) and pato (duck) dishes are excellent.

A Special Choice

Teatro Nacional Restaurant

For unique and special dining, try the restaurant in the National Theater. Take in the view of the city from the terrace; to the left is the Television Tower and to the right the rest of the city. There is a piano bar and the seating is comfortable in felt chairs. The range of meat and poultry dishes served here includes steak au poivre, osso buco, and pato furestier (duck with onions and wine).

Sightseeing

The city's highlights, of course, are its modern structures — the architecture and the design of the city. A hearty day's walk from any point will ultimately take in all, or most, of the city's highlights. The best place to start, though, is Television Tower, which offers a visible map from its observation deck. Start there to figure out the layout and get in touch with the design.

The city's stomach is the most interesting. The eastern tip, Lake Paranoá, is the only part of the city that was unplanned and is allowed for private housing.

Television Tower

Television Tower is the tallest structure in Brasília and offers the greatest view of the city. From that vantage point the airplane shape of the city becomes evident. Directly below the tower is the musical fountain. Right beyond this is the bus station, at the right angle of Eixo Monumental and Eixo Rodoviario. Forming a large circle around the bus station are the sectors for hotels, business, and culture. To the left is the *National Theater,* shaped like an Aztec pyramid. On the right, looking east, is the *Cathedral of Brasília,* in its wine-cup shape. Then, still looking east, the parallel row of government buildings is visible, with its end the twin towers. Beyond the *Three Powers Square,* made up of the twin towers and the buildings of the executive and judicial branches, is the lake. Turning west, the most immediate site is the JK Monument, then the municipal government buildings and the military sector.

The tower itself is 715 feet high, but the observation deck is at 246 feet. At sixty-five feet is a restaurant, Paranoá Churrascaria, a pub, and a gift shop. There is a constant stream of children from the suburb of Cristalina, selling jewelry. The elevator is open from 8 A.M. till 8 P.M. and has a sign reading "It is easier to live if you have a friend," which is obviously an anti-suicide message.

Catedral de Brasília

On the south side of Eixo Monumental is the Catedral de Brasília, a magnificent structure. With sixteen arched spires, representing heaven-stretched hands, circling the structure, the church is shaped in the form of a wine cup, with wide bottom and skinny top. The entrance to the church is marked by four bronze statues by Halinn Alfredo Ceschiati which symbolize Christ's disciples. The entrance curves down and passes through a totally dark passage called the Meditation Zone; the darkness symbolizes the time before creation. The sanctuary itself is underground and is illuminated only by natural light that is filtered in through the stained glass windows. The twenty-two columns forming a frame around the windows represent the twenty-two states of Brazil

There are paintings by Brazilian artist Di Cavalcanti and three flying angels that announce the arrival of Christ. The church is built with concave walls that enable sound to carry to opposite sides. The marble is Italian, the crystal French, the bells a gift from Spain, and the organ German.

There are no seats in the church. It is open from 9 A.M. to 11 A.M. and 2 to 5 P.M.

Praça dos Três Poderes

Three Powers Square forms the eastern end of the long line of government buildings along Eixo Monumental. On the other side of the square is the lake. The square is made up of the twin towers of the legislative branch, the Federal Supreme Court, Planalto Palace, two statues, and a large flagpole.

If seen as a clock, the twin towers would be the six, the Supreme Court building the four, the clothespin statue the two, the flagpole the 12, the two warriors statue the 10, and the Presidential Palace the eight.

The twin towers are flanked by a saucer and a bowl. The saucer is used by the Senate and the bowl by the House. Near the top of the 28-story buildings is a ramp between the two forming an H for humanity (*humanide*). Open 8 to 12 and 2 to 5.

The Federal Supreme Court has a monument to justice in front of it.

The clothespin statue was built to create equilibrium in the square. It is now a bird's paradise.

The flagpole, *Mastro da Bandeira,* was originally built by the military when they were in power. When the civilian government took over, they asked Oscar Niemeyer to make the flagpole look less macho. He designed twenty-two tubes circling the pole, which represent the twenty-two states of Brazil. A new flag, donated each month by a different state, is hoisted at the beginning of the month. The flagpole is 328 feet tall.

The two warriors statue was made to honor the laborers who built Brazil.

The Planalto Palace has a marble and glass exterior and is introduced by columns. There is a changing of the guard and, like the White House, when two flags fly, the President is present, when there is one flag, he is absent. One is allowed in only in formal attire.

Itamarati Palace

Located in the Esplanade of the Ministries, just west of Three Powers Square, Itamarati Palace houses the Foreign Ministry. The building sits in a large pool of water, surrounded by flora, with a statue of a meteor in the middle. Built in contrasting antique and modern styles, the building also contains many paintings. Admission is only with a one-day notice.

Palácio do Ministerio da Justiça

Opposite Itamarati, the Palace of Justice is one of the most striking structures in Brasília, with artificial waterfalls emanating from its columns in Roman arches blending with the glass in a rectangular shape. Open Monday through Friday 8–5.

Teatro Nacional de Brasília

Located just east of Eixo Rodoviario on the north side of Eixo Monumental is the remarkable Teatro Nacional de Brasília, shaped like an Aztec pyramid.

Construction on the theater began in 1960 but was suspended in the beginning of 1961. By this time, though, the general foundation was laid and use of one of the theater's auditoriums was possible. The Martins Penna auditorium was first used in 1966.

In 1976 construction resumed to complete the theater. Another brief stasis occurred, but by 1979 construction was rolling toward its end. During the two years before its opening on April 21, 1981, all the rooms were finished. There is space for theater administration, headquarters for the Fundacâo Cultural (Cultural foundation), rehearsal rooms, two art galleries, a printing press, and a library for the arts.

In May of 1980 the National Theater Orchestra was set up by the government.

The theater, in its triangular shape, equals about fifteen stories. The three main auditoriums are: Villa Lobos Theater, seating 1,307; the Martins Penna hall, seating 399; and the Alberto Nepomuceno Hall for 96 persons.

The theater has computerized lighting and state-of-the-art recording equipment. There are extensive indoor gardens, with sculptures by Alfred Ceschiatti and Mariane Peretti, a panoramic restaurant, and a bar. On the northern and southern façades are carvings by Athos Bulcão, who also has work inside the theater.

JK Monument and Museum

Behind Television Tower, toward the western tip of the city, is a monument and museum dedicated to the founder of Brasília, Juscelino Kubitschek. The monument itself is a tall pole that has a statue of JK inside a crescent moon.

The museum is entered through an underground area built by Niemeyer. In one room there are the original plans of the city, as composed by the people working on it. In a second room is the personal library of JK. In another room are his clothes and medals and finally there is a room lined with pictures and documents of JK from his infancy to his death. I particularly enjoyed the photos of JK with Eisenhower, Louis Armstrong, and JFK in Washington, D.C. Upstairs is the tomb of JK, *O Fundador*, "the founder."

Igreja Dom Bosco

Dom Bosco sanctuary is dedicated to the saint who predicted Brasília in 1883. He said, "Between the fifteenth and twentieth parallels, in the place where there shall be a lake, there shall be born a great civilization and this shall happen in the third generation. This shall be the promised land." This quote is written on a plaque on the entrance doors.

Inside, the only light is provided by a huge candelabrum that hangs from the ceiling. The windows are of sixteen different colors of crystal; there are 7,200 pieces of crystal in the huge hanging chandelier. The ceiling is blue and the sanctuary contains a sculpture of Christ done in wood. The floors are marble. The church is located at Av. W3 Sul, at Quadra 703.

Nossa Senhora de Fatima

The first church built in Brasília was constructed as a promise to Sara Kubitschek, fulfilling her desire that the first building in Brasília be a church. It was completed in 1958, two years before the city officially opened. Designed by Oscar Niemeyer, the church is shaped like a nun's hat.

It is located between superquadras 307 and 308, right in front of Local Commercial sectors 107 and 108.

Museu de Valores do Banco Central

Located in the South Banking Center is one of Brasília's most interesting museums, Museu de Valores do Banco Central. The museum was opened in 1981 and is an off-shoot of the Central Bank Museum in Rio.

The museum is on the second floor of the bank building, which has twenty-two floors, eight of which are underground. Divided into three rooms, the museum has a collection of bills, documents, and securities of the National Treasury, the Conversion Office, The Stabilization Office, and the Regional Office of the Ministry of Finance of Brazil's many states. It also has a collection of some 15,000 items from the Brazilian mint and 34,000 coins from the gold reserve. All in all, the museum has 109,000 items that chart Brazil's economic history.

The Brazilian Room exhibits coins, bills, and printed securities since Brazil's discovery. The gallery of colonial Brazil features the monetary systems from the Portuguese and Dutch occupations. The Brazilian Empire room highlights the year when Brazil first started issuing bills and coins. The Republican Brazil gallery displays tender from modern Brazil.

The Currency Room highlights currency from around the world, and portrays the experimentation that has taken place with tender and money for ages. Finally, the World Room displays modern currency from around the world.

Identification is needed to enter the museum. It is open from 10 A.M. to 4 P.M. Tuesday through Friday and from 2 P.M. to 6 P.M. on Saturday.

Caixa Econômica Federal

Another museum in a bank is Caixa Econômica Federal, which also documents the economic history of Brazil. This museum exhibits banking facilities throughout the years. There are replicas of antique branches, ledgers, typewriters, adding machines, desks, safe rooms, lottery machines, and conference rooms. There is also an exhibit of the centennial promotion of 1922.

The museum is located across the street from Banco Central and is open from 9 A.M. to 9 P.M. Monday through Friday and 1 P.M. to 6 P.M. on Saturday.

Superquadras

The superquadras, the residential sections for government workers spanning each side of Eixo Monumental and running north and south along Eixo Rodoviario, are worth seeeing because of their symmetry and order.

Each superquadra (block) is a self-contained square surrounded by trees, lawns, and hedges. Each block has eleven buildings that all follow the basic architectural pattern— an open ground floor and no more than six stories. Each building has seventy-two apartments; two to three thousand people live in one superquadra.

Each neighborhood, made up of four superquadras, has its own elementary school, playground and sports facilities, shops, cinemas, and supermarket.

Buriti Palace

In front of the Praça da Municipalidade (Municipal Plaza) is the administrative seat of the federal district, the Buriti Palace. This palace houses the governor's office and the offices of his staff. There is an illuminated fountain in the square. It is open to visitors on weekdays from 8 till 6.

Military Zone

Sequestered from the offices of the civilian government, the military sector is past the JK monument toward the western end of Brasília. The buildings are long and expansive. Inside there is an auditorium shaped like an *M* for *military*. In front of the buildings are extensive landscaped gardens done by Burle Marx, who did the landscaping for the whole city, and a giant flagpole in the shape of a sword.

Palácio da Alvorada (Palace of the Dawn)

At the tip of Eixo Monumental, at the shores of Lake Paranoá, is one of Brasílian's first structures — the home of the president. The building has white triangular-shaped columns. The palace can be visited when the president is not there. Permission should be obtained from security. There is a small church on the left side of the palace created by the only non-Brazilian architect, Le Corbusier.

University of Brasília

Located along an extensive strip of land on the northern side of the lake, the college was founded in 1961 and has over 9,000 students. The architecture here is wonderful.

Medici Sports Center

With facilities for car racing, swimming, diving, tennis, soccer, basketball, and track, the center is worth stopping at. There is also a stadium for 116,000, a gym for 20,000, and a convention center, one of the five largest in Brazil, that has an archive containing over 400 years of history.

Satellite Cities

Most of the workers of Brasília live in the satellite cities. As mentioned, the population in the cities is much poorer and is now dominated by the culture from northeastern Brazil, Bahia. A city's distance from downtown Brasília identifies greater poverty.

The main city is *Planaltina,* oldest of the satellite cities, dating back to 1859. It has 60,000 people and is twenty-five miles west of Brasília. It is probably the most important of the cities and has nice colonial streets.

Taguatinga, the first city built as a direct outcome of Brasília in 1958, is the largest and most developed. It has light industry of its own and has a population of 300,000.

Guará, nine miles away, has many modern apartments for the workers of Brasília.

Tours of the satellite cities are available.

Walking Tour

The best way to take in Brasília is on foot. Start at Television Tower to familiarize yourself with the layout of the city.

From there, walk east on Eixo Monumental toward Three Powers Square and past all the governemnt buildings lined up so neatly. Initially you will pass the bus station, the central marking point for the ordered city, and the superquadras will be on either side.

On the right, or south, side will be the cathedral. The next noteworthy site is Itamarati. Continue until you reach Three Powers Square. In the square is the Museu Histórico, which traces the many steps, from 1898 to 1956, in Brasília's ultimate formation. On the square is also the two warriors sculpture.

On the other side of the Eixo, which is reached by turning round the Three Powers Square, and a little further west, is the Aztec pyramid of the National Theater.

Leave your feet for a moment and take a cab to Palácio da Alvorada on the lake. From there, ask the driver to let you off at the strip of the embassies on the Lago Sul.

From there, delve into the superquadras and get yourself to the eight-mile strip near the Television Tower called W3S—the main shopping street.

Brasília Nightlife

Nightspots do not proliferate in Brasília in the same way that restaurants do, so the city's nightlife does not offer a lot of variety. Apart from Corte, in the St. Paul Park Hotel, the best nightclubs are in the shopping centers near the airport on the south side of the lake. They are L'Escalier and Grog. There are a few piano bars and some pick-up places.

Corte Club Privé
St. Paul Park Hotel
Quadra 2, Bloco H
Phone 226-1515
8 P.M.–4 A.M.
Closed Sunday

Corte Club Privé, in the St. Paul Park Hotel, is a discotheque only. There is a large dance floor with modern equipment and sound. As you make your way downstairs, take note of the disc jockeys in their transparent booth. Plenty of air conditioning and couches and hassocks arranged around tables keep you comfortable whether dancing or sitting. There are lots of mirrors to enhance the effects of dimness combined with flashing colored lights. The entrance, separate from that of the hotel, is canopied and easily recognizable.

Grog
Gilbertinho Shopping
Center
Quadra 11, Bloco F
Phone 248-5641
9 P.M.–4 A.M.
Closed Sunday

Live music plays at the Grog on Friday and Saturday nights, and Tuesday night features the Brazilian music called "Cara-okê." The club is dark and intimate, with romantic corners and plenty of space for those who love to dance. Leather couches and hassocks are set against the walls. One wall is a glassed-in garden of hanging plants and flowers, lit with spotlights. A spiral staircase leads to the rest rooms. Outside, a brass railing and lighted window filled with flowers decorate the exterior. Entrances, at the front and sides, are mirrored.

L'Escalier
Gilberto Salomão
Shopping Center
Quadra 5, Bloco E
10 P.M.–4 A.M.
Wednesday–Sunday

There is a lot of action at L'Escalier which has dancing on two levels. This is a discotheque only; the disc jockey can be seen as you enter. There is dancing below, but the main level is upstairs. A large room with mirrored walls is lined with leather couches. If you're nostalgic, you'll enjoy hearing Sinatra's "New York, New York" given a spin.

Papillon
Centro Comercial
Gilberto Salomão
Quadra 5, Bloco E
Phone 248-0987
10 P.M.–4 A.M.
Wednesday–Sunday

Also in the Salomão shopping center, Papillon has live music on Wednesday and operates as a disco during the rest of the week. There are two rooms; in the center of each is a sunken dance floor with psychedelic flashing lights that sweep across the crowd. Placed against the walls, which are mirrored to reflect the lights, are couches with tables in front of them.

Chez Levi
Centro Comercial Sul
Quadra 109, Bloco E
Loja 1260
Phone 248-5799
10 P.M.–4 A.M.

Chez Levi has live music and dancing. Although not as elegant as GAF (both establishments are owned by the same man), the shows here are unique in that they feature popular singers from Brasília (most of them happy to sing requests). Opened in 1986, this place is the best in town for live shows. Intimate, dark, and highly recommended.

Piano Bars

GAF
Gilberto Salomão
Shopping Center
Quadra 5, Bloco E
Phone 248-1754
7 P.M.–4 A.M.

The piano bar at GAF offers live music in an elegant setting. Even if you eat elsewhere, this is the best place to spend a quiet evening. The couches are comfortable, and the bar, although connected to the restaurant, is secluded to maintain a more relaxed atmosphere.

For Men Only

Men on the prowl have plenty of opportunities here. The streets in the hotel area are full of prostitutes. *Le Bateau Wisqueria* in the Setor Recreativo Sul (Southern Recreation Sector) is a pickup joint with dancing girls doing either strip-tease or go-go. Some are here to be picked up, some just to be danced with (this is in exchange for a drink). *Stalão*, Setor Hoteleiro Sul, is another pick-up joint for men and is next to the Brasília Imperial Hotel. Here you will find mostly professionals.

Shopping

W3S, the eight-mile strip near Television Tower, is the longest undesignated strip for shopping, and the one most used by residents.

The southern peninsula, across the lake, has two shopping centers: Gilberto Salomão and Gilbertinho. Both are known more for their nightclubs and restaurants, but shopping can be done there.

Like the rest of Brasília, there is also a designated shopping area. On the north side of Eixo Monumental near the bus station and across from the National Theater, is Conjunto Nacional Shopping Center, also called Eixo Rodoviario Shopping Center.

Located in the mall are many shops, restaurants, and fast-food joints. There is an H. Stern and a Sears, shops for records and muscial instruments, and supermarkets, of which the Jumbo chain is the largest. Jumbo's logo is an elephant with a raised trunk.

The restaurant *Snob* offers quiet lunches and so does the *Stalinho* on the second floor.

With rooms for videos and popcorn vendors, there are many fast-food places. One is *Pizza & Pizza*, another is *Fast Jacks* (like McDonalds), which serves hamburgers, chicken salad sandwiches, and hot dogs, and has a menu with fifty items.

Brasília Potpourri

Air Shuttle

Varig/Cruzeiro operates shuttle flights to Rio (Ponte Aérea); the flight takes about an hour and fifteen minutes. You can buy your tickets on the plane. Varig/Cruzeiro is

located at CLS 306 BLB, Loja 20 (phone 242-4111).
They also maintain an office at the Hotel Nacional.

Brasília Flag

The four crossed arrows in yellow against a green back-
ground are intended to signify Brasília's position at the
center of Brazilian policy.

Bus Station

The largest architectural complex in Brasília is the bus
station, located at the actual center of the city.

No Show

Lucio Costa, the designer of Brasília and its Plano Piloto
(Pilot Plan), never came to Brasília during its construction.
He sent advisors who reported to him.

Prairies

The federal district is huge (about 3,600 square miles), but
consists mainly of prairies (chapadas).

The Fourth Musketeer

JK, Lucio Costa, and Oscar Neimeyer each acknowledge the
efforts of Israel Pinheiro, who became the commanding offi-
cer of the labor force (candangos) that built Brasília.

Iguaçú
Falls

Like a Mighty
Warrior

guaçú Falls is a natural wonder, comparable to Mt. Everest in its overpowering effect. Its force and singularity make you feel enlightened, privy to something, like a great idea. It is also romantic. The falls plunge into the mighty Iguaçú River, which separates Brazil from Argentina and junctions eighteen miles downstream with the Paraná River, Brazil's border with Paraguay. You can effortlessly visit all three nations within one day.

Unlike Niagara Falls, though, Iguaçú Falls (great waters) is not an international commonplace. Although part of the trio of great waterfalls—Niagara and Victoria Falls in southern Africa are the others—Iguaçú has been confined in its reputation to Latin America and experts.

The falls, which were discovered in 1542, lie on the Iguaçú River and are eighteen miles from the Paraná River (Rio Paraná), the seventh largest river in the world. Iguaçú is twice as large as Niagara, and is broken up into 275 inlets and drops, making it a lot more complex than Niagara, which has two straightforward spills. (The most violent drop is called *Garganta do Diabo*, "Devil's Throat.")

The falls were discovered by Álvaro Núñes Cabeza de Vaca. Seventeen years before he came upon Iguaçú Falls, de Vaca explored North America. Unlike Columbus, de Vaca went inland, exploring the Mississippi River, the Great Lakes, the Salt Lake Desert, and the Colorado River. In 1537 he returned to Spain. Soon after that he was appointed Royal Overseer of the new Jesuit community on the Paraguay River. Eventually he severed his ties with the Jesuits and in his further explorations, found the falls.

Although de Vaca's is the first documented sighting of the falls, they were allegedly created centuries earlier by the force of a young Indian couple's love. Taroba, the son of Igobi, chief of the Caigengue tribe, which ruled the area between the present Iguaçú and Paraná Rivers, was inseparable from the blind princess Naipi. Naipi was beautiful and sharp-witted; Taroba was as strong as an ox.

One morning they were walking in the Valley of the Butterflies, thought to be adjacent to the rivers, and Naipi was asking Taroba to describe the sights they passed. His narrative was constant, until they came upon a small hill. Naipi, patient as long as she could be, finally burst out with curiosity. Taroba described the "I-guassu" river in front of him. "It's rounding the valley like a mighty warrior," he said. Naipi, at that moment, felt the unkind censorship of her blindness, and screamed. Taroba felt her anguish, kissed her hand, and walked away from her. He went to the edge of the river and stood in contemplation. He prayed to Mboi for Naipi's sight. With his pleadings, the river stopped. A strange roar emanated from the earth. Then there was an earthquake, which ripped up the ground. When the earth had quieted, there was a deep gorge that the now-running river dropped into. The creation of the falls took Taroba's life, but it gave Naipi her sight and she became the first human to witness the Iguaçú Falls. The legend states that now, in a full moon, the falls will echo the painful cry of Naipi, hoping for her lover's return.

The falls, after de Vaca's discovery, attained a high stature—Niagara was discovered in 1678 and Victoria Falls in 1885. Jesuit missionaries who made their home near the falls kept up its reputation internationally, with news going back to Europe. But the Jesuits' expulsion in 1740 brought immediate amnesia upon Iguaçú.

Iguaçú stayed forgotten until activity in the area started again in the late nineteenth century. In 1889 military engineer Joaquim Firmino established a military colony at Iguaçú (the town near the falls had 340 people at the time). By 1912 the military colony had been terminated and was transformed into Guara Puava municipality. Two years later the town Foz do Iguaçú (Junction of Iguaçú) was created and was officially named in 1918 by Colonel Jorge Schimmelpfeng.

In 1939 South America's largest national park was created around the falls. It covers 250,000 hectares of forest. In 1946 the town of Foz do Iguaçú became part of the state of Paraná, whose capital Curitiba is 630 kilometers away.

The area is now underscored by tourism (the abundance of hotels in such a small city highlights Foz's dependence on tourism), with Foz do Iguaçú having grown to its present size of 145,000. Aside from tourism, there is also industry in beans, manioc, rice, coffee, wheat, and soy beans in the area. A bridge connecting Brazil and Argentina (it was only reachable by boat before) was completed and opened November 29, 1985. Named after Tancredo Neves, Brazil's president-elect who died before taking office, the bridge is thirty-five feet high and half a kilometer long.

With the near completion of Itaipu Dam and hydroelectric plant, north of the city, the area surrounding the falls has been altered. The dam is the largest in the world and was begun in 1975, in a joint effort between Brazil and Paraguay. It is massive and powerful—one half of one turbo generator supplies Paraguay with all its electricity. The dam is also a monument to Brazil's modernity, while its neighbor, the falls, is a puissant symbol of nature.

The dam has obviously transformed the landscape on the Paraná, but it has also altered the lifestyle of the area. Iguaçú Falls and Foz do Iguaçú are still based on tourism, but the presence of the plant now creates an industrial edge. The two towering formations are a double lure to the area.

Spelling Bee

Iguaçú is one of those names spelled several ways. In English there are two different variations: Iguasu and

Iguassu. In Argentina it is spelled Iguazú and in Paraguay it is spelled Yguazu. This book uses the Brazilian spelling, Iguaçú (*pronounced: Ih-gwa-soo*).

Orientation

The town of Foz do Iguaçú is seventeen miles from the falls, to the south, and nine miles from Aeroporto Internacional das Cataratas, connected by Estrada das Cataratas; many of the hotels we have recommended are on this road. Itaipu is twelve miles north of Foz do Iguaçú.

The town itself has three main streets: Av. J. Kubitschek, Av. Brasil, and Av. Paraná. The southern end of the town where Rio Iguaçú and Rio Paraná join, is the point where Argentina, Brazil, and Paraguay come together and is marked by a monument.

Av. Brasil is parallel to Av. J. Kubitschek and Av. Paraná. Av. Paraná at its south end connects with Estrada das Cataratas and on its north end connects with Av. Costa E. Silva, the road that leads to Curitiba, the state capital. Av. J. Kubitschek connects, at its northern point, to the road heading toward Itaipu Dam. The main street that cuts all the streets named above at right angles is Av. Rep. Argentina.

Estrada das Cataratas is twenty-eight kilometers long and is the main stretch joining Foz do Iguaçú and Iguaçú Falls. All hotels and restaurants on the highway are numbered by their distance from Foz. For example, the Hotel Bourbon is at km. 2.5, two and a half kilometers from Foz. Hotel das Cataratas, at the falls, is at km. 28.

Argentina was previously only reachable by boat from the Porto Meira, six kilometers from Foz do Iguaçú. Now there is a bridge, Ponte Tancredo Neves, connecting the two countries, which is linked to Av. Cataratas. On the Argentina side is Ciudad Puerto Iguazu, which can eventually be the starting point for a trip to Buenos Aires, 1,700 kilometers away. An airport in Argentina is thirty-one kilometers from Foz do Iguaçú.

Paraguay and the town of Puerto Stroessner, six kilometers away, can be reached by Ponte Internacional da Amizade (Friendship Bridge). Puerto Stroessner has the only convenient casino, Casino Acaray, in the area. (Another casino is in the Hotel Internacional on the Argentinian side of the falls, but it is far from Foz.)

The falls is boxed by the national park, three quarters of it on the Brazilian side. Views of the falls can be had on either the Brazilian or Argentinian side; both should be tried, neither being the same.

The Tropical Hotel, Hotel Cataratas, is in the park next to the falls on the Brazilian side. Hotel Internacional is in the Argentinian side of the park.

The two government tourist information centers (PARANATUR) in town are located in the Hotel Cataratas and near the Ponte Internacional da Amizade.

The most crowded times in Foz do Iguaçú are December through February and July. The tropical weather provides for all-year-round swimming.

Arrival

The airport, as stated, is nine miles from both the falls and Foz, just off Estrada das Cataratas. Customs is perfunctory. Cabs are available for about $8 to $10. There are fancy buses for about one dollar, but there is not much space for luggage.

Hotels

In view of its size, there is an incredible number of hotels in Foz do Iguaçú, which indicates the importance of tourism here. The hotels will be found concentrated in three main areas: near the falls, along the Estrada das Cataratas, which runs between the falls and the town of Foz do Iguaçú, and within the town. As throughout Brazil, hotels are rated on a government star system and include breakfast in the rate.

Hotel das Cataratas 4*
Estrada das Cataratas,
Km. 28
Phone 0455-742666
Telex 0452-113

Hotel das Cataratas, located in the Iguaçú National Park opposite the falls, offers a spectacular view of the falls. Hotel das Cataratas is operated by Tropical/ Varig, the owner of Hotel Tropical in Manaus, and follows a design similar to that of the Manaus Tropical. Several long wings are built in a square, sprawled out in a lush and exotic natural setting that includes wild animals roaming around. The grounds offer a variety of outdoor facilities including tennis courts and a pool of varying depths. There are 200 rooms, equipped with TV, minibar, music, and air conditioning. There are also two restaurants, a piano bar located near the pool, a lounge, and a game room. The hotel is fifteen kilometers from the airport, and twenty-eight kilometers from town. Expensive.

Hotel Bourbon 5*
Estrada das Cataratas,
Km. 2.5
Phone 0455-741313
Telex 0452-247

The quaint Hotel Bourbon is located on the highway near the town of Foz do Iguaçú. Outside, there are tennis and basketball courts, a soccer field, two swimming pools, and extensive grounds. A plaza at the Restaurante Taroba also has a coffee shop, Naipi, as well as a piano bar (Boicy) and a game room. The hotel is nine kilometers from the airport, twenty-two kilometers from the falls, and two and a half kilometers from town. Expensive.

**Hotel Internacional
Foz 5***
Rua Alm. Barroso, 345
Phone 0455-734240
Telex 0452-574

The Hotel Internacional was only recently erected in town (1984). The round seventeen-story tower contains 211 rooms and has two swimming pools, one for children and one for adults. There's a discotheque called Skorpius. The grounds include tennis courts and extensive gardens. Moderate.

**Continental Inn
Hotel 4***
Av. Paraná, 485
Phone 0455-731329
Telex 0433-370 RADZ

Also newly opened, the Continental Inn Hotel is a glass and concrete structure of three floors. There are seventy-six rooms, equipped with remote control color TV and a refrigerator. The hotel has a pool as well. It's on the way to Cataratas on Av. Paraná. Moderate.

**Hotel Internacional
(Argentina) 5***
**Parque Nacional Iguazu
3370 Pcia. de Misiones
Centro de reservas
Av. Madero 1020, P.B.
1106 Buenos Aires**
Phone 311-4259
Telex 79600

The Hotel Internacional, on the Argentinian side of the river, is built within sight of the falls and offers a beautiful view. It is located, like Hotel das Cataratas, within the national park that surrounds the falls. The hotel has a nightclub, two bars, two restaurants, and a coffee shop, as well as a room for playing music and video cassettes. The grounds include three tennis courts and a pool. The hotel is six kilometers from the Argentinian airport, and thirty-six from the Brazilian airport. Its only drawback is distance from town. There is a casino here too. Expensive.

Hotel Panorama 4*
Estrada das Cataratas,
Km. 12
Phone 741200
Telex 0452-257

The Hotel Panorama is located on the highway that runs into Foz do Iguaçú. It has 160 rooms and three stories, built in a perfect semicircle around the pool, which is round also and set in a tropical garden. The hotel also has a convention hall. Moderate.

Hotel San Martin 4*
Estrada das Cataratas,
Km. 17
Phone 742577
Telex 0452-248

Another hotel on the highway — this one closer to the falls — is San Martin. The hotel has one story, with 142 rooms. Wooden floors and wood-beamed ceilings within, and outdoor facilities that include tennis courts, soccer fields, and a miniature golf course create a country club effect that's enjoyable. A travel agency in the lobby arranges tours that focus on different aspects of the area. Moderate.

Dom Pedro I Palace
Hotel 3*
Estrada das Cataratas,
Km. 3
Phone 742011
Telex 0452-473

The Dom Pedro I Palace, on the same strip of highway as the Hotel Bourbon, is a low building made up of five wings that radiate out from a central point. There are 182 rooms with air conditioning and color TV. The hotel has a pool and a nightclub. Moderate.

Hotel Carimã 4*
Estrada das Cataratas,
Km. 10.5
Phone 743377
Telex 0452-256

Hotel Carimã, located on the highway on the way to town, calls itself the largest hotel in Paraná state. Its two floors contain 340 motel-style rooms. There's a huge lobby, a game room, and several large meeting rooms, including an auditorium that seats 560. A winding staircase connects the floors. The restaurant seats 250, and the American bar seats 40. Moderate.

Hotel Colonial
Iguaçú 3*
Estrada das Cataratas,
Km. 16.5

Phone 741777
Telex 0452-299

The Hotel Colonial Iguaçú is located toward the falls on the Estrada das Cataratas highway. It has a country-style decor, and is similar to the Hotel San Martin in feeling and design. There are 200 apartments in its two stories. Spacious both inside and out, the hotel includes four acres of grounds as well as a game room, a TV room, a reading room, and a chapel. There are two pools. Moderate.

Rafahin Palace Hotel 4*
Rod. BR-277, Km. 727
Phone 733434
Telex 0452-453

Hotel Rafahin, on the road to Curitiba, has three floors, sixty-eight rooms. The pool is on the lower level. This is a moderate hotel with a somewhat drab exterior. The restaurant is on the main level, and serves excellent food, popular with locals. Moderate.

Mirante Hotel 4*
Av. Rep. Argentina, 892
Phone 731133
Telex 0452-296

The Hotel Mirante, in Foz do Iguaçú, has sixteen floors, 148 rooms. There are two pools, one on the roof, and one at ground level. The hotel also has a discotheque. Moderate.

Bogari Palace Hotel 3*
Avenida Brasil, 106
Phone 732411
Telex 0452-250

Bogari Palace, on the main street of Foz do Iguaçú, is a comfortable two-story building with a large, well-lit lobby and sixty rooms. The pool is to the rear of the lobby. Inexpensive.

Estoril Hotel 3*
Av. Rep. Argentina, 892
Phone 731322
Telex 0452-296

The Estoril Hotel is adjacent to the Mirante on the Av. Rep. Argentina. There are three floors, 118 rooms, and a small pool. Inexpensive.

Hotel Salvatti 4*
Rua Rio Branco, 577
Phone 742727
Telex 0452-237

Hotel Salvatti is a hotel in town that offers some of the advantages of the larger hotels. It's a fourteen-story building with 117 rooms. There's a sauna and a pool, a restaurant, a bar, a beauty parlor, and a garage. Moderate.

Hotel Foz do Iguaçú 3*
Av. Brasil, 97
Phone 0455-732511
Telex 0433-223

Across from the Bogari Palace, Hotel Foz do Iguaçú has two floors, 140 rooms. There is no pool. Inexpensive.

Hotel Rafain 3*
Rua Marechal Deodoro, 909
Phone 742635
Telex 045-2270

The 81-room Rafain in town is an excellent choice if price is a consideration. Located in a four-story building, it offers the amenities of a four-star hotel including a bar, a restaurant, color TV, carpeted floors, air conditioning, and a stocked refrigerator. Inexpensive.

Restaurants

Truly first-class restaurants do not abound in Foz do Iguaçú; they are rather few and far between. The best restaurants outside of the hotels are the churrascarias scattered about. We will recommend to you the best available.

Continental

Restaurante Tarobá
Hotel Bourbon
Estrada das Cataratas,
Km. 2.5
Phone 741-1313
Moderate

Restaurante Tarobá, in the lobby of the Hotel Bourbon, features live music, with musicians who perform Paraguayan-style, without hats. If you can, get a booth at the end where you'll have a view of the pool and the surrounding trees. Seats are upholstered leather, the lighting is dim, the menu is bilingual and offers a number of typical Brazilian dishes — duck l'orange (pato ao molho de larangja) and peixe ao molho de camarões (boiled fish), for example. Spaghetti and steaks are also included on the menu. For dessert there are crêpes suzettes and bananas flambados. If you like to, join in and clap your hands to the music. You'll have fun here.

Restaurante
Internacional
Hotel Internacional
Rua Alm Barroso, 345
Downtown
Phone 734-240
Moderate

The Restaurante Internacional, on the main floor of the Hotel Internacional, is a large room with modern furnishings. The walls, done in brown, are hung with etchings. Entrées include duck (pato com laranja), ravioli with four cheeses, lombo á brasileira (breaded steak with banana), and surubim á brasileira (catch of the day with shrimp sauce).

Cataratas Hotel
Restaurant
Estrada das Cataratas,
Km. 28
Phone 741-200
Inexpensive

The Cataratas Hotel Restaurant offers a slightly more internationalized brand of Brazilian cooking. Several large rooms with wood floors and high beamed ceilings are reminiscent of the Cuzco Turista Hotel. In the center of the dining room, a table is spread with salads and fruit. Supreme de frango cubana, chateaubriand ao asparago, stroganoff de filet with cream sauce, and marsala with mushrooms are some selections. Menu is bilingual (Portuguese/English).

Chinese

Restaurante China
Estrada das Cataratas, Km. 7
Phone 74-1314
Inexpensive

Typical Chinese fare will be found at Restaurante China. The main dining room is large with bare floors; two other rooms are visible behind the glass doors. Shrimp, chicken, and duck dishes, as well as other kinds of meat, will be cooked any way you like. Selections from the menu include frango passarinha, breaded shrimp, peixe com molho de lagosta (fish with lobster sauce), and vegetable chop suey.

Spanish

Restaurante Abaeté
Rua Almirante Barroso, 893
Downtown
Galeria Viola
Phone 74-3084
Moderate

Owner Paquito Serrano calls his restaurant "a cantina of Spain in Iguaçú." The restaurant is located in a red brick Spanish-style house with a tile roof. Several large rooms with wooden floors open into a Spanish-style patio and thence to an alleyway. The food here is great, and the atmosphere is congenial. Highly recommended.

Churrascarias

Rafain
Estrada das Cataratas,
Km. 6.5
near Hotel Bourbon
Phone 74-2720
Moderate

Rafain, near the Hotel Bourbon, is one of four restaurants of the same name in the Foz area, but this one is the prettiest and the largest—it seats up to 1,500 people comfortably. There are ten varieties of meat, roasting before you on an open oven, and thirty different salads, with an average meal costing approximately $15. The chef, all in red and wearing a red hat, prepares the food before you. The music (live) alternates between Paraguayan, Gaucho-style, samba, and Argentinian. Occasionally, on request, a popular U.S. tune too. Lots of fun.

Rafahin
Br. 227, Km. 727
Phone 73-3434
Inexpensive

Of the same chain as Rafain, Rafahin is located in a large brick hacienda next to the hotel of the same chain and name. There is music and a show every night. The churrascaria serves ten different types of meat and thirty salads; the salads are arranged on a salad bar. The dining room within is a huge L-shaped room with wood beams rising to a peak overhead.

Churrascaria Novo
Mundo
Av. J. Kubitschek, 3,550
Phone 73-4796
Inexpensive

Churrascaria Novo Mundo offers an abundance of food and a very simple atmosphere. The dining room is huge, with a bare floor. Fourteen types of meat, twenty different cold salads, and twenty-seven combination plates provide all you can eat. All this at a reasonable price.

Rafain
Av. Brasil, 157
Downtown
Inexpensive

At Rafain, Av. Brasil, the drink menu is complemented by an extensive salad bar. The large interior is pretty, with white cloths on the tables; there are tables outside as well. Although not as large-scale as the others in the chain, this Rafain is quite pleasing.

Santa Felicidade
Estrada das Cataratas,
Vila Yolanda
Phone 74-3384
Inexpensive

Santa Felicidade is another churrascaria, located across from Restaurante China. There is live music played inside a large room with wooden floors. Ovens are visible. A dinner selected from eight varieties of meat and thirty salads will run approximately $3.

Churrascaria Charrua
Estrada das Cataratas,
Km. 2.5
near Hotel Bourbon
Phone 72-2169
Inexpensive

Of the same type, Churrascaria Charrua is located just up from Rafahin near the Hotel Bourbon. The large, well-lighted room with wooden floors, has a center table where cold dishes are placed. Tables with cloths and paper napkins maintain a simple churrascaria atmosphere.

Cabeça de Boi
Av. Brasil, 1325
Phone 74-1164
Inexpensive

Live music plays at Cabeça de Boi, a churrascaria opposite the Salvatti Hotel. This is a large place with high wood-beamed ceilings. Open ovens cooking the meat can be seen from where you sit. The food is good, but the atmosphere somewhat crude. Look for the cow's head in the driveway.

Coffee Shops

There are several good places for fast food, whether for lunch or a late-night snack.

Restaurante Interlanch The Restaurante Interlanch in
Hotel Internacional Foz the Hotel Internacional is a large
Rua Alm. Barroso, 345 and attractive coffee shop that
Phone 734-240 serves omelets and sandwiches
Inexpensive as well as canja, a kind of chicken
soup, and sardinhas com cebola
(sardines with onions).

Aquarius Even less formal, the Aquarius
Hotel Internacional Foz coffee shop, also located in the
Hotel Internacional, is open
twenty-four hours. This is a
good place to enjoy coffee and
dessert or a light sandwich. Usually crowded, even late at night.

Fast Food in Town

In the town of Foz, at the square opposite the Bogari Hotel on Av. Brasil at the corner of Rua Rebouças, are a number of fast-food restaurants. A delightful ice cream parlor is *Baloon,* which is usually crowded with young and old. Nearby is the *Via Pizzeria,* which has indoor and outdoor tables. At *Falls Burger* you can order from the photos hanging on the walls—hot dogs, hamburgers, cheeseburgers, and batatas fritas (French fries) in all shapes and forms.

Sightseeing

The main reason anyone comes to Foz do Iguaçú is to view the falls, from both the Brazilian side and the Argentinian side. Itaipu Dam should be your second priority, with the option open for short visits to Porto Iguazu, the town of the falls in Argentina, and Puerto Stroessner in Paraguay.

There are three ways to reach the falls from Foz do Iguaçú. If you have a car, take Estrada das Cataratas south to the end. Taxis are available, of course, and there is bus service along Estrada das Cataratas, with two buses an hour. The bus stops will be marked *paradas*.

The bus will let you out at the Hotel das Cataratas in Parque Nacional do Iguaçú; the pounding of the falls becomes immediately apparent. The houses passed upon entry are where the park workers reside; there is a school for their children in the park. There is also a museum on the right at the entrance.

Helicopter rides over the falls (and over Itaipu Dam) are available. The ride lasts six minutes and tickets can be obtained outside the hotel.

The rim of the falls is shaped like a horseshoe, with Brazil the near leg and Argentina the far one. The two countries meet at Devil's Throat (the most violent of the many spills and in Portuguese called Garganta do Diabo). Actually, eight-five percent of the falls lies in Argentina.

A yellow raincoat should be rented before beginning on the walkway (*passarela*), which is one mile long and made of metal with green rails. The walkway starts at the hotel and as you walk, the sound of the falls becomes more haunting, more fierce.

Making your way toward the curve of the horseshoe, approaching Devil's Throat, the real nature of the falls becomes apparent and dramatic. At this point, down a few steps, you are actually under the falls and almost feel a part of it. The falls are not fluid and continuous, but channeled by many rocks and trees.

It is the vantage point, under the falls, that separates the view from the Brazilian side as compared to that of the Argentinian side. With the falls actually falling by you, and being jutted out on the walkway, you really see the entire spectacle. Its force is dumbfounding and scary.

Behind the ramp there is an elevator that takes you to an observation deck. From this point the whole formation of the falls—the water's entry into the drop, the drop itself, and the river below—becomes clear. This again differs from the Argentinian side, which is a little behind the actual drop, on the upper part of the river. On a sunny day rainbows form over the falls and can be seen wonderfully from this point.

Lunch in the Hotel Cataratas or a picnic are both nice. The rest of the day should be spent in the National Park, which is rich in wildlife and flora.

The Falls from Argentina

To reach the Argentinian side of the falls, you should cross the Tancredo Neves bridge three miles from Foz do Iguaçú. (You can cross the bridge by bike, car, or taxi, and you also have the option of going to Argentina by boat from Porto Meira.)

The bridge, half a kilometer long and twelve meters high, offers a bird's eye view of Paraguay, Argentina, and Brazil. The joining of Rio Iguaçú and Rio Paraná is at Marcos das Tres Fronteiras, and the three countries are marked by monuments on their respective banks: blue and white for Argentina; red, white and blue for Paraguay; and green and yellow for Brazil. Rio Iguaçú separates Brazil and Argentina and Rio Paraná separates Brazil and Paraguay.

A passport is not necessary, but it is safer to have it along; it necessary for a greater trip into Argentina.

The bridge exits onto a road, dirt and clay, that forks one way to the falls and the other way to Puerto Iguazu. On the road to the falls is a military camp, Ejército Argentina. Eventually the road leads to Parque Nacional Iguazu, which has a small entrance fee.

The Argentinian side also has a walkway, about the width for two abreast, that follows the falls. The railing and walkway lead right up to the water itself.

The violent rush of the water will, aside from getting you wet, create a heavy mist, almost impenetrable by sight, that looks like a cloud. There are live fish visible in the water, and a small island, San Martin, divides Argentina and Brazil.

The view from here is more precise than from the Brazilian side. As in Brazil, the park has a five-star hotel (described in the Hotel section) that's a good place for lunch. It's beautiful and worth stopping at. There is also a casino on the premises that is open from 9:30 P.M. to 3 A.M.

Puerto Iguazu

A stop in Puerto Iguazu on the way back to Foz do Iguaçú might be worthwhile. There is an Indian museum and an excellent store for shopping (the shopping here is better than in Foz) called Casa Macarmann on Av. Brasil, 370. The town also has stores that sell fine sweaters, leather goods, antelope, and souvenirs.

Itaipu Dam

The area around the falls has taken on greater importance with the building and near completion of Itaipu Dam and hydroelectric plant, thirty-six kilometers from the falls. It is worth seeing (even if you're not an engineer) because of its size, which is astonishing.

The dam is the largest in the world and was a joint effort between Brazil and Paraguay, the result of a treaty signed in 1973. The dam is named after an island in Rio Paraná and cost an equivalent of U.S. $25 billion to build, with most of it financed by Brazil.

Construction started in 1975 with the artificial diversion of the water of the Paraná. More than twenty-two million cubic meters of rock had to be removed. The main body of the dam is 1,234 meters long. The rockfill and earth dams on the banks of the river total over seventeen million cubic meters and extend for over five kilometers.

The length of the dam is about eight kilometers and the height is an equivalent of a 62-story building. The spillway is 390 meters wide and can discharge 62,000 cubic meters of water a second. The total capacity of the dam and plant is 12,600,000 kilowatts.

The construction of the dam was so massive that a town for the workers was set up adjacent to the plant. At peak levels of construction and work, up to 40,000 workers were needed, but the town houses only 9,000, with schools and a hospital on the premises.

The first rotation of the first turbogenerator took place on December 17, 1983. The reservoir created by the dam contains twenty-nine trillion liters of water. The dam will be able to supply, through eighteen turbo generators, seventy-five million kilowatts an hour. Only half of the generators are working now, but one half of one generator supplies all of Paraguay with electricity.

The dam, reached by bus or cab, is open to the public four times a day: 8:30 A.M., 10 A.M., 2:30 P.M., and 4 P.M. There is a public-relations center that shows a film documenting Itaipu's history. It is shown ten minutes after your arrival. The tour that follows is an hour and a half and takes in the actual dam and water release; the control center; and the lake created by the stanching of the water on the Paraná.

After the official tour, a stop at the town built for the dam's workers is recommended (cars are not allowed in).

Shopping

There are three main areas to shop in and around Iguaçú. There are some shops in the town of Foz do Iguaçú, some on the Estrada das Cataratas. Other fine shops are located in the Argentinian town of Puerto Iguazu and in Puerto Presidente Stroessner, Paraguay's border town.

Iguaçú Shopping

The best place to shop is the arcade at the Hotel das Cataratas. You can browse through shops selling local handicrafts, souvenirs, and artifacts. A well-stocked *H. Stern* jewelry shop has a magnificent selection of Brazilian gemstones, including some local specialties. On Estrada das Cataratas is the *Artesanato Três Fronteiras,* which sells local candy, wines, perfumes, ceramics, copper objects, and other souvenirs.

Shopping in Argentina

Argentina is famous for its fine leather, which is used in men's and women's clothing and household furnishings. Argentinian sweaters are stylish and well made and in top fashion designs. While in Puerto Iguazu on your way to the Argentinian side of the falls, you should stop and browse the shops in town. The supply naturally is limited and cannot compare with what is available on Calle Florida in Buenos Aires. The best shop I found is *Casa Macarmann* at Av. Brasil, 370. Here you will find leather and suede jackets, stylish wool sweaters for women and men, and cowhide rugs, as well as leather bags. Browsing is encouraged and if nothing else, you can pick up a souvenir of Argentina.

Shopping in Paraguay

The main lure of going into Paraguay is its casino, but there are a number of stores that might be worthwhile visiting.

The ride over the Friendship Bridge is very pretty. Immediately upon arriving in Paraguay, you will find hawkers in the street and many stalls set up for shopping.

The main business corner is Carlos Lopes and Av. Rodriguez. The huge Mona Lisa billboard introduces Galleria

MonaLisa. At MonaLisa you can buy liquor, ponchos, handicrafts, shawls, records, tapes, and gaucho artifacts.

Right behind MonaLisa is the Fouad center, a three-story complex of stores and galleries. Casa Y Pacarai, Av. Carlos Lopes, 250, has antiques, woodworks, records, mate (tea) sets, wooden handicrafts, shawls, hammocks, and gold items for sale. We recommend it.

Nightlife

Since the falls themselves form the main tourist attraction in the surrounding areas, there is not a lot to do here at night. By far the most popular spot is the casino located across the border in Paraguay. A few discotheques and clubs are the alternative.

Hotel Casino Acaray
Paraguay

The Hotel Casino Acaray is just across the Paraná River. A cab will take you there via the Ponte de Amizade; there are no tolls, and no passports are necessary. Outside there are slot machines; inside, blackjack and roulette. The main room, large and well-lit with tile floors, has a bar at one end for coffee and drinks. Dress is not fancy. Minimum bets are about $1.50. The size of the chips, rather than their color, indicates their value. Unfortunately, most games, particularly blackjack, are stacked against the client. The casino should be visited for the experience rather than the hope of winning money—your chances of winning are slight. I played blackjack until I discovered that the dealer's first two cards are closed. If you have ever played blackjack, you will realize that in such a game you can't win.

A Taberna
Av. República Argentina, 500
Phone 74-3112
9 P.M.–4 A.M.

A Taberna, in front of the Hotel Estoril, is a student hangout that has live shows nightly. The main room is large, with a wood-beamed ceiling. The club, which is much frequented by older people as well, is hip and loud and Eduardo, the owner, is a well-known man about town.

Skorpius
Hotel Internacional

Skorpius is the discotheque in the Hotel Internacional and is open Tuesday through Saturday till 4 A.M. There is a cover charge.

Wiskadão
Alm. Barrosa
Tuesday through Saturday
11 P.M.–4 A.M.

Wiskadão, in front of the hotel San Rafael, is a large four-room club for dancing with music to accommodate every taste. You'll find disco, romantic, country, and Brazilian music here.

Sambalão
Av. J. Kubitschek
Foz
Closed Monday
10 P.M.–4 A.M.

Sambalão, in front of the Praça da Paz, features live Brazilian music. There's a small round stage where the musicians perform their music, which is dominated by trumpets and drums. Packed.

Salvatti Hotel Disco
Foz
Tuesday through Sunday
11 P.M.–3 A.M.

The Salvatti Hotel's discotheque is popular with young people.

Iguaçú Potpourri

Bus Station

The main Estacão Rodoviário is located at Av. Brasil, 99, phone 73-3959. Buses leave from this terminal to all parts of the country.

Post Office / Airline

The main branch is at Getulio Vargas, 72. *Varig/Cruzeiro* is located at Av. Brasil, 821, phone 74-3344.

Sauna Clubs

There are several "sauna clubs" around town. Be aware that this is a euphemism for houses of ill repute.

Travel Agency

My favorite travel agency in Iguaçú is STTC at Av. Brasil, 268, phone 732-044. They have excellent guides who speak English and can whisk you around in comfort in private cars.

São Paulo

*A Large Place
for Business*

ão Paulo is, more than anything else, a business center. A city is always identified by one or two predominant features—New York is known for Wall Street and for its culture, Detroit for its cars, Los Angeles for the movies, Rio for its beaches and nightlife, Paris for its art, and Rome for the Vatican—and São Paulo is most thoroughly a place, a large place, for business. It is apparent, when here, that the city's single common denominator and motivator is work, and that pushes the city along through any time.

To grasp São Paulo's dimensions and its production, one must merely cite statistics. The city has a population of over thirteen million, making it between the fifth and the seventh largest city in the world (there are differing opinions). In 1872, São Paulo had 31,385 people. In 1920, it was up to 579,033. By 1970, there were 5,978,977. São Paulo's population makes up ten percent of Brazil's total population, but over fifty percent of its tax base. There are over 28,000 avenues, 50,000 factories, 116,000 retail stores and 12,000 wholesale businesses. The city accounts for forty percent of Brazil's industrial production.

The state of São Paulo, of which the city of the same name is capital, has twenty-five million people and is larger than the states of New York and Pennsylvania. The state produces sixty-five percent of the country's industrial output and has 114,000 factories. It produces fifty percent of the country's cotton, sixty-two percent of its sugar, thirty-three percent of its coffee, over fifty percent of its fruit, sixty-five percent of its paper and cellulose, sixty-five percent of its machinery and tools, and ninety percent of its cars (over one million vehicles a year). The state also consumes sixty percent of the country's electric energy used for industry.

The city, a melting pot of monumental status, has the largest community of Lebanese in the world, larger than the population of Lebanon. It is also home to the largest community of Japanese outside Japan and has more Italians than Venice.

São Paulo's relentless expansion, though, happened almost wholly in the last century. Before that time, it languished as a small town that survived mainly on its coffee crop.

São Paulo's roots, like the rest of the country's, actually started in the eastern state of Bahia. In 1549, the Jesuit priest Manoel da Nóbrega and some of his followers landed in Bahia on a missionary expedition, with the intention of setting up a school. His attempts were largely unsuccessful. In 1553, Father José de Anchieta arrived and was soon sent south by Father Nóbrega to search out a new location for the school.

Father Anchieta arrived at Piratininga Plateau, between the Tamanduatei and Anhangabaú rivers, about thirty-five miles from the coast, in 1554. To the priest and his travelers the climate was perfect; it resembled Spain's.

Father Nóbrega was sent for and he lived with Father Anchieta in a house built by the Indian chiefs Tibiricá and Caiubí. Their house served, initially, as both church and school and was called São Paulo.

In 1556 a new church, called Colégio, was built. Around it, the original house, and the Indian settlements that protected the village, São Paulo grew. The village also had three convents surrounding it.

The seventeenth century changed the texture of the town. Its economy was based on sugar exports, but that didn't garner much wealth. Unable to afford slaves, the people of São Paulo began to hunt Indian slaves, selling some and keeping others. At that time the international slave trade was very much on the rise, and São Paulo became Brazil's headquarters for slave traders, *Bandei-*

rantes. Treks to the countryside for Indian slaves were begun in São Paulo, and some of these treks led to unexplored territory that was evenutally claimed for Portuguese Brazil. Yet the slave trade economy was transparent, without substance, and did not create sturdy foundations for the city.

In 1711 the village of São Paulo became a city which transformed its economic base from slave trading to gold. It became the chief center for gold exploration, attracting a great number of people. Explorations originating from São Paulo led to gold discoveries in Minas Gerais, Goiás, and Mato Grosso. Yet, like the slave trading before, gold was a transitory economy, and thus did not really root São Paulo more heavily nor expand its population greatly after the rush ended.

In 1759 the Jesuits were banned from Brazil. By that time São Paulo again was slimmed down to its original base of sugar farmers. Not until the early decades of the nineteenth century did São Paulo experience any significant events. Brazilian independence was declared here by Dom Pedro I, from the original Jesuit Colégio, making São Paulo a provincial capital. A few years later a school of law was extablished here, giving the city new vitality, a larger population, and greater commercial activity.

The city itself — its physical framework — also grew; streets were widened and created. This was paralleled by the growth of newspaper and book publishing and by the expansion of the theater. The law school increased the city's number of intellectual residents, who gave the city a new importance and eventually spurred it to become the country's biggest cultural center.

The end of the nineteenth century was the turning point in São Paulo's history, and the city did not look back. Some historians call this period the Second Founding. Three factors led to this: the extraordinary rise in coffee cultivation in the state, the construction of the state's first railroads, and a massive European immigration into the city known as the Great Migration.

On May 7, 1900, fifteen electric tram cars were installed, as was the first electric power plant in South America. The city, pushed on by the new energy brought by the immigrants, grew inexorably. The city's borders were constantly swelled and its infrastructure constantly expanded.

Yet in its sweaty, almost blind growth, São Paulo destroyed all of its historical structures. Colégio, the city's founding house, was largely demolished and so were most of São Paulo's past foundations. To see any of the area's history one must leave the city and go to towns like Carapicuíba, the Convent of Embu, the Bandeirantes, and Santana do Parnaíba.

In the 1920s, the 25-story Martinelli building was constructed, and in a way that is truer testimony to São Paulo than Colégio. The city is huge, tall, work-minded, and most thoroughly modern.

Getting There

São Paulo has three airports: Guarulhos, fifteen miles from the city; Congonhas, within the city limits; and Viracopos, sixty-five miles away.

Guarulhos, the newest, most modern of the three, has taken over all the international flights from Viracopos. Guarulhos is served by all of the international airlines, most prominently by Varig.

At Guarulhos, there is a place to change money, a duty-free shop, and a red and green light immigration system, like Rio's. The maximum of goods upon entry, without being checked, is $300.

The airport has on the premises a government tourist office and information center, car rentals, and two banks.

The taxi service is on the right as you exit. *Guarucoop* is its indicator. The purchase of a white ticket is for a normal ride into the city, and is about $5. The purchase of a blue ticket is for a deluxe ride, which is in a larger car with air conditioning and is about fifty percent more.

Congonhas, in the city itself, is used only for some domestic flights. The buses to downtown, Congonhas, are anywhere from $2 to $3. Tickets for the buses are bought inside the airport and the buses themselves are air-conditioned and have T.V.

The subway, another option, goes to both downtown and Congonhas frequently, with midday departures every 15 minutes.

Viracopos, sixty-five miles away, is still used by many airlines because of the prevalent thick smog in São Paulo. (It is so heavy that one's eyes and nose are usually troubled.)

The massive city is spread out on 2,400 square miles. The major streets that you should familiarize yourself with are:

Av. São João was the first street in São Paulo. It has the city's first buildings, hotels, original squares, main post office, and Hotel San Raphael.

Av. Ipiranga is a wide street that connects the Praça da República. It is home to the Hilton, the city's tallest building, Edifío Itália, and many stores.

São Luiz is the Fifth Ave. of São Paulo. Most of the airline offices are here—Air France, KLM, Varig, SAS, Swissair.

Av. Paulista was formerly the site of wealthy mansions but is now the home to many international conglomerates like Citibank and Bank of Tokyo, and is the location of the art museum, MASP, which is a highlight of the city. Many consulates and the Assis Chateaubriand art museum are on this street of skyscrapers.

Rua Augusta is where much of the less proper nightlife is located, on one end, and the best boutiques, clothing shops, pubs, and bars are located, on the other.

Av. Faria Lima is still being constructed, but is and will be a wealthy residential street.

Praça da República is a district for shopping, for hotels, and for restaurants. It is a central district in São Paulo, especially for the tourist. The streets are tree-lined and there is a park, with small lakes and bridges. The district is home to many artists and their works; there is a handicrafts fair there on Sunday morning.

The city's largest building, Edifício Itália, is in the Praça da República on the corners of Av. Ipiranga and Av. São Luis. The bus terminal is also in Praça da República, as well as H. Stern's headquarters and shop.

Barão de Itapetininga, near Praça da República, is also a section for shopping, for books, and for walking. The Municipal Theater is here.

Largo do Arouche has many flower stands and markets that are open twenty-four hours a day. It is also near Praça da República.

The Japanese district is home to all races of Oriental people. It is riddled with stores, restaurants, nightclubs, hotels, and markets for food and other goods.

In this city of parks, Ibirapuera is the largest, and is to São Paulo what Central Park is to New York. There are two large lakes, and every weekend there are concerts.

The park also has many buildings: an Oscar Niemeyer exhibition hall, a planetarium, a velodrome for car racing, an indoor sports stadium, a museum of contemporary art, and various government buildings. The park is also home to the museums of modern art, aeronautics, folklore, and science.

The city, in its modernity, is the largest cultural center in Brazil, with many film festivals, shows, museums, galleries, etc.

Getting Around

A subway system was completed in 1975, with one line and a second expected. The completed line runs north and south, linking the districts of Santana and Jabaquara, passing through downtown. The east-west line will connect Itaquera to Barra Funda. All the subway stations, except for Sé and São Bento, have bus terminals. The city offers an integrated ticket that is good for bus/subway crossovers. The subway runs from 5 A.M. till midnight.

Taxis in São Paulo work in two ways: by radio call and by roving the street. Some people are wary of hailing a cab because they have a reputation for swelling the price, but in our experience this is not true. The safety of a radio taxi is that the price is decided upon before pickup.

Trains for around the country leave from Estação da Luz station.

São Paulo is just under the Tropic of Capricorn and so is not as hot as the rest of the country that is closer to the Equator. The rainy season is between December and April. São Paulo can be cold at times, but the weather is generally the same, which is hot.

Hotels

As a major convention center, São Paulo of course has many luxury, top-notch hotels, most of which offer a wide range of facilities, from pet-sitting to heliports to large convention halls. All hotels here, like the rest of Brazil, are rated by the government on a star system. All prices include breakfast. Prices for São Paulo's hotels equal those of Rio's.

São Paulo Hilton 5*
Av. Ipiranga, 165
Centro
Phone 256-0033
Telex 011-21981

The São Paulo Hilton is located across from the Edifício Itália. A round tower of thirty-two floors rises from a triangular base; there are 407 rooms, with air conditioning and American TV programing broadcast via satellite. On the tenth floor is the pool (outdoors, on the roof of the base building), barbershop, sauna, and massage. A coffee shop and restaurant, The Harvest, may be found on the fourth floor. The London Tavern is on the lower level, as is a shopping arcade, where the jeweler H. Stern may be found. The hotel has a built-in garage. Expensive.

Maksoud Plaza 5*
Al Campinas, 150
Bela Vista
Phone 251-2233
Telex 011-30026

The Maksoud Plaza, with twenty-two floors, 420 rooms, is among the largest of the luxury hotels. Rooms have videocassette players as well as music and TV. The pool (indoors, with a glass roof), is on the second floor. The hotel has four bars, its own nightclub, the 150 Club, and an H. Stern jewelry outlet. Its restaurants, Vikings and La Cuisine du Soleil, are both worth a visit. Sports facilities include a sauna, squash courts, and a solarium. There is also a heliport. The hotel provides the best security and is the most private in the city. Expensive.

Grand Hotel
Ca d'Oro 5*
Rua Augusta, 129
Centro
Phone 256-8011
Telex 011-21765

The Grand Hotel Ca d'Oro in center city has unique facilities — two pools, one a large rooftop pool with arching glass roof, the other a round, open-air pool in a garden setting, along with squash courts and a billiards room. The hotel has its own antenna, so the American Armed Forces Network can be seen in private rooms, and you may find yourself watching the Superbowl in Brazil. There are 350 rooms. The lobby, bar, and restaurant have the feeling of a first-class hotel, created by plush furnishings and a predominantly natural wood decor. Ca d'Oro also has a kennel. Expensive.

Caesar Park 5*
Rua Augusta, 1508/20
Cerqueira Cesar
Phone 285-6622
Telex 011-22539

The Caesar Park is a top-notch hotel in the Cerqueira Cesar section. Its 177 rooms have TV and videocassette players. There's an open-air pool with a sauna and a bar on the roof. The Chariot Bar in the lobby has great live music and a friendly atmosphere, created by the musicians, who stroll around and talk to drinkers. The Japanese restaurant

Mariko and the Caesar Restaurant, with live music, are both superior. The hotel has a heliport too. Expensive.

Mofarrej Sheraton 5*
Av. Santos, 1437
Cerqueira Cesar
Phone 285-3837
Telex 011-34170

The Mofarrej Sheraton is a newly built luxury hotel in the center of town, with twenty-three floors, 247 rooms. There's a shopping arcade on the level below, which also contains a restaurant with its own waterfall. The lobby is a huge room with glass walls that looks like a hothouse with large round couches and marble floors covered with Persian rugs. One of the hotel's two pools is in this lobby. Expensive.

Hotel Transamerica 5*
Av. Nações Unidas, 18591
Santo Amaro
Phone 523-4511
Telex 011-31761

Twelve miles from the center of São Paulo in Santo Amaro is the Hotel Transamerica, with extensive facilities for tourists and businesspeople. The hotel has eight floors and 218 rooms. There are two lobbies; the lower one contains the pool. Health club facilities include ballet and jazz classes, shiatsu and hydrojet massage, jogging track, and sauna. There's also a squash court and an eighteen-hole putting green, as well as tennis courts. The piano bar is spacious and ornate. Transamerica also has two restaurants, Antarius and Blooming, on the recommended list. There's a heliport and a kennel. This hotel's only drawback is its out-of-town location. Expensive.

Hotel Bourbon 4*
Av. Vieira de Carvalho, 99
Centro
Phone 223-2244
Telex 011-32781

The Hotel Bourbon was erected in 1982, in the center of town. Other branches are in Iguaçú and Curitiba. The hotel was built in the style of the 1930s, with black and white checkered sidewalk and street lanterns outside; its graceful, molded architecture is a welcome contrast to the ultramodern exteriors of São Paulo's other luxury hotels. There are eleven floors, 122 rooms, each with a videocassette player, color TV, and air conditioning. The hotel has no pool. The lobby, furnished with leather upholstered chairs, is quite elegant, as is the restaurant, which is located off to the side of the lobby. Moderate.

Othon Palace 4*
R. Líbero Badaró, 190
Centro
Phone 239-3277
Telex 011-30448

The Othon Palace, centrally located in the financial district, is another large luxury hotel with a more pleasing exterior than most of the others. A long, thin, austere building twenty-five stories high, it has 250 rooms with air conditioning, TV, and music. There is no pool. There are several restaurants and a bar. Car rental is available. Moderate.

Nikkey Palace 4*
Rua Galvão Bueno, 425
Liberdade
Phone 270-8511
Telex 011-35187

The Nikkey Palace is a Japanese hotel located in the heart of São Paulo's Oriental section. There are 102 rooms with air conditioning, color TV, video channel, and AM/FM radio. A wet and dry sauna with jet shower and massage takes the place of a swimming pool. There's a Japanese restaurant, Tsubaki, and an international restaurant that serves French and Brazilian dishes. Moderate.

Augusta Palace 4*
Rua Augusta, 467
Consolação
Phone 256-1277
Telex 011-37956

The Augusta Palace Hotel is in the Consolação section of the city. There are ten floors, 159 rooms. The hotel has a pool, a sun terrace, and a sauna. The lobby is full of plants and has an indoor waterfall. Moderate.

Brasilton São Paulo 5*
Rua Martins Fontes,
330
Phone 258-5811
Telex 011-25558

A Hilton Hotel, the Brasilton has everything a Hilton is known for: modern, efficient decor and plush business setting. Centrally located, Brasilton has 250 rooms, a rooftop pool on the nineteenth floor, and meeting and secretarial facilities. Many of the recommended restaurants are within walking distance. Expensive.

Metropolitan Plaza
Hotel 4*
Av. Campinas, 474
Cerqueira Cesar
Phone 287-4855
Telex 011-35667

A short distance from the Sheraton is the Metropolitan Plaza, a comfortable hotel of bright, bold design. There are thirteen floors and ninety-four rooms. The pool and sauna are on the first floor, as is the restaurant. The hotel is one block from the Japanese restaurant Suntory. Moderate.

Crowne Plaza 4*
R. Frei Caneca, 1360
Consolação
Phone 284-1144
Telex 011-33096

The Holiday Inn Crowne Plaza is one of the seventeen Holiday Inns in Brazil. Its 223 rooms have air conditioning, TV, and radio. The pool is on the roof of the building in open air, and there's a sauna, a steam bath, and an exercise room as well. There are a number of bars and restaurants. The hotel is also equipped with a heliport. Moderate.

San Raphael 4*
Lgo. do Arouche, 150
Centro
Phone 220-6633
Telex 011-22457

The San Raphael is a white twenty-story building of imposing design, located off São João near the Largo do Arouche and its flower market. There are 200 rooms. Decor in the lobby and corridors is simple but fairly elegant. There is no pool, but the suites have huge round bathtubs for couples. Moderate.

Hotel San Michel 4*
Lgo. do Arouche, 200
Centro
Phone 223-4433
Telex 011-22457

Across the street from the San Raphael, the San Michel is another white building of modern design with an adobe look. There are seven floors, seventy rooms. Like San Raphael, the hotel has a barbershop and beauty parlor. No pool. Moderate.

El Dorado Boulevard 5*
Av. São Luis, 234
Centro
Phone 256-8833
Telex 011-22490

The El Dorado is another large luxury hotel located in the center of town. There are fourteen floors, 157 rooms. There is an outdoor pool on the main floor and several bars and a restaurant. Moderate.

Hotel Bristol 4*
R. Martins Fontes, 277
Centro
Phone 258-0011
Telex 011-24734

The Bristol Hotel is a fifteen-story glass and concrete structure in center city. There are ninety rooms, with color TV and videocassette players. No pool. The hotel has an American bar where live music is played, as well as a restaurant. Moderate.

Eldorado
Higienópolis 4*
R. Marques de Itu, 836
Higienópolis
Phone 222-3422
Telex 011-30546

The Eldorado Higienópolis is located on a pleasant tree-lined street in a neighborhood not far from center city. There are thirteen floors and 142 rooms with color TV, air conditioning, and minibar. The outdoor pool is on the main level. Restaurant, coffee shop, and shops are on the ground level. Moderate.

Restaurants

Some Paulistas like to say that São Paulo has the largest menu in Latin America. São Paulo's restaurants reflect its size and great ethnic diversity. There are restaurants to please the palate of every nationality, including French, Italian, Swiss, German, Scandinavian, Kosher, Arabic, Japanese, Chinese, and Brazilian. The city's enormous Oriental population has given rise to an especially rich variety of Chinese and Japanese restaurants.

French

Ca d'Oro
Hotel Ca d'Oro
Rua Augusta, 129
Phone 256-8011
11:30–2:30; 7–10:30
Expensive

Ca d'Oro is a fine restaurant for French and Italian dining. The dining room is spacious, with large windows beside each table, and beautifully decorated, with elegant hanging lamp fixtures seen above as you enter the bar. Fresh flowers are at every table, and the table service has the restaurant's own crest marked on each plate. An appetizer tray with lobster and shrimp is brought round. Daily specials include leg of veal roasted in rosemary and duckling roasted in a delicate herb gravy. You may also have steak Diane, spaghetti carbonara, and giant shrimp flamed with pernod prepared at your table. Desserts include selected cheeses, Italian ice cream, crêpes suzettes, and flaming cherries served with liqueurs and ice cream. Service is superb.

La Cuisine Du Soleil
Maksoud Plaza Hotel
Alameda Campinas, 150
Phone 251-2233
Noon–2:30; 7:30–1 A.M.
Closed Sunday
Expensive

La Cuisine du Soleil serves French and Portuguese dishes at a fixed price ($20 and up). Somewhat like the restaurant in the Rio Palace, round tables surrounded by semicircular couches and chairs dot the dining room. Côte de veau poêlée (sauteed veal chop), canard au miel et citron vert (duck with honey and green lemon), and river trout in julienne strips are some of the choices. For lunch try poulet roti (grilled chicken) or entrecôte bordelaise de filet mignon de boeuf. La Cuisine du Soleil is right next door to the 150 Club.

Marcel
Rua Epitácio Pessoa, 98
Phone 257-6968
Noon–5; 7–midnight
Expensive

Marcel is an authentic French restaurant that serves excellent traditional French dishes such as, for starters, escargots, paté du campagne, and saumon fumé. There are excellent soufflés (soufflé de fruits de mer, soufflé de crevettes); fish filets and shellfish (filets belle meuniere, crevettes champagnes); chicken dishes (poulet en papillote — chicken with vegetables wrapped in aluminum paper); and steaks (chateaubriand moutarde). Specialties are lapin au vinaigre or aux pruneaux (rabbit with vinegar or prunes) and canard a l'orange. Desserts include fruit tartelettes, meringues, and mousse au chocolat. This is a small restaurant (about twelve tables) where the preparation of the food is supervised by the owner. It has consistently been awarded three stars by the Guia Quatro Rodas.

Continental

Paddock
Av. São Luis, 258
Phone 257-4768
11:30–4; 6–11
Moderate

Other location:
Rua da Consolação, 222

Paddock, near the Eldorado Hotel, can be recognized by its mascot—the metal racehorse that hangs outside. Owned originally by members of the Jockey Club, the restaurant offers continental dining in an elegant setting with excellent views of the city. The three rooms are small, but use of rows creates three separate dining areas. The bar, hung with awnings, is surrounded with leather couches. Dining is in booths on leather chairs. Try bacalhau ao forno or filet de sole; other suggestions are trout with estragão, peru (turkey) roti with arroz a Milaneza, and pato (duck) bonne femme.

Terraço Itália
Edifício Itália
Av. Ipiranga, 344
Phone 257-6566
11:30–3 A.M.
Expensive

Terraço Itália is located on the upper floors of the Edifício Itália, the tallest building in São Paulo. Take the elevator to the thirty-seventh floor and change for the forty-first floor. The bar, reached by a spiral staircase, is on the forty-second floor. The restaurant has four rooms, two on each floor. Those on the upper floor are most intimate. Each has a different type of decor and live music, but all offer a splendid panoramic view of the city. Menu offerings include feijoada, camarão a grega (shrimps cooked Milanese style with mozzarella), chateaubriand fettuccine a terraço Itália (with fresh cream and parmesan cheese).

Japanese

Suntory
Alameda Campinas, 600
Phone 283-2455
Noon–2:15; 7:30–11:45
Expensive

Suntory is a Benihana-style restaurant where food is cooked at your table by a chef and served sizzling hot. There's also a sushi bar and an American bar for drinks. Situated in a house of dark brown wood, the restaurant has a Japanese garden with a waterfall in the back for guests to wander in or to gaze at as they sit at the bar. The restaurant is extensive, with separate rooms for boiled, fried, or grilled dishes, and private dining in the traditional manner—seated shoeless around a low table. All the rooms are carpeted and decorated in the spare but elegant Japanese manner. Choose from Shogun-yaki (shrimp, chicken, or pork), sukiyaki (meat and vegetable), Ishi-yaki (shellfish, chicken and vegetables grilled), and others, all cooked to taste.

Tsubaki
Nikkey Palace Hotel
Rua Galvão Bueno, 425
Liberdade
Phone 270-1420
Noon–3; 7–11:30
Moderate

Tsubaki, in the Nikkey Palace Hotel, has created an authentic Japanese ambience. At the center is a glassed-in waterfall surrounded by plants. There are several private dining rooms, as well as tables that have had a wok and a grill built into them, where all food is cooked by a chef at your table. There is also a sushi bar for sushi and sashimi. Tempura, sukiyaki, teppan-naki (prato a chapa), and Tsubaki-habe (prato a caçarola) are all specialties of the house. There's also a bar area, where four types of sake are served, as well as Suntory and Scotch whiskies.

Eno Moto
Rua Galvão Bueno, 54
Phone 279-0198
11–2; 6–10
Moderate

Eno Moto, in the center of town, is top of the list for Japanese food. Try sukiyaki, prepared at your table; batayaki (meat, bean sprouts, vegetables fried at your table); or teishoku (a complete meal with selected dishes). The restaurant's reputation is based solely on its food, since its interior is simple.

Italian

Carlino
Av. Dr. Vieira de
Carvalho, 154
Phone 223-1603
Noon–Midnight
Moderate

Carlino is a large Italian restaurant owned by Mr. Lucca, an Italian from the north of Italy, who also owns Tocanina. The decor is simple, with bare floors and travel posters of Italy decorating the walls, but the food is tops. Pizza, ravioli, and spaghetti of all types may be had here. Spaghetti com frutos do mar (with shellfish) and paglia e fieno ao gorgonzola (green and white pasta with gongonzola) are recommended. You may also want to try trutas grelhadas with risotto tropicale (grilled trout with tropical rice), or fettuccine gratinati com camarões (fettuccine with shrimp).

Gigetto
Rua Avanhandava, 63
Phone 256-9804
11:30 P.M.–3:30 A.M.
Moderate

Gigetto is an after-theater restaurant with a sophisticated air. Frequented by directors, singers, artists, and their fans, who come just to stargaze and drink in the atmosphere, its simple decor—wooden walls and bare floors—gives the feeling of a good restaurant. The menu is large, offering mainly Italian and some regional dishes ranging from minestrone and cappelletti a romanesca to filet de peixes grilhadas with batatas (grilled filet of fish with potatoes) or camarão (shrimp) ao Paulista. Pizzas, pasta, omelets, steak, salads, and other assorted dishes are served to satisfy all kinds of late-night appetites. Prices are reasonable.

Famiglia Mancini
Rua Avanhandava, 81
Phone 256-4320
11–3 A.M.
Moderate

Next door to Gigetto, Famiglia Mancini is a fun and colorful place for southern Italian food—mainly pasta—in varieties that cover a menu seven pages long. Decorated in red and green, with a wood ceiling, its walls are decorated with masks, hanging wine bottles, and photos of celebrities. Waiters in long aprons scurry to and fro. There's an antipasto table, where you can help yourself, and an amazing array of pasta dishes—spaghetti, fettuccini, ravioli, gnocchi, tortellini, lasagna with cheeses, shellfish, meat, vegetables, pesto sauce, and more. Omelets, soups, fish, and meat dishes are also available. Dine outside on the veranda or inside one of the many rooms.

Bongiovanni
Av. 9 de Julho, 5505
Phone 280-1355
11 A.M.–midnight
Inexpensive

Italian cuisine will also be found at Bongiovanni, along with some regional entrées. Fettuccine with mushroom cream, fresh-water fish with coconut milk, and meat escalope with madeira sauce are dishes to try here.

Churrascarias

Dino's Place
Av. Morumbi, 7976
Phone 542-5299
Largo do Arouche, 246
Phone 221-2322
Alameda Santos, 45
Phone 284-5333
11:30–1 A.M.
Inexpensive

Dino's Place is one of the most famous of the churrascarias, and with good reason. There are three locations in São Paulo. Spacious and sunny, with wood ceiling and rounded walls, it offers a terrific salad bar and à la carte menu. Try rump steak (alcatra) or contra filet. The asparagus, tomato, and broccoli salad, palmito salad, or the tuna and olive salad, served with five different dressings, make great complements to steak dishes, and are all part of the salad bar, included in the meal.

Baby Beef Rubaiyat
Av. Brigadeiro Faria Lima, 533
Phone 813-2703

Alameda Santos, 86
Phone 289-6366

11:30–midnight
Inexpensive

Baby Beef Rubaiyat, with several locations in the city, is another fine churrascaria. Chefs may be seen from the dining room, roasting the meat. Filet mignon contrafile and mixed grill (misto a Rubaiyat) are recommended. There is also an ample selection of fish, fowl, and shellfish. Salads are available, but celery, carrots, and olives will be at your table. Fresh pineapple, strawberries, and papaya may be ordered for dessert. The three dining rooms are large, with wood ceilings and white cement walls.

Another branch of Baby Beef can be found near Restaurant La Trainera; this one has a larger menu. Inside, large windows look out on a garden. From the dining room, meat may be seen cooking on the ovens. The steaks here have been garnered from the restaurant's own cattle farm.

Bassy
Rua 13 de Maio, 334
Phone 34-2375
11–4; 7–1 A.M.
Inexpensive

Bassy is a most popular lunch spot for businessmen; on weekdays you'll see them lined up here. A diagram of a cow on the menu shows the cuts of meat that can be selected. Tomato and cucumber, eggplant and red pepper, or potatoes and onions marinated in vinegar serve as delicious antipastos. The dining room is large and rectangular with high ceiling and wood-paneled walls decorated with wine bottles; seating is in wooden booths. A small bar in the front accommodates those waiting to be seated.

Continental Hotel Choices

The Harvest
Hilton Hotel
Av. Ipiranga, 165
Phone 256-0033
Noon–3; 7–midnight
Moderate

The Harvest offers continental dining with a regional touch in a luxurious and romantic setting. There's a pianist, and the food is delicious. Try filet of sole in ginger sauce, prawns in coconut sauce, or their surf and turf combination, with steak and lobster. Smoked trout and duck with almond sauce are specialties. There's an open salad bar on which a delicious cucumber salad and palmito will be arrayed, as well as fruits and cheeses. Dining is in a large room lined with mirrors; service is elegant. Take the elevator or escalator to the fourth floor—one flight up from the lobby.

Blooming
Hotel Transamerica
Av. Nações Unidas, 18591
Phone 523-4511
Noon–3; 7–midnight
Moderate

Another hotel restaurant that offers elegant dining is Blooming, in the Hotel Transamerica. The restaurant overlooks the hotel pool and the tennis courts and golf courses. Inside there are latticework walls and ceiling, bouquets of flowers in abundance, and tables with high-backed chairs placed around a polished bar in the center of the room. Appetizers are especially exotic, ranging from duckling paté with sour apple salad to shrimp or lobster cocktail with golf sauce and asparagus tips. There is also a cheese tray. The table service is fancy, with elegant stemware and embroidered cloths and napkins. For an entrée, try steak au poivre vert, served on a silver dish. Fish dishes include trout au bleu and milk-poached haddock. There is also a series of dishes prepared at your table: curried lobster flambée and veal scallops sautéed in white wine sauce. This restaurant is well worth the twenty-minute taxi ride from the center of town.

Scandinavian

Viking
Maksoud Plaza Hotel
Alameda Campinas, 150
Phone 251-4233
Noon–3; 7–midnight
Moderate

Viking, in the Maksoud Plaza, offers a buffet that includes sixty hot and cold Scandinavian dishes, ranging from fish with various dressings to different kinds of meat—smoked trout and marinated herring, as well as chicken salad, pork livers, and roast beef, not to mention the myriad forms of salad. After choosing from the buffet you'll be seated at a round table. A word to the wise: eat slowly, and do not mix fish, meat, or cheese. The restaurant is on the lower level of the hotel.

Brazilian

O Profeta
Alameda dos Aicás, 40
Indianópolis
Phone 549-5311
11:30–midnight
Moderate

At O Profeta, enjoy a typical Brazilian meal in a comfortable and elegant setting that is the closest you'll come to a hacienda. Specialties from the region of Minas Gerais—turkey, roasted suckling pig, and chicken stew—are served at a fixed price, and the food is good. Enter through the bar area, handsomely decorated, to the dining room, which is huge, with wood ceilings reminiscent of an old ranch house. Next door is a tea room, a real colonial café, where the serving of tea is a slow ritual, as in the old days.

Swiss

Chamonix
Rua Pamplona, 1446
Jardim Paulista
Phone 287-9818
7–1 A.M
Expensive

Chamonix serves Swiss food with slightly Gallic undertones: quiche Lorraine, pheasant dans son nid (with champagne and paté canapés), and various fondues. Sauerkraut, favorite of both French- and German-speaking Swiss, is served with different kinds of meat. The restaurant has its own wine cellar. Its ambience is pleasant, and live music is featured at night.

Chalet Suisse
Rua Libero Badaró, 190
Othon Palace Hotel
Phone 239-3277
Noon–3; 7–12:30
Expensive

If raclette is what you crave, try Chalet Suisse in the Othon Palace. Cheese, chocolate, or shrimp fondue and veal with mustard and mushroom sauce are special dishes, as well as an authentic raclette with potatoes. The restaurant is on the twenty-fifth floor and offers fine views of the São Paulo skyline.

German

Windhuk
Alameda Dos Arapanes,
1400
Indianópolis
Phone 240-2040
5–1 A.M
Moderate

For German dishes such as trout, pork shin (eisbein), and smoked ribs (kassler), head for Windhuk in the Indianópolis section, a short cab ride from downtown.

Spanish

Don Curro
Rua Alves Guimarães,
230
Pinheiros
Phone 852-4712
11–midnight
Weekends 11–1 A.M
Moderate

For real Spanish paella, try Don Curro. You may also want to try camarão ao alho e champignon (shrimps with garlic and mushrooms), lagosta com manteiga (grilled lobster with butter), or zarzuela de pescado (fish stew).

Hungarian

Hungaria
Alameda Joaquim
Eugenio de Lima, 766
Cerqueira Cesar
Phone 289-2251
Noon–3; 8–2 A.M.
Closed Sunday
Moderate

Hungaria is an outstanding Hungarian restaurant. At night a typical Hungarian orchestra plays and customers sit at candlelit tables to enjoy the music. Entrées include goulash made with veal, chicken, or mixed meats and cabbage; and gypsy filet, which is stuffed with Hungarian sausage and served with paprika sauce. The sausage is homemade, and the fruit strudel is excellent.

Piroska
Alameda Jau, 310
Phone 289-2251
11–3; 7–1 A.M.
Moderate

Piroska also serves a pork, beef, or veal goulash that is worth dipping into. Beef with paprika and mushroom sauce and Hungarian shishkebab with red cabbage and potato are other specialties.

Greek

Zorba O Grego
Rua Henrique
Monteiro, 218
Pinheiros
Phone 211-9557
1–3:30; 8–4 A.M.
Closed Sunday
Moderate

For typical Greek dishes like moussaka (eggplant, tomato, and meat casserole) or lamb with sauce and potatoes, try Zorba the Greek. Another dish served here is rabbit stew with cinnamon and cloves.

Kosher

Europa
Rua Correia de Mello,
56
Bom Retiro
Phone 221-7348
11–6:30
Closed Friday night,
Saturday lunch
Moderate

Europa serves Jewish food, all of it kosher, including gefilte fish, marinated herring with vinegar and sugar, and roasted duck with whole wheat. On Friday and Sunday, it's open for lunch only.

Arabic

Almanara
Rua Brasilio da Gama,
70
Phone 257-7580

Rua Oscar Freire, 523
Phone 280-2724

Av. Brigadeiro Faria
Lima
Shopping Center
Iguatemi
Phone 212-6990

For quick and tasty dining, there is Almanara, an Arabian restaurant with several locations. There is counter service here, with a separate dining area. Hummus and kibes asado sandwiches, chicken or steak platters (michui de frango or carne), and charutinho de uva or repolho, served wrapped in a leaf, are all highly recommended.

Galeto (Chicken) Restaurants

Galeto's
Alameda Santos, 112
Cerqueira Cesar
Phone 289-4240

Av. Dr. Vieira de
Carvalho, 176
Central
Phone 221-8978

Rua Desembargador
Eliseu Guilherme, 49
Paraiso
Phone 284-6492

Galeto's specializes in chicken. The Galeto that is pictured on the menu, is a small fowl which is known in the United States as a Cornish hen. In spite of their name, the restaurants serve pork, lamb, and filet mignon of beef too. Red wallpaper, wood ceilings, and bare floor make up the interior. Not fancy, but good.

Fast Food

An antidote to haute cuisine is fast food, which in São Paulo, as in any modern city, is spread throughout the metropolis. For quick, cheap eating, McDonald's can be found throughout the city, as can Dunkin Donuts, and Bob's, a hamburger and hot dog chain popular in Brazil. For a somewhat less generic taste, you might try the Brasserie Victoria, whose owner, an 82-year-old Lebanese man, serves fast food with an Arabic flavor. Next door is the rotisserie, where sit-down meals are served in a fancier setting. The restaurants are located at Av. Juscelino Kubitschek, 545, in Vila Olimpia (phone 282-0209).

Another good lunch place is the Promenade Café, on the lower level of the Eldorado shopping center. It's an open-sided restaurant that's great for people-watching. It looks out on the fountains in the mall's center and the activity around the elevators. The interior, though not fancy, is comfortable. Plants and flowers abound, and seating is on leather chairs. Although the menu offers a range of sandwiches and pizzas served European-style with lots of different toppings, and larger steak and fish entrees, only the buffet is available for lunch.

A Special Choice

Clyde's
Rua da Mata, 70
Itaim
Phone 852-1383
Noon–2 A.M.
Moderate

Clyde's is a singles bar that combines the features of a piano bar, a disco, and a good restaurant. Executive lunches are served here, along with tea in the mid-afternoon. House specialties are shrimp with blue cheese, trout with almonds, and chicken filled with cheese. On the Patio (a courtyard in the rear), a pianist plays from 6 till 10 P.M., after which there are live bands, usually jazz. On the upper level, designed for greater intimacy, old U.S. films and videos of World Cup events are shown continuously. Clyde's is the only restaurant/club of its kind. Its food and entertainment are equally praiseworthy. Clyde's is one of our Nightlife recommendations.

Sightseeing

As a modern city with a large, ethnically diverse population, São Paulo has many resources in the way of cultural activities. Museums, university centers, sports arenas, parks, and monuments abound. Its principal art museum, MASP, houses Latin America's most complete collection of modern art. Its soccer stadium, Morumbi, was home to Pelé, the world's greatest soccer player. There's a horse-racing track, and one for car racing. Ibirapuera, São

Paulo's central park, and the Praça da República and flower market in center city are sights not to miss. For a more organized tour, try one of the many city tours offered through the cultural circuit.

Butantã Snake Institute

Of all the sightworthy places in São Paulo, Butantã is the first on the list. It's an oddity unlikely to be found anywhere else. The institute was founded by Dr. Vital Brazil, a Brazilian scientist, for the purpose of preventing snakebite-related deaths. One of its original purposes was the invention of a vaccine against the bubonic plague, which at the time was appearing on the coast. The institute now distributes vaccines and medical products to medical units throughout the state, as well as running the Hospital Vital Brazil, which offers free treatment to victims of venomous animal bites. The museum contains examples of venomous snakes and spiders, while outside there are pens where live snakes may be seen. At feeding time, live frogs and hamsters are released into the pens. Inside the museum, there's a skeleton of an anaconda sixteen and a half feet long, a rattlesnake (cascavel), a cobra (cipo), and a water cobra, as well as some spiders (scorpions and black widows). Basic advice about what to do for bites is given. For instance, tourniquets should not be used, as they could result in amputation of the affected area. Not to be missed are the public demonstrations of venom extraction, given at 9:30, 10:30, and 11:30 A.M., and 2, 3, and 4 P.M. daily.

The Butantã Institute is on the grounds of the city university (Cidade Universitaria), although it has a separate entrance marked Serpentario, and is administered by the Ministry of Health rather than the university. The largest university in Brazil, Cidade was established in response to the need to improve education in São Paulo. The unification of several research institutes, schools, and colleges and the establishment of a law school brought about the formation of the university. The grounds, originally called Fazenda Butantã (Butanta Farm), are extensive, and offer a beautiful view of the city. The university is in the Pinheiros section. Many tour buses stop here.

Ibirapuera Park

Ibirapuera Park covers one and a half million square meters and houses several important city buildings, such as City Hall, the Legislative Assembly, the Planetarium, and a gymnasium as well as two museums—the Aeronautics and Folklore Museum and the Museum of Nativity Scenes. The park also houses some important monuments. The Monumento as Bandeiras is here, sculpted by Victor Brecheret to honor the original settlers from Santos who found the plain that is now São Paulo. The obelisk honors the heroes of the city's founding, with inscriptions written by the Brazilian poet Guilherme de Almeida. No cars are allowed in the park. There is a Japanese pavilion with typical gardens and lakes, and a garden for the blind.

Museums

The *Museu de Arte de São Paulo,* or MASP, was founded by Assis Chateaubriand, an eminent journalist. While serving as the Brazilian ambassador to Britain, Chateaubriand sought out a famous Italian art professor, Pietro Maria Bardi, to help him in establishing the museum. An 80-year-old man, Bardi became a Brazilian citizen in order to dedicate himself fully to the establishment of the museum.

Since its inception, the museum has moved to an extraordinary structure, a large building on four columns, on the Avenida Paulista. The interior was designed by Lina Bo Bardi, the curator's wife. A series of terraced gardens, waterfalls, and small reflecting pools grace the grounds in the back. Artworks are suspended by wires secured in tempered glass placed in reinforced concrete blocks. This practice, criticized at the time, is currently used in many American museums.

The permanent collection, of 750 artworks, includes paintings by Botticelli, Raphael, Velazquez, Rembrandt, Franz Hals, El Greco, and Picasso. There is an extensive collection of Impressionist works by Degas, Cézanne, Renoir, Van Gogh, and Modigliani. This is a good place to introduce oneself to the Brazilian masters Portinari, Di Cavalcanti, Anita Malfati, Tarsila do Amaral, Guignard, and Aldemir Martins. Recent acquisitions of import are *War*, the monumental painting by Lasar Segall, and a sculpture by Bruno Giorgi. There is also a collection of Italian ceramics from the fifteenth, sixteenth, and seventeenth centuries, and a rare collection of English art.

MASP was originally conceived as an art promotion and education center, in addition to its function of preserving Western art. To that end, much space is dedicated to new artists who work in a variety of less traditional genres, such as photography, cartoons, and engraving. The first floor is used for exhibitions; on the basement level are two auditoriums, used for plays, lectures, and nightly concerts, as well as an international film festival.

Museu de Arte Contemporanea, with 5,000 works of modern art encompassing Cubism and Futurism, is one of São Paulo's twelve art museums. Open Tuesday through Sunday from 1 till 6. Ibarapuera Park, Bienal Pavillon.

Museu de Arte Moderna, Brazil's oldest art museum, created Brazilian Cinematheque and Plastic Arts Biennial. Open Tuesday through Friday from 1 till 7 and Saturday and Sunday from 1 till 5. This museum is in Ibarapuera Park too.

Museu Lasar Segall houses most of Segall's work: 130 oil paintings, 375 watercolors, and 207 engravings. Tuesday, Wednesday, Thursday, from 2:30 till 6:30; and Saturday and Sunday from 2:30 till 8. Rua Alfonso Celso, 388.

Museu de Arte Sacra, at Av. Tiradentes, 676, is worth visiting for its architecture alone. The Convent da Luz, in which it is located, is a beautiful example of a colonial building. The museum's collection counts over 11,000 objects, as well as 9,300 numismatic pieces and medals. Open Tuesday through Sunday from 1 till 5.

Casa do Bandeirante is a museum exhibiting typical artifacts of the eighteenth century, such as flour mills and water-driven engines. A typical residence itself, the museum is open Tuesday through Saturday from 10:30 till 5 and Sunday from 9 till 5. It is located at Praça Monteiro Lobato.

The Cultural Center

Inaugurated in 1982, the Centro Cultural São Paulo sponsors a whole range of cultural events. Its library on the second floor contains 50,000 books on the subjects of literature, philosophy, science and technology, religion, and the arts. On the third floor are a discotheque with 23,000 records, two theaters, and a cinema that is open to the public at 7:15 P.M. daily. Tuesday through Friday at 4:30 there are audiovisual presentations sponsored by the research center for contemporary art. There is also a Juvenile Center where classes are given for children on photography and the plastic arts. The center is located at Av. Dr. Enéas Carvalho de Aguiar, 23.

Sports

Soccer (Futebol)

Soccer is Brazil's biggest and most popular sport. Originally brought over from England and practiced in the empty lots of São Paulo, it's become the country's national pastime. The three largest soccer stadiums in the city are Pacaembu, Canindé, and Morumbi. Of these, Morumbi is the biggest, capable of seating 160,000 to 200,000 people. It's an open-air stone structure somewhat like Shea Stadium in New York. Five of the most popular teams that play here are the Palmeiras, the Corinthians, the São Paulo Club, Portuguesa, and Santos. Santos was made famous by its illustrious one-time member, Edson Arantes do Naciemento, or Pelé, the star of the three-time world champion team, who was credited with over 1,000 goals.

Horse Racing (Hipódromo)

Horse races are held at the Paulistano horse track of the Hipódromo de Joquei Club, Cidade Jardim section, south of downtown. Races take place on Monday, Wednesday, and Thursday at 7:30 P.M. and Saturday and Sunday at 2 P.M. There's a special red-carpeted entrance for members of the club, who wear jackets and ties. It's a good flat track where bets can be placed for a minimum of 25 cents. Exacta and Dupla (Trifecta) betting is available.

Sections of the City

Japanese Section

The Oriental district, predominantly Japanese, has been built up by São Paulo's large population of Chinese, Japanese, and Korean immigrants. The section is a bustling district where the Oriental motif is followed in pagoda-shaped buildings and streetlights of red poles with white lights that look like Japanese lanterns. The Cultural Brazil-Japan Association is a center for cultural events. The inhabitants of the section own almost every establishment, whether restaurant, bakery, grocery store, or newsstand. Restaurants and nightclubs abound here, as do Karaoke places. The Nikkey Palace Hotel is here, as well as the restaurant Taizan. There are plenty of stores where you can buy souvenirs and items such as incense or Buddhist religious objects that would be difficult to find elsewhere.

Praça da República and Largo de Arouche

Praça da República is a large square in the center of the city brimming with tourists, shops, and vendor stands. There's a park with grand old trees, small lakes with ducks swimming in them, benches, and a bandstand. There are rows of small stands where arts and crafts objects, leather bags, paintings, and clothes are sold; on Sunday mornings there's a hippie fair. Just across the street is the tallest building in the city, the Edifício Itália; adjacent is the flower market on Largo de Arouche, open twenty-four hours.

Historical Buildings

Among the historical buildings that you may want to visit are the *Catedral Metropolitana* and the *Municipal Theater.* The *Catedral de São Paulo* is a Gothic-style cathedral built to replace the Church of São Pedro de Pedra of 1740. The cathedral was completed in 1954. An immense structure with a capacity for 8,000 people, the cathedral is quite beautiful, with two spires and a dome. At the main entrance statues of Old Testament prophets face those of the New Testament. There are thirty stained-glass windows, an Italian organ with five keyboards, and a crypt which is open to the public on weekdays from 2:30 till 4:30 P.M. Stone was imported from Siena, Galdana, Egypt, and the Congo to construct the interior of the church.

The *Municipal Theater* is one of the most beautiful buildings in São Paulo. It was built in 1903 by Ramos de Azevedo in seventeenth-century baroque style with art nouveau touches. The theater, which seats 1,632 people, is located off Barão de Itapetininga, a few blocks from Praça da República.

The Circuito Cultural

The Circuito Cultural is a series of bus tours designed to acquaint the tourist with different points in the city. There are eight different routes to choose from, including, for instance, a visit to the Capela Imperial Museu Paulista, ending at the Botanical Gardens. Another route begins in Ibirapuera Park and visits the Cultural Center and the Museum Lazar Segall. The tours operate on Sunday and start from the Iguatemi Shopping Center. Tickets can be purchased at the Sé Metro Station or at Information Posts of the Secretariat of Sports and Tourism.

Fairs

Fairs are a way of life in Brazil, but they are more intense in São Paulo because the city is such a business center; all handicraft and industrial products exhibits and all national congresses are held in São Paulo. There are many individual fairs, but the conventions and fairs that take place at Anhembi Park, the city's largest convention center, are festivals in and of themselves, with selling and dealing going on at a breakneck pace. São Paulo's second convention center is Convention Palace.

The Hippie Fair, Praça da República, is held on Sunday from 8 A.M. to 1 P.M. and features handicrafts, paintings, stamps, coins, gemstones, clothes, and leather goods. All prices are reasonable.

The *Antique Fair,* Av. Paulista, 1578, under MASP, takes place Sunday from 10 A.M. to 3 P.M. Antiques from all periods are on sale here.

Liberdade Fair, Praça da Liberdade, which is held on Sunday from 1 P.M. to 9 P.M., features Oriental goods, plants, handicrafts, and Japanese fast food.

Embu Fair, in the city of Embu, twenty-eight kilometers from São Paulo, is open for the whole day; paintings, ceramics, gemstones, leather goods, and handicrafts are for sale.

Carnaval and Samba

Not known for its version of Carnaval, São Paulo nonetheless has a grand festival, with four days of efficient beauty and play. The main spectacle is the samba march on Av. Tiradentes, which involves over 50,000 participants. Some samba schools are:

Grêmio Recreativo e Cultural Escola de Samba Unidos do Peruche, Av. Ordem e Progresso, 1061.

Grêmio Recreativo e Cultural Escola de Samba Mocidade Alegre, Av. Casa Verde, 3498.

Grêmio Recreativo e Cultural Escola de Samba Nene de Vila Matilde, Rua Julio Rinaldi, 220.

Grêmio Recreativo Cultural Esportivo e Beneficente Escola de Samba Barroca da Zona Sul, Rua Paulo Figueiredo, 173.

Grêmio Recreativo Escola de Samba Camisa Verde e Branco, Rua James Holland, 663.

Nightlife

Because São Paulo is a large city, there are many options for things to do at night. There is a diverse selection of places to go—shows, discos, pubs, piano bars, cinemas, and bars. Diversity is also reflected by the city's many cultures, with different spots having particular ethnic slants. The city stays open late, and the average closing time is 2 or 3 A.M.

Bars

Clyde's
Rua da Mata, 70
Itaim
Phone 852-1383,
883-0300
Noon–2 A.M

Clyde's is a singles bar that combines the features of a piano bar, a disco, and a good restaurant. Executive lunches are served here, along with tea in the mid-afternoon. One of the house specialties is shrimp with blue cheese. On the Patio, a courtyard in the rear, a pianist plays from 6 to 10, after which there are usually live jazz bands. Upstairs, past the bar and restaurant, the third floor combines dancing with U.S. films and soccer videos. The first floor is generally for singles; the upper floors are for couples. Owned by an Oriental family, Clyde's is the only restaurant/nightclub of its kind in the city.

Roof
Av. Cidade Jardim, 400
Jardim Paulista
Phone 212-3006
7 P.M.–4 A.M

Atop the Edifício Dacon, on the twenty-second floor, Roof (not to be confused with the bar atop the Hilton) has a large bar area, and is good for either singles or couples. The building itself is round and all glass, and offers a spectacular view. There's dancing. Popular with the young crowd.

A Baiúca
Praça Franklin
Roosevelt, 256
Phone 255-2233
Noon–4 A.M.

This 30-year-old establishment, which is a restaurant during the day, features a diversity of live music at night—jazz, Brazilian, and Italian—usually presented by a band of four musicians and three singers. There is no cover charge. The design of the bar, which is extremely attractive, is modern, with a touch of the homey (there is a stone fireplace). A Baiúca is one block from the Hilton.

Terraço Itália
Av. Ipiranga, 344
Phone 257-3365

Atop the Edifício Itália, the city's tallest building, this bar/restaurant is intimate, with candlelight dinners. On the second level there is a live six-piece band. There are leather chairs and small round tables and a mirrored ceiling in the bar. Of course, the view is great. Take the elevator to the thirty-seventh floor and change for the forty-first floor.

Lattitude 3001
Av. 23 de Maio, 3001
Ibirapuera
Phone 212-8698

A wide bar with a restaurant, a live band, and a dance floor, Lattitude 3001 is an old pirate ship, anchored at its own dock. There are three levels. On the upper level a band plays, and there's a deck overlooking Ibirapuera Park, the obelisk, and the bridge. Head out to the deck, beyond the bandstand, for a great view.

Clubs and Shows

150 Night Club
Hotel Maksoud Plaza
Al Campinas, 150
Bela Vista
Phone 251-2233
9 P.M. – 2 A.M.
Closed Sunday

Dinner is available at this club, which has live piano music and its own band and show, with room for dancing. Many famous musicians have played here, like Frank Sinatra, Dizzy Gillespie, Billy Eckstein, and more. There is a private club downstairs. Say hello to the hostess Elzi, a young lady who speaks English.

Showdays Saloon
Av. Rebouças, 3970
Eldorado Shopping
Center
Phone 814-9372,
815-7006
11:30–4; 8 P.M.–3 A.M.
Closed Monday

On the third floor of the Eldorado Shopping Center, Showdays Saloon is an authentic saloon of the 1800s. With a Gay Nineties touch, a huge bar, and two levels, Showdays has live country, rock, or Brazilian music and cancan shows (Tuesday through Thursday). There is an international restaurant on the premises. Friday and Saturday, women can enter at half price, and on Sunday there's a disco for the under-18 set.

Palladium
Eldorado Shopping
Center
Av. Rebouças, 3970
3rd Floor
Phone 813-8713, 9045
Monday–Thursday
8 P.M.–4 A.M.
Friday–Saturday
11 P.M.–4 A.M.
Closed Sunday

The Palladium seats up to 1,100 people and has two floors, a foyer, and a dance floor, and serves dinner. It is a classical showcase theater, with decor recalling the 40s and 50s, but with ultramodern sound and lighting; there is a mobile chandelier and a revolving stage. There is a cover charge. The Palladium has its own troupe and the show I saw was an homage to São Paulo, "São Paulo Night and Day."

O Beco
Rua Bela Cintra, 306
Phone 259-3377
8 P.M. on
Closed Sunday

After eighteen years of success in São Paulo, O Beco burned down. But is has opened again at a new address. The club has samba, live music, dancing, and a theme show. The club seats 300 and serves dinner.

Plataforma I
9–11
Closed Sunday

With the original Plataforma in Rio, this one, although large, is smaller than its sister. Shows stay for a year and are an hour and a half long.

Via Brasil
Av. 9 de Julho, 5710
Jardim Paulista
Phone 883-2951
9–5 A.M.
Closed Sunday

This samba club is purely for dancing, live and sometimes furious.

Barracão de Zinco
Av. Ibirapuera

This is another samba club.

Piano Bars

L'Ultimo Romantico
Rua Avanhandara, 40
Phone 258-6523
7 P.M.–3 A.M.

Across from the Brasilton Hotel, L'Ultimo is a large room with a friendly atmosphere, where customers often come to play piano. Owner/pianist Daniel Perola plays romantic, popular, and classical music.

Trianon Piano Bar
Hotel Maksoud Plaza
Al Campinas
Phone 251-2233
6 P.M.–2 A.M.

In the same hotel as the 150 nightclub, the Trianon Piano Bar is intimate and dark, with a huge bar.

Executive Bar
Hotel Ca D'Oro
6–midnight

This elegant bar has a singer and piano and is right next to the restaurant.

Big Bar
Rua Avanhandava, 16
Phone 258-2674

In front of Hotel Brasilton, Big Bar features popular Brazilian music. Definitely worth a try.

For Men Only

Upscale

Biblos Boite
Rua Augusta, 647/657
Phone 258-3571
8 P.M.–4 A.M. 7 days

A 20-year upscale establishment, Biblos is both a pick-up joint-striptease show and a place to relax. The bar is in the front room, and the show in the ante-room, and there is a restaurant downstairs. There are up to 60 girls at a time in the place, and the bar shows porno cartoons. The Japanese wife of the owner keeps a close watch on all people and events and can arrange anything.

La Licorne
Rua Major Sertório,
661 Vila Buarque
Phone 256-8724
8 P.M.—4 A.M.
Closed Sunday

With flags of all nations at its entrance, this large place, with thick carpeting and leather chairs, has erotic shows. There are striptease shows every half hour, a disco, and many girls. There is a three-drink minimum, with drinks going for about $3.50. There are also professional girls just off the premises that have their own apartments. The club is popular with Japanese businessmen.

Scarabocchio
Rua Araújo, 244
8 P.M.—3 A.M.
Phone 259-1290
Closed Sunday

Opposite the Hilton, Scarabocchio is dimly lit, and has a bar, tables, and chairs for food and a stage for erotic shows. There is also a disco, and couches for relaxing upstairs. There is no sign outside marking the place, but it is near Banco de Tokyo. Scarabocchio has the same owner and set up as Licorne.

Less Classy

Club Paris
Rua Araújo, 155
Phone 259-2447

A small place, across from the Hilton, Club Paris has go-go dancers and striptease. A small and bawdy place. Look for an Eiffel Tower at the entrance.

Michel
Rua Major Sertório, 106
Phone 259-2257
9—4 A.M.

Another bawdy place, Michel's features go-go dancers and striptease acts. Larger than Club Paris, it is also lively. Look for a blue sign with stars at the entrance.

G Ben
Rua Major Sertório, 678

Similar to Michel and Club Paris, but raunchier and tackier.

Kilt/Puma Chalet
Rua Nestor Pestana,
227
Phone 258-6152
8:30—4 A.M.

Nestled one after another in a line of bathhouses are Kilt/Puma Chalet. They are places to relax and have a sauna, as well as watch erotic shows. Prostitutes do frequent the place.

The lower numbers of Rua Augusta would be considered the red light district of São Paulo. There are many prostitutes and establishments flashing signs saying "Relax" or "Sauna."

Culture

Teatro Municipal
Praça Ramos de
Azevedo

Teatro Municipal has been home to ballet, opera, and concerts, attracting some of the finest companies in the world. There are six floors and 1,632 seats. Peak season is May through December; tickets range from $17 to $50.

Cinema

There are many movie theaters in São Paulo, showing current feature films from the U.S., Brazilian films, Latin American films, and revivals. The Cultural Center of São Paulo, Rua Figueira, 77, has two theaters and a cinema, showing Brazilian films, and opens at 7 P.M.

Shopping

Like any large city, São Paulo offers many options for shopping; one needs only to stroll. There are nearly one million stores spread out within its boundaries.

There are many markets and fairs throughout the city. Food markets are held once a week in separate neighborhoods, where fruits, meats, and more exotic foods can be purchased. There is an antique market every Sunday from 10 till 5 at MASP. In Praça da República there is an arts and crafts fair every Sunday from 8 till one.

Many streets and certain districts are noted for their shopping and abundance of stores: *Rua Barão de Itapetininga, Rua Augusta, Rua 25 de Março, Rua João Cachoeira, Ipiranga,* and *São Jão.* The districts of *Quadrilátero, Liberdade,* and *Praça da República* are also good for shopping.

Being a business and corporate city, conventions are part of São Paulo's routine. Most conventions are held at the large Anhembi Park, with its two halls, Exhibition Pavilion and Convention Palace. Bienal Pavilion in Ibirapuera Park is also a large and regularly used convention hall. Items ranging from computers to clothes to cars to electronics to furniture are sold and displayed at these conventions.

São Paulo also has a number of large and modern shopping centers.

Morumbi Shopping Center, Av. Roque Petroni Junior, 1089, is a large horizontal mall. It is fully air conditioned and has a solar ceiling for heat. Aside from many stores, including an H. Stern for jewelry and a Sears, Morumbi has several restaurants, three cinemas and a skating rink. Trees and colorful flowers add to the decor.

Iguatemi Shopping Center at Av. Brigadeiro Faria Lima, 1191 is an emporium of over 230 fine shops selling wares of every type. It was São Paulo's first major shopping center and perhaps the most modern; with free computerized shopping available. There are cinemas, restaurants, a post office and even a huge supermarket.

Ibirapuera Shopping Center at Av. Ibirapuera, 3103 features modern sculptures and fountains amidst its 280 shops of every type imaginable. This tri-level shopper's paradise has several fine restaurants and is worth your browsing.

Eldorado Shopping Center at Av. Rebouças, 3970 is extremely attractive and the largest. Note the smoked glass walls and the numerous fountains with flowers galore. The parking lot is the site of frequent Sunday morning concerts. The Palladium and Showdays Saloon; two recommended night spots are located on the top (third) level.

Shopping Center Norte, next to the Tietê River and bus terminal, offers fine buys and sponsors a free shuttle bus. There are over 250 stores, some restaurants, three movie theaters, and amusement park, and parking for 4,000 cars.

Aside from the shopping centers, there are sections in the city that are known for specific goods.

Rua 25 de Março, downtown, is known for its wholesale trade, its discount fabrics, and hats.

Rua José Paulino, in the east zone, is the oldest shopping district in the city for discount goods. The area is dominated by Israelis and Koreans now.

Rua Teodoro Sampaio, in the west zone, has shops selling clothes and furniture.

Rua Santa Efigênia, downtown, is the area for electronic goods.

Rua Dr. Mário Ferraz, in the south zone, is an elegant strip of expensive boutiques.

Av. Cidade Jardim, in the south zone, is also a fancy shopping district for the wealthy.

Galeria de Artes, Av. Dr. Vieira de Carvalho, 1202, is a shopping center for the visual arts. Closed Sunday, it is open weekdays from 9 A.M. to 7 P.M. and Saturday from 9 A.M. to 1 P.M.

There is a Gucci in the *Eldorado* and *Morumbi* shopping centers.

There are thirteen H. Sterns in São Paulo. The main office is at Praça da República, 242. Stores are located in Iguatemi, Ibirapuera, and Morumbi shopping centers, the Brasilton, Caesar Park, Eldorado São Luis, Hilton, Maksoud Plaza, Othon Palace, and Transamerica hotels, the Guarulhos airport and Rua Augusta, 2340.

Excursions

The state of São Paulo is as productive as the city. It is covered with farms and factories; a Mercedes factory, a VW factory with 45,000 people, which is a city to itself, and the Union Carbide factory in Petrobrás are all open to the public. The state is also expansive and diverse, its topography having both beaches and mountains.

Just outside the city are towns that reflect São Paulo's early history. Carapicuíba, the Bandeirantes, Santana do Parnaíba, Pindamonhangaba, and Silveiras have all preserved many of their historical structures and foundations and give a good picture of the past.

The city of Campinas, with one million inhabitants, is a university town, with over 200,000 students. It is north of São Paulo.

Guarujá

The coast provides wonderful beaches and resorts only an hour and a half from the city of São Paulo.

Santos, Brazil's chief port, is on the Atlantic. We recommend a trip to glimpse the coast and spend a day or a weekend at gorgeous Guarujá, one of the first beaches.

The saying in Brazil is that Paulistas work to spend in Rio—perhaps, but they also spend in Guarujá. Here many well-to-do Paulistas own condominium apartments, relax on spotless beaches, and enjoy weather suitable for swimming almost all year round.

During the summer months (December through March), the island is packed with Paulista vacationers. It is by far the most popular weekend resort of São Paulo.

Getting to Guarujá

The coast and Guarujá can be reached by the Anchieta highway, the four-lane, twelve-tunnel Immigrantes highway, or by public transportation. We recommend taking the bus. Jabaquara station, reached by subway or cab, has buses leaving for the coast, and specifically Guarujá. The bus goes directly to the Guarujá terminal.

Along the route in Ipiranga, there is a monument celebrating Emperor Dom Pedro I's declaration of independence from Portugal. Built in the centennial year of 1922, the monument is the largest in Latin America and is now a museum.

On the highway, you will pass a Mercedes factory, a Scania factory, a Karmann factory, and a large VW factory that employs 45,000 people. From the highway there are beautiful views of Santos and you will find many places to stop and take pictures. Near Santos, in Petrobrás, the most polluted town in Brazil, is Union Carbide.

The city of Santos, which has the Balneário shopping center, is the central location on the coast, dividing it north and south. The south is not developed and retains its rustic appeal. The north, where Guarujá is located, is the most developed part of the coast in Brazil. There are hundreds of tiny bays and beaches, and the towns, especially Guarujá, are luxurious, with apartment buildings, summer houses, yacht clubs, restaurants, nightclubs, and hotels. Guarujá is for São Paulo's rich and has some of the finest beaches on Brazil's Atlantic coast.

Orientation

Guarujá is an island reached by bridge or ferry from Santos. Its main street is Dom Pedro I and the beach street is Av. Miguel Stefano. There are many beaches; Astúrias and Pitangueiras are the central ones. The center of Guarujá is filled with tall white buildings that can be seen from the beach. Morro Muluf hill divides the downtown area with its tall white buildings from the beach area, where no apartment house can exceed three floors. The Old Chapel of Slaves, dating from the eighteenth century, is on Pereque Beach. Guarujá also has many forts from the past, the main one being Barra Grande (1884).

There is shopping at the Balneário Shopping Center in Santos, a city of 650,000 people.

Bring a bathing suit and enjoy the beaches.

Hotels

There are many lovely hotels in Guarujá; there is even one five-star choice. Our favorites follow. Again, all hotels are rated by the government and breakfast is included.

Casa Grande Hotel 5*
Av. Miguel Stefano, 999
Phone 86-2223
Telex 013-1746

This expensive and luxurious hotel has 160 private apartments on the beach and offers air conditioning, two restaurants, three bars, a disco, a sauna, a pool, three tennis courts, golf, a garage, and a slew of stores on the premises. The apartments have a colonial touch, with wooden furniture, carpets, and wooden floors. The grounds are huge and lush, made especially exotic by the presence of tropical birds. There are a beauty parlor and a barbershop downstairs. The hotel also has a children's dining room. Advanced reservations should be made in São Paulo. Expensive.

Delphin Hotel 4*
Av. Miguel Stefano
Phone 86-2111
Telex 131738-
HDSABR

The Delphin is a spread-out, two-story building with 120 rooms, and the option of suites, deluxe and presidential. The hotel also has a pool, bar telephones, meeting and convention space, and straw huts on its private beach. There are a boutique, a hairdresser, a restaurant, a game room, a nightclub, and a garage on the premises. Moderate.

Guarujá Inn 4*
Av. da Saudade, 170
Phone 87-2332
Telex 013-1500IGJA-
BR

With the same owners as Delphin and one and a half blocks from the beach, this hotel has a pool, a restaurant, a coffee shop, a churrascaria, a bar, TV, a game room, a jewelry store, a boutique, air conditioning, and 116 rooms.

Gávea Palace Hotel 4*
Av. Marechal Floriano
Peixoto, 311
Marro do Maluf
Phone 86-2212

Atop the hill in the center of town overlooking the beach, Gávea Palace has 66 apartments, a restaurant, and a bar. Moderate.

Jequitimar Hotel and
Spa 4*
Av. Major Prado, 1100
Phone 0132-53-3111
Telex 013-1683

With its own separate beach and island across from Guarujá, Jequitimar is a resort and spa that offers aerobic classes, massages, saunas, facials, cardiograms, and other facilities for good health. There is a gymnastic center and soccer, golf, tennis, volleyball, and water sports. Very modern in its look, furnishings, and decor, the hotel also has meeting facilities. Moderate.

Restaurants

There are many small, some excellent, restaurants scattered around the island. We are partial to *Il Faro Restaurant*, Rua Mário Ribeiro, phone 86-1112, for international cuisine, and *Micheluccio*, Av. Dom Pedro I, for pizza.

São Paulo Potpourri

Newspapers

English-language newspaper is the *Daily Post*, which is published Tuesday through Saturday and distributed free in many of the first-class hotels. Editions of New York and Miami papers are also available on newsstands. Caderno 2 section of the *O Estado de São Paulo* lists events of the day.

Telephones

Public telephones can be identified by the big yellow ore-lhões (big ears) and require a token (ficha), which can be purchased at newsstands, bars, and shops. A token is not needed for information, 102 on the dial, or operator assistance, 107. Special tokens are required for international booths, which are colored blue.

Tipping

When not included in the bill, a tip should be between ten and fifteen percent.

Traffic

Traffic is heavy in São Paulo, so give yourself plenty of time for meeting a deadline.

Water and Milk

Though chlorinated, water is not advised for drinking; drink only bottled water, *agua mineral*. Milk is fine.

Recife

A Tropical Venice

uilt around a river and on the ocean, with a network of canals and rivers serving as main arteries and with myriad bridges, Recife is a tropical Venice. The city, whose culture is tied to its fishing and seafood, is one of the oldest in Brazil and has an interesting history. Boa Viagem, an almost Copacabana look-alike, sports beaches lined with palm trees, deluxe hotels, and high-rise condominiums.

You will definitely want to visit nearby Olinda, a sister city four miles north, which today is a living museum of its colonial past. Recife, named after the offshore reefs (*recifes*) is now the capital of the state of Pernambuco. It is also the home of two Afro-Indian Portuguese folk dances, Frevo and Maracatu, which explode in clubs and, on occasion, spontaneously in the streets. But the region's beauty and excitement do not diminish its economic importance.

Recife is the principal financial and transportation center in the northeast. It is by far the most important port, with 3,000 meters of docks. It is the gateway to and from Europe and the nucleus for train travel throughout the northern part of Brazil.

History

Born out of conflict, Recife was originally called Povoação dos Arrecifes. It was, in 1627, a minuscule fishing town of two hundred, entrapped in the shadow of its northern neighbor, Olinda.

Duarte Coelho, the first captain of Pernambuco, wanted to make Olinda the New Portugal. Vastly more picturesque than Recife, Olinda was, nonetheless, completely landlocked. Coelho was resistant to Recife's receiving any importance, and thus Olinda prospered, deriving its economy from sugar. Olinda's success produced a community of wealthy men who came to be known as Sugar Lords.

In February of 1630, the Dutch successfully captured and burned Olinda and transferred the seat of power to Arrecifes. Utilizing its natural harbor, they built an extensive port with docks and canals, simultaneously building up the city. Conde de Nassau, head of the Dutch forces, changed the name of Arrecifes to Mauritzstadt. The expulsion of the Dutch ten years later saw the stripping of the name, but not of Recife's newly gained importance.

The middle class that grew out of the Dutch occupation attempted, after the departure of the Dutch, to consolidate the city's, and their own, stronghold on the entire state. The aristocrats of Olinda, quiescent during the Dutch occupation, began attacking Recife in an attempt to regain their lost power. The fighting spiraled into a full-blown, although localized, war called Guerra dos Mascates in 1710.

Although victorious in the Guerra dos Mascates, Recife had to withstand three separate rebellions in the first part of the nineteenth century: the Confederacão do Equador in 1824; the Guerra dos Cabanos in 1832; and the Revolução Praieira in 1848.

In 1706, during the Guerra dos Mascates, Brazil's first printing press was installed in Recife. More than a century later, Brazil's oldest daily newspaper, *Diário de Pernambuco* was established there in 1825.

Now Recife is a major city. Although in 1872 Recife was the third largest city (after Rio and Salvador) with 116,000 people, it grew at a subdued pace for years. It has for decades been a small city—like Portland in the U.S. Its inheritance from the Dutch, though, was a sturdy economic network. With that as a foundation, Recife, with almost

1.2 million people—mainly black—is expanding beyond its already important base.

Born because of its proximity to the ocean, Recife is molded and twisted around it. Boa Viagem beach is spectacular. Formed and constructed like Rio's, with tall modern buildings shadowing the beach, Boa Viagem is narrower than Copacabana. The beach always smells of fish and is lined with coconut trees.

Olinda, with its colonial architecture and narrow antique streets, is spectacular. It is now an artists' city and is dominated by its history.

Carnaval here is not as large as either Rio or Salvador, but is equally vigorous. It is underlined by its dancing and costumes. *Frevo* is defined by its frenzied style and is broken into three divisions: *frevo de rua,* street dance; *frevo de bloco,* group dance; and *frevo-canção,* song dance. Each region has its own style. *Frevo* has been compared to breakdancing in America. *Maracatu* is also a bit crazed, and is reminiscent of the old conga. *O caboclinho* is the oldest dance in Brazil, originating from the Indians.

Orientation

Officially only Santo Antônio, Boa Vista, and Recife make up the city. But the exclusion of Olinda and Boa Viagem would make it incomplete.

Downtown, made up of three separate sections, is immediately recognizable by its bridges. As mentioned, Boa Vista, Santo Antônio, and Recife are cut by water. Santo Antônio is the heart of downtown, with the railroad station, Forte dos Cinco Pontas, and Praça da República. A former municipal prison here was transformed into what is now the Casa da Cultura, with many cells housing exhibits, shops, and small theaters. The most important churches and markets are also in Santo Antônio.

The River Capibaribe partitions Santo Antônio from Boa Vista, which is on the mainland. At the end of Santo Antônio, on a peninsula, is Recife, marked by Fort do Brum. The state tourist center, EMPETUR, is in Santo Amaro, on Av. Cruz Cabugá, 533.

Olinda is four miles north of the city. It is a colonial town, with many old mansions with balconies. There is a large population of artists there and with that comes museums, art shows, cafés, and bars. The city, which has been named a national landmark, is not to be bypassed.

Arrival

Guararapes International Airport is in Boa Viagem. The finest residential quarter in the area, Boa Viagem is the name of both the suburb and the long promenade that parallels the ocean. The best beaches and hotels are in this section. It resembles Rio in both its look—a long strip sliced by looming buildings and ocean—and its zones. It is divided by six Postos that get higher as they get farther from downtown. It is also marked by its visible reefs, which are reachable during low tide. The streets directly behind the Av. Boa Viagem, are Rua Dos Navegantes, Av. Cons. Aguiar, and Av. Domingo Ferreira.

At the airport, cabs are readily available and will whisk you to your hotel in less than a half hour. Rates are reasonable.

Hotels

The best hotels in Recife are in the Boa Viagem section, in the south of the city and part of the residential area. Although the beach is reminiscent of Rio's Copacabana, it is not as wide. The best restaurants are also in Boa Viagem.

Like all hotels in Brazil, those in Recife are rated by the government on a star system. All hotels have air conditioning and refrigerators and all prices include breakfast. Hotel prices are generally forty percent less than those in Rio or São Paulo.

Recife Palace 5*
Av. Boa Viagem, 4070
Phone 325-4044
Telex 081-4528 REPH BR

The Palace is a brand-new luxury hotel in Boa Viagem. It has a high-tech design, with 300 rooms on twenty floors and two small pools on the top floor. The hotel offers an assortment of services: babysitting, sauna/steambath, massage, laundry, car rentals, unisex beauty salon, and newsstand. There are three bars—at the pool, in the lobby, and a piano bar—three restaurants, and an H. Stern jewelry shop. Each room has air conditioning, radio, TV, closed-circuit TV, minibar, refrigerator, and a marble bathroom complete with telephone. For business travelers there is meeting space with translation facilities, 16 mm. projectors, slide projectors, videos, photographer, secretarial services, typewriters, and computers. A choice of continental or Brazilian breakfast is offered. The Rio Palace in Rio is under the same management. Moderate.

Hotel Miramar 4*
Rua dos Navegantes, 363
Phone 326-7422
Telex 081-2139

One block off the beach in Boa Viagem, this deluxe hotel has similar amenities to those at the Recife Palace. Shaped like a box with three sides, the hotel has a pool in its courtyard. There are 173 rooms (with some suites available), a sauna, a beauty salon, a restaurant, a coffee shop, a nightclub, a bar, and shops. Moderate.

Hotel Quatro Rodas 5*
Av. José Augusto Moreira, 2200
Olinda
Phone 431-2955
Telex 081-1324

Surrounded by palm trees, this hotel is one of the nicest resorts in Brazil and could be the prettiest in Recife. It is made up of one large white building, a small art deco one-story building, and a sprawl of cabañas. Completely self-contained on its own grounds by the beach, the resort offers many leisure possibilities: two pools (one under a thatched roof and another atop the main building), tennis, sauna, a bar, and a restaurant. There are also meeting facilities. Expensive.

Hotel Savaroni 4*
Av. Boa Viagem, 3772
Phone 325-5077
Telex 081-1428

A sparkling structure, very modern outside and very slick inside, with furniture that is almost futuristic, this hotel is in the same area on the beach as the Recife Palace. There are seventy rooms on ten floors, a pool, and a good restaurant (one of our recommendations). Rooms have TV, refrigerators, and air conditioning, and the hotel also offers a convention hall for two hundred people, a beauty salon, souvenir shops, and two bars. Moderate.

Hotel Othon Palace 4*
Av. Boa Viagem, 3722
Phone 326-7225
Telex 081-2141

Part of a deluxe Brazilian chain, this hotel has seventeen floors and 264 rooms. There are two pools, a beauty salon, a coffee shop, a restaurant, and a bar with a simulated waterfall. The rooms have TV and refrigerators. Moderate.

Hotel Jangadeiro 4*
Av. Boa Viagem, 3114
Phone 326-6777
Telex 081-1502

Directly on the beach, this hotel has one hundred moderately priced rooms with TV and air conditioning. There is a pool on the top floor, a sauna, and a good restaurant overlooking the ocean. Moderate.

Hotel Vila Rica 4*
Av. Boa Viagem, 4308
Phone 326-5111
Telex 081-1903

Conveniently situated on the beach, the hotel has twelve floors and 118 rooms with TV, air conditioning, and mini-bars.

There are convention facilities, as well as a playroom, a pool, a restaurant, a coffee shop, and a garage. Moderate.

Park Hotel 3*
Rua dos Navegantes, 9
Phone 325-4666
Telex 081-1903

Sister to the Vila Rica, with similar facilities, the Park is a little larger, with fifteen floors and two hundred rooms with TV and mini-bars. The Hippie Fair is held nearby every Sunday in the Praça Boa Viagem. Inexpensive.

Hotel Boa Viagem 4*
Av. Boa Viagem, 5000
Phone 341-4144
Telex 081-2072

Each room in this hotel has TV, air conditioning, and a stocked refrigerator. The hotel also offers a sauna, a pool, a beauty salon, a disco, and a restaurant. The bar on the second floor affords panoramic views of the ocean. Moderate.

Mar Hotel 5*
Rua Barão de Souza Leão, 451
Phone 341-5433
Telex 081-1073

This two-floor, 112-room hotel, three blocks from the beach, has a restaurant in the lobby and TV and stocked refrigerators in the rooms. Moderate.

Hotel Casa Grande e Senzala 4*
Av. Conselheiro Aguiar, 5000
Phone 341-0366
Telex 081-1669

This quaint, 21-room hotel has colonial decor and architecture. Each room has air conditioning, TV, and a stocked refrigerator, and there is an excellent restaurant (recommended) that serves authentic Pernambuco fare served by waitresses in typical costumes. Inexpensive.

Hotel do Sol 3*
Av. Boa Viagem, 978
Phone 326-7644
Telex 081-1337

This beach-front hotel has seven floors, 73 air-conditioned rooms, and a restaurant that is popular with local residents. The price is definitely right. Inexpensive.

Downtown Choices

Grande Hotel 4*
Av. Martins de Barros, 593
Downtown—Santo Antônio section
Phone 224-9366
Telex 081-1454

Located in the center of Recife, this regal-looking hotel offers babysitting service, a barbershop, a cocktail lounge, a restaurant, laundry service, parking, a pharmacy, and meeting facilities. There are 108 rooms on six floors. Its one drawback is its distance from the Boa Viagem. Moderate.

Hotel 4 de Outubro 3*
Rua Floriano Peixoto, 141
Phone 224-4477
Telex 081-2065

This downtown hotel is colonial-style, with 53 rooms. There is no pool, but it's near the Casa da Cultura. Only in a pinch. Inexpensive.

Another Olinda Choice

Mar Olinda Hotel 3*
Av. Beira Mar, 1615
Phone 429-1699
Telex 081-3249

This modern hotel offers comfortable surroundings and a pool for cheap prices. There are 48 rooms with air conditioning, TV, and mini-bars. The hotel is on the beach and the views, especially at sunrise, are spectacular. Inexpensive.

Restaurants

Recife's many excellent restaurants offer all types of food: continental, Brazilian (Bahian) including typical dishes, and fast food, all of these served in a variety of settings. Like hotels, most of Recife's restaurants are in Boa Viagem.

Pernambuco, the region, has its own distinctive style of cuisine. Such dishes as buchada, sarapatel, galinha de cabidela, charque assado com farofa, and carne de sol make up the varied list of Pernambuco's unique diet. Fried needlefish, fish stew, and foods made from manioc and corn also underscore the region's cuisine. Fruits abound in the tropical climate, of course, and some are unique: caja, umbu, jaca, mangaba, jambo, sapoti, carambola, romã, and araçá. All in all there are nearly seventy-five different types of fruit available in Recife.

Regional

Senzala
Av. Conselheiro Aguiar, 5000
Boa Viagem
Phone 341-0366
Noon–3, 7–midnight

An excellent place to sample typical regional food is Senzala, next to the Hotel Casa Grande. Both the carne de sol and the charque a mucama represent the best typical Pernambuco fare. Camarão a Maurício de Nassau Casagrande, camarão a casa grande and logosta ao molho de coco (lobster with coconut sauce) are also highly recommended. The restaurant tries to re-create a Pernambucan dining experience in appearance as well; the decor is that of an old ranch, with leather, antiquarian artifacts, and ikons. Waitresses in native *mucama* (slave) dress will serve you.

Lapinha
Praça Boa Viagem, 16
Boa Viagem
Phone 326-1914
Noon–4, 7–midnight

A must here is the carne de sol. There is also an excellent selection of regional fruits and juices. On Saturday the feijoada is excellent. Maître Adalberto is an institution here.

Ceia Regional
Restaurante
Rua Prof. Andrade
Bezerra, 1462
(near the Convention
Center) Olinda
Noon–3, 7–11
Tuesday-Sunday

Regional specialties here are the linguiça and cuscuz platters. A perfect spot to dine while visiting Olinda. Remember, the views from here are memorable and will make your visit to the restaurant worthwhile.

O Sobrado
Rua José Osório, 234
Madalena
Open 24 hours

This simple restaurant serves excellent carne de sol.

Seafood

Restaurante Lobster
Av. Boa Viagem, 2612
Boa Viagem
Phone 326-7593
Noon–4:30, 6–1

You can enjoy open-air dining in a private house at Restaurante Lobster, where the specialty is, of course, lobster—grelhada (grilled), ao termidor (sauteed), or ao molho de coco (with coconut sauce). Lobster prices are a bargain, but if you would prefer another dish, try camarão do molho de coco (shrimp with coconut and white wine sauce). Enter by walking through the outdoor garden. The antique-style roof, and large, religious carvings within enrich the decor.

Churrascarias

Churrascaria Rodeio
Av. Boa Viagem, 4780
Phone 325-2276
Noon–4, 6–midnight

An informal and excellent spot for lunch is Churrascaria Rodeio, located on the beach-front street near the Park Hotel. This is a steakhouse that also offers dishes like brochete misto and more. Outdoor tables make this a great place for watching the beach scene, but you can also choose to eat inside, where a large ceiling fan will keep you cool.

Churrascaria Parque Rodeio
Av. Boa Viagem, 1864
Phone 326-1864
Noon–4, 6–midnight

Churrascaria Parque Rodeio is another restaurant under the same management that you may want to visit.

Boa Viagem Churrascaria
Av. Boa Viagem, 4250
Beira Mar
Phone 326-1186
Noon–3, 6–midnight

There will be dancing as well at Boa Viagem Churrascaria. The building that houses the restaurant is made of red stone, and overlooks the ocean. The entrance is impressive, gained after climbing an interminable flight of red steps. Both indoor and outdoor seating is available, although there is no air conditioning.

Churrascaria Laçador
Rua Visconde de Jequitinhonha, 138
Boa Viagem
Phone 326-3911
11–midnight

For dining entertainment, Churrascaria Laçador is a good bet that offers music and a show most nights. This is mainly a steak place; t-bone steak and baby beef are possible entrees, as well as galetos ao primo canto (chicken with rice salad). The ranch atmosphere is created inside by the wood floor, walls, and pillars.

Continental

L'Atelier
Rua Bernardo Viera de Melo, 91
Olinda
Phone 429-3099
7–midnight

Another fine choice in Olinda is L'Atelier, located in the heart of the city. The restaurant offers a beautiful view and an antique interior, with colorful and pleasing tapestries for sale. The building is a restored colonial house with a garden in the rear. Menu options include smoked trout (truta defumada), coq au vin, fondue, and a delicious filet mignon au poivre.

Kartier
Av. Domingoes Ferreira, 4215
Boa Viagem
Phone 325-5563
Noon–3, 7–midnight

Kartier, in Boa Viagem, offers a show with dinner; on weekends, there is a cover charge. The whole experience takes place in an immense room equipped with a stage. A large selection of fish dishes is offered, along with a variety of steak dishes.

Sambura
Av. Beira Mar, 1551
Olinda
Phone 429-3466

For a change, you may want to venture out to Olinda, where there are a number of fine restaurants. One of these is Sambura. The restaurant is entirely circular, has many windows, and looks out at the ocean, so dining here may feel a little like eating on a ship. The seafood is excellent; file de peixe with shrimp sauce is highly recommended. An outdoor dining area is attached, so open-air dining is available as well. The menu is on the door.

Restaurante Marruá
Centro de Convenções
Phone 241-2111
11:30–12:30 A.M.

A good steakhouse is Restaurante Marruá, located in the convention center. Within, white tablecloths, a high ceiling, and lots of plants give the place a refreshing feel. The restaurant has a great variety of steak dishes.

Hotel Savaroni
Av. Boa Viagem, 3772
Phone 352-5077

Another somewhat more sophisticated dinner showplace is the Restaurante Hotel Savaroni. Off from the lobby, a pianist plays, and the dining room offers a beautiful view of the ocean. The menu here includes a comfortable variety ranging from shrimp and lobster dishes (lagosta ao molho coco; camarão ao molho de coco/tomate) to beef Stroganoff.

French

La Maison
Av. Boa Viagem, 618
Phone 325-1158
7 P.M.–1 A.M.

Open for dinner only, this unpretentious French eatery serves excellent fondues and êntrecote dishes. Live music livens the ambience.

Chinese

Restaurante Canton
Rua Desembarg-João Paes
Near Palace Hotel
Phone 326-6709
Noon–3, 6–12:30

A good Chinese restaurant is Restaurante Canton near the Palace Hotel, which offers Chinese cuisine with some Brazilian influence. Try frango picado com pimenta e caju (chicken with pepper and nuts) or camarão cozido ao molho de tomate (shrimp cooked in tomato sauce). Typical Chinese dishes are offered as well, such as sliced beef in lobster sauce, lobster in Chinese sauce, and chop suey. The decor is thoroughly Chinese with lanterns and a Chinese door, and the menu is bilingual.

Shanghai
Av. Boa Viagem, 5262
Boa Viagem
Phone 341-0953
11:30 A.M.–2:30 A.M.

Not as pretty as Canton, but worth a visit for the best sweet and sour pork (porco agridoce) in Recife.

Fast Food

Mr. Pizza
Cons. Aguiar, 3500

For fast food and/or lunches try Mr. Pizza, two blocks from the beach. It's located on a great walking street, overlooking the ocean.

Beliscão
Av. Boa Viagem
Across from
Churrascaria Rodeio

Overlooking the beach is another open-air restaurant suitable for lunch or even a light dinner. Beliscão offers pizzas, sandwiches (steak or cheese), and the usual fast food—cheeseburgers and hot dogs (cachorro quente)—at low prices.

Recife Sightseeing

Recife has many sites worth visiting. Its beautiful beach strip, almost rivaling Rio's Copacabana, is the Boa Viagem, with its international hotels (one of which you might be staying in) and modern buildings.

Recife has many relics of its rich history. Its architecture is intriguing, and many ancient customs and traditions have survived. The State Tourism Calendar lists over one hundred annual festivals in Recife. The more historical parts of Recife are the areas of São José, Boa Vista, Recife, and Santo Antônio.

A thorough listing of events, by the day, can be found in Recife's *Diário de Pernambuco.*

Casa da Cultura was, for most of its existence, a prison. In 1848, it was built as a jail for two hundred. Designed with a central courtyard and with all the cells visible from one central point, the floor plan is that of a crucifix. The building was named a national monument and was restored in 1973. Now, the Casa da Cultura houses small handicraft stores in its three levels of cells, and has a museum, classrooms, and a restaurant. On Rua Floriano Peixoto. Open from 9 A.M till 9 P.M; Saturday and Sunday 3 P.M till 8 P.M

Mercado de São José, a genuine hustling and hassling Old World market, was constructed during the second half of the nineteenth century; since its opening in 1875 the market has never been closed. All materials for construction were imported from France. It was declared a national monument in 1973. Open 6 A.M til 5:30 P.M

Forte das Cinco Pontas, the Five Pointed Fort, was built by two Dutch architects using wood and clay. In 1684 the fort was rebuilt by the Portuguese, who reshaped it into a square. Declared a national monument in 1938, the fort was used as a prison in 1977. Now it houses the Museum of the City of Recife. Open Monday through Friday 8 A.M till 6 P.M; Saturday and Sunday 2 P.M till 6 P.M

Matriz de Santo Antônio, begun in 1753, is on the site of the old gunpowder factory, used during the Dutch invasion. The center of the church, the chapel, and the pillars were completed and the final touches were made in 1790. The interior designs took another twenty years to finish and now the church stands as one of the few unadulterated structures in Brazil. The main chapel and the church's paintings are fine. The church is located in the Praça da Independência and is open from 8 A.M till noon and 2 P.M till 5 P.M

Convento Franciscano was built by Franciscan Friars in 1606 on land donated by a plantation owner. Six years later, the military took over the convent, which was located by a river, for the purpose of fighting the Dutch. In 1654 the Friars restarted their work. Completed finally in 1770, the convent has several chapels, a school, a cloister, and a hospital. The convent is decorated in tile and rosewood. Located on Rua do Imperador Pedro II, 206 and open 7 A.M till 11 A.M and 2 P.M till 5 P.M.

Igreja e Convento do Carmo is a mid-seventeenth century convent and church, built mainly through the financing of Captain Diogo Cavalcanti de Vasconcelos. Originally started in 1663, the main chapel was finished in 1685. The final product was unveiled in 1767. The church has six altars and two lateral chapels, with fine rosewood carvings and is considered one of the finest representations of Baroque style in Brazil. The convent and church were remodeled in 1857, in 1898, and in 1938. During the period from 1817 to 1846, the Carmelite nuns were forced out so that the military could use the premises for barracks and a hospital. It is now considered a national landmark. The church is on Pátio de Nossa Senhora do Carmo and is open from 8 A.M. till noon and 2 P.M. till 5 P.M.

Capela Dourada da Ordem Terceira Franciscana is the product of the convent of the same name in Italy. The cornerstone was laid in 1696 and the chapel was finished in 1724 and has a fabulous gold inlay. On Rua Imperador Pedro II, 371, and open 8 A.M. till 7 P.M.

Pátio e Igreja de São Pedro dos Clérigos was constructed in the eighteenth century by the sisterhood of the same name. The church highlights Brazilian Baroque architecture and is the first of Recife's buildings to be designated a national monument. On Pátio de São Pedro and open 7 A.M. till 11 A.M. and 2 P.M. till 6 P.M.; Saturday 8 A.M. till 11 A.M. and Sunday 10 A.M. till noon.

Capela de Nossa Senhora da Conceição da Jaqueira was constructed on property owned by Henrique Martins in 1766. The chapel is a national monument. Located on Av. Rui Barbosa.

Liceu de Artes e Ofícios had its origins in the Society for Mechanical and Plastic Artists of Pernambuco. The building was started in 1841 and finished in 1880. The society taught mathematics, architecture, and writing. The president of the society, in 1871, authorized space for a museum/library, which now houses books, porcelains, furniture, and paintings. In 1950, the society terminated and was taken over by the Catholic University. On the Praça da República and open 8 A.M. till noon and 2 P.M. till 5 P.M.

Teatro Santa Isabel was begun on April 1, 1841. It was the baby of French architect Louis Leger Vauthier, who was in charge of public buildings at the time. Finished in 1850 by a Brazilian architect, the theater burned down nineteen years later. Rebuilt in 1876, the theater is famous for attracting world-renowned artists. On the Praça da República and open from 8 A.M. till noon and 2 P.M. till 5 P.M.

Estação Central is the historic railroad station for Recife, built in 1890, and still in use today. On Praça Visconde de Mauá.

Fort do Brum was originally designated Diogo Pais by the governor of Recife, Matias de Alburquerque. Construction started in 1626 and was taken over by the Dutch in 1630. With the Portuguese return, Antônio Correa Pinto redesigned the fort in 1670 and it was completed in 1690. Now a national monument, it was considered the most important strategic structure in Recife. The fort now includes a chapel. On Praça do Brum. Open 8 A.M. till noon and 2 P.M. till 5 P.M.

Faculdade de Direito was the first law school in the country, part of the initial wave of law courses that were begun in Olinda and São Paulo. The school moved from Olinda in 1854 and in 1889 the president of Pernambuco built a permanent building. It was finished in 1911. Praça Adolfo Cirne. Open 8 A.M. till noon and 2 P.M. till 6 P.M.

Casas de Arquitetura Purista are the only examples left in Recife of post–World War I cubist architecture called Purismo. Located at numbers 292, 305, 311, and 323 on Av. Visconde de Suassuna, they were built around 1940. The style was identified by its powerful use of straight, hard lines.

Walking Tour

A tropical Venice, a city of rivers and bridges, Recife must be seen on foot to take in its beauty. Even if not to see specific sights, the city is wonderful to stroll, particularly across the bridges in Boa Viagem. The bridges connect the city, and tell the story of Recife through their locations.

The historical center of town, though, is made up of the districts of Recife, São José, Boa Vista, and Santo Antônio.

Starting in Recife, Forte do Brum will lead to Estação do Brum, which was used by the Great Western Brazil Railroad Company from 1881 to 1934. Following a straight path, you will come upon the Church do Pilar, 1680, which is decorated in tiles. Right beyond is Catedral da Madre de Deus.

Santo Antônio is where Praça da República is located. On the square are the royal palm trees brought from Africa and the Governor's Palace from 1814. Also located there is the Teatro Santa Isabel, dating from 1850. On Av. Dantas Barreto is the Church of Santíssimo Sacramento. On Rua Nova is the Church do Rosario dos Pretos. The whole area is filled with churches that tell of Recife's past. The Pátio de São Pedro, a complete preserved estate from the eighteenth century, is also in Santo Antônio.

In São José is the Casa da Cultura and the Mercado de São José. On the same street with the Casa da Cultura is the Museu do Trem. The Church N.S. do Terço is on Rua Vital de Negreiros, and nearby is Forte das Cinco Pontas. The Palacio da Soledade, on Rua Oliveira Lima, was the seat of the revolutionary government in 1817, and now houses the Law School.

Jangadas

Jangadas, which means "fishermen," has become the name of the boats used and built by the local fishermen of Recife. Long their means of gliding on the water, jangadas are only to be found in Pernambuco.

Rides on the long, skinny boats—really sturdy rafts because they are made from logs strung together in six pieces, and include a sail with an advertisement on it—are available just beyond the Praça Boa Viagem.

Rides are advertised by the boaters and the excitement of the ride is in watching the reefs and the people on the beach.

Carnaval

Carnaval is a national institution, and its merriment is no less in Recife. The exception in Recife is a six-day Carnaval festival called Semana Pre-Carnavalesca. Hence Recife parties for close to a month before Ash Wednesday.

The celebration is underlined by the dances frevo and maracatu. Frevo, wild and contagious, is broken down into three main divisions—frevo de rua, street dance; frevo de bloco, group dance; and frevo canção, song dance. The music and rhythm carry you, and the crowd, into a state of intoxication. The better dancers are constantly improvising and leading the pack.

Maracatu is also wild and resembles the old conga. Dancers are dressed in Indian garb and bounce throughout the city.

For the people not willing or unable to dance, there is the corso, the art of the parade that involves floats and cars.

Similar to all parades, corso originally involved a procession of horse- or donkey-drawn carts or carriages. Now cars are done up in wild styles, and specific groups stand atop to engage other cars in confetti fights.

Convention Center

On the road linking Recife with Olinda, the Convention Center plays an important role in Recife's life. Host to many conventions, shows, and seminars, the center is always busy due to Recife's importance as a business center. There is parking for two thousand cars.

Olinda

The most important site outside of Recife is Olinda, its historic arch rival. Founded before Recife and the center of life in the seventeenth century—before the Dutch cultivated Recife and elevated it to its present status—Olinda is now a beautiful colonial city, considered a cultural monument by UNESCO due to its Baroque architecture.

Founded in 1535, the city, originally called Nova Lusitania, was supposed to be the New Portugal according to its founder, Duarte Coelho. Its beauty is unsurpassable, but it has no natural harbor and hence lost out to Recife in importance.

Now though, centuries after the war with Recife over power and sugar, Olinda is a city of artists, old mansions, museums, cafés, and bars.

The *Alto da Sé,* the point of origin, highlights Olinda's beauty, showing off its reefs and beaches. From this point, the houses and streets of four hundred years ago are evident.

The *Museu de Arte Sacra,* dating from the seventeenth century, and the *Academia Santa Gertudes* are wonderful buildings from Olinda's colonial heyday. The Museu de Arte Sacra, formerly the Episcopal Palace, has an important collection of art picturing the early periods of the city's history.

Not far from the museum is a street that has to be visited for its colonial authenticity. *Bonsucesso,* beginning at Amparo Church, is the oldest street in Olinda, where the houses are colored in the red, green, blue, and yellow of the past. The mansions highlight the Moorish and Portuguese influence of the time; they are all built with balconies, detailed verandas, and archways. Towering windows, known as *muxarabis,* adorn the façades.

On Rua Bernardo Vieira de Mello, toward the hills of the city, is the *Mercado da Ribeira,* the former slave-auction site and market. Now, Mercado da Ribeira has many stores.

In front of the market is the old *Olinda Senate House,* where Bernardo Vieira de Mello began the first push toward Brazil's becoming a republic. Now, on every November 10 there is a commemoration of his speech.

At Carmo Square is Nossa Senhora do Carmo, the first Carmelite church built in Brazil in 1588.

On Rua São Francisco is *Nossa Senhora da Neves Convent/ São Roque* chapel, the first Franciscan chapel in the country, built in 1585. The inside is lined with frescoes and wood carvings. Olinda Seminary and Nossa Senhora da Graça Church, on Rua Bispo Coutinho, constructed between 1584 and 1592, are beautiful examples of sixteenth-century architecture.

At Largo da Misericórdia is *Misericórdia Church,* built in 1540, where you will find finely carved wood and gold engravings and paintings.

The *Contemporary Art Museum,* on Rua 13 de Maio, has a large collection of Brazilian art. The building was constructed in the eighteenth century as an ecclesiastical prison for the Grand Inquisition and ultimately became a jail. It was transformed into a museum by the journalist Assis Chateaubriand, then the publisher of Brazil's largest newspaper chain.

There are many other churches and sites in the city. Its beautiful beaches, beginning at Av. Beira Mar, have cafés and restaurants and are hangouts for artists. Some of the beaches are do Farol, Casa Caiada, Rio Doce, and praia do Pau Amarelo, where a fort of the same name is located.

Walking Tour

The starting point for any walking tour of Olinda is Alto da Sé, the location of the city's birth. From this point the beauty of Olinda's beaches and view of the north coast is realized. On the other side is Olinda's historical past, from its founding to its colonial period.

Some examples of Olinda's past are the Museu de Arte Sacra and the Convento da Conceição. The only modern structure in Olinda is Oscar Niemeyer's watertank.

Making a right from the sqaure you come to the Church
of Amparo and Church of São João. Continuing, the
churches of N.S. do Rosario and the Fonte do Rosario
emerge on Bonsucesso, the oldest street in Olinda, in
which the houses are painted in red, green, blue, and yellow. The Moorish influence is obvious in the houses.

Rua Bernardo Vieira de Mello takes you to the hills of
Olinda where the Mercado da Ribeira, the old slave-auction house, and the senate house can be visited.

On Rua São Bento there are many art galleries and the
700-year-old city building. Going down Rua 27 de Janeiro,
toward the Praça João Alfredo, you will see the church of São
Pedro and the house where Count Mauricio de Nassau lived;
it is now a tavern and nightclub. A little farther away is the
Church do Carmo, which begins the Av. Beira Mar, where all
of Olinda's famous beaches are located.

Excursions

Pernambuco's coast has many beaches worth visiting. Just
south of Recife are Piedade, Venda Grande, Candeias, and
Barra da Jangada, all in the town of Jaboatão. In the town
are many clubs and restaurants. Off the beach of Barra da
Jangada, where the Jaboatão and Piedade rivers meet, is an
island called Ilha do Paiva, Love Island. Boat trips are
available.

In the town of Cabo, the major industrial site in Pernambuco, there are many beaches. The most beautiful vista
in the state is located at Santo Agostinho.

The district of Ipojuca, still farther south, also has wonderful beaches, and the Pernambuco Tourism Company
has built modern campsites there.

Two more towns along the southern coast are passed
before reaching the final district before the State of Alagoas.

São José da Coroa Grande is a traditional summer resort with good hotels, restaurants, and houses for rent. It is called Saint Joseph of the Big Crown because of the many rock formations that look like crowns. Immense natural pools have been formed by the reefs and São José is considered one of the best places in Pernambuco for diving and underwater fishing.

North of Recife there are also a number of beaches. Past Olinda are the beaches of Rio Doce, Janga, and Pau Amarelo, site of the first fort built by the Dutch. The next beach in line is Maria Farinha, considered one of the five most beautiful beaches on the Brazilian coast. Wind surfing is offered there.

Finally, the island of Itamaracá is recommended. Linked to the mainland by Getulio Vargas bridge, the island is located fifty kilometers from Recife in the town of Itapessuma. With beautiful beaches, a fort, hotels, restaurants, and a shopping area, the island offers many options for a weekend trip to the beach.

Nova Jerusalem

Nova Jerusalem, one hundred miles from Recife in the district of Brejo da Madre de Deus is a mini duplicate of Christ's Jerusalem. The town is most famous for its Passion Play during Easter week, which is considered one of the three major tourist attractions in Brazil.

With five hundred actors on twelve stages surrounded by stone walls—the largest open theater in the world—the Passion Play is reenacted. The stage is also made up of seven gates and seventy towers, equal to one-third of 33 A.D. Jerusalem.

There are ten scenes in the play. The first highlights the important events in Christ's life. Scene two depicts his entry into Jerusalem, the expulsion of the money lenders and the infidelity of Judas. Scene three is the last supper. The fourth through seventh scenes portray the kiss of Judas, Christ's arrest, Herod, and Pontius Pilate. Scene eight is Christ carrying the cross. The ninth is Judas' death and Christ's crucifixion. And the tenth is the resurrection.

There are many hotels and restaurants and space for camping outside the city.

Nightlife

The traveler who enjoys nightclubs will not be disappointed in Recife. The city's discotheques are on par with those of Salvador. Recife also has its own form of African-based religion, Macumba, which is seen at night. At Carnaval, outlandish costumes and several dances unique to Pernambuco (frevo and caboclinhas) still flourish. The beaches of Olinda are cool and refreshing at night for walking, and after dusk, the Alto da Sé becomes a street fair with crafts, makeshift bars, barbecue stands, and music.

Discotheques

New York Discotheque
Av. Boa Viagem, 4308
Phone 326-6111

Downstairs in the Hotel Vila Rica, New York Discotheque is open seven days. The lights whirl around mirrored walls; inside, the club is small and not particularly elegant. Small round tables and couches are set against the wall.

Happy Ending
Hotel Recife Palace
Av. Boa Viagem, 4070
Phone 325-4044

Happy Ending is found on the main level of the Hotel Recife Palace, one of the newest and best hotels in Recife. Within months of its opening, the club was the most popular in town.

Cavalo Dourado
Rua Carlo Gomes, 390
Prado Section
Tel. 227-4805

For a more local flavor, visit a North-Eastern Forró where music and costumes typical of Pernambuco will be seen. Cavalo Dourado is one. It is open only on weekends, and is best reached by cab.

In Olinda, the Auto da Sé, up on a hill, offers a gorgeous view. From there, a truly enjoyable evening may be spent walking along the beaches. There is a plethora of restaurants and bars, some with music, that are places to sit and enjoy the scenery.

Dinner With Shows

Kartier
Av. Eng. Domingos
Ferreira, 4215
Boa Viagem
Phone 325-5563

Kartier, in Boa Viagem, offers a show with dinner. On weekends, there is a cover charge for a show. The whole experience takes place in an immense room equipped with a stage. A large selection of fish dishes is offered, along with a variety of steak dishes.

Hotel Savaroni
Av. Boa Viagem, 3772
Phone 352-5077

Another somewhat more sophisticated dinner showplace is the Restaurante Hotel Savaroni. Off from the lobby, a pianist plays, and the dining room offers a beautiful view of the ocean. The menu here includes a comfortable variety including shrimp and lobster dishes.

Copus & Copus
Centro Sul Shopping
Center

Other nightclubs include Copus & Copus, in the Centro Sul shopping center, which is open only on weekends.

Club 363
Hotel Miramar
Rua dos Navegantes,
363 Boa Viagem
Phone 326-7422
10:30–4 A.M.

Club 363 offers weekend shows. Pyschedelic lights hover over a small crowded dance floor.

Disco 34
Jagandeiro Hotel
Av. Boa Viagem, 3114
Phone 326-6777

Open on weekends only. Similar to Club 363, only a bit smaller.

For Men Only

Club Twenty
Rua Luiz de Farias, 20
Boa Viagem
Phone 326-6033
4-1 A.M.

There are a few bathhouses in Boa Viagem that any cab driver will be able to take you to. This is a lovely bathhouse, almost a health spa in its style and look. Aside from the amenities of any bathhouse the club offers gambling along with an array of anxious ladies.

Club Scandinavian
Candiso Ferreira, 387
Boa Viagem
Phone 341-2207

This club is similar to Club Twenty.

Olinda

Sete Colinas
Hotel Quatro Rodas
Phone 431-2955

A lovely club in Olinda well worth a visit is Sete Colinas in the gorgeous Hotel Quatro Rodas.

Gay

Misty
Rua dos Ninfas, 125
Boa Vista

A gay bar in Recife is Misty.

Macumba

Macumba is the African religion brought over to Salvador by slaves. Although repressed for years, Macumba survives today because of its ingenuity; Macumba gods are linked with Christian gods for the original purpose of deception. Over time, though, the religion became more integrated into mainstream society, with almost ten million Brazilians practicing it and a lot more taking it seriously.

For visiting Macumba ceremonies, the best places are in Olinda; Pai Edu, an Iemanjá temple is your best bet. Check with your concierge.

Shopping

Handicrafts in Recife are considered the finest in Brazil by many people. Artists here work with wood, straw, leather, clay, or any other natural material to be found. Baskets, hats, mats, and bags are made from straw. Leather hats, coats, bags, and chairs are produced.

Pernambuco is famous for its work with clay. The clay dolls of Caruaru, the largest figure art center in the Americas, according to UNESCO, are absolutely magnificent.

The products made from wood are more structural, reflecting certain themes: flowers, fruit, animals, and human figures.

Shopping areas in Recife are located in the center of the city, in the districts of Boa Vista, Santo Antônio, and São José. The main shopping center in Recife is centered in Boa Viagem.

Mercado São José

Begun in 1875, Mercado São José is a true Rastro. It is completely uncensored in its style, with a crazed sense to it. Infused with the smells of meats and fruits, the market offers also sweets, drinks, medicinal herbs, crustaceans, records, and handicrafts. It is located near the Flower Market on Rua do Porado in Santo Antonio.

Casa da Cultura

The Cultural Center in Santo Antônio, the transformed prison with levels of cells now shops, is the largest center for handicrafts in Recife. There are stores for statues, paintings, linen, jewelry, pottery, antiques, and clothes. In the center of the building is a theater with an endless schedule of shows and events ranging from dance to plays, a museum, and small bars.

Hippie Fair

Held every Sunday in the Praça Boa Viagem in front of the Park Hotel, the handicraft market has many goods on sale. As in Rio, there are many fine leather goods, handicrafts, lamps, and paintings all over the sidewalk.

Recife Shopping Center

Like an American mall, the shopping center has many different stores, including a Mesbla Department store, an H. Stern jewelry shop, supermarkets, video shops, pharmacies, boutiques, and fast-food restaurants. A good place to just meander, and there are rides for kids.

Other Fine Shops

H. Stern
Recife Palace Hotel
Recife Shopping Center
Mar Hotel

The famous jewelry chain, the largest in Brazil, has three fine branches. You can pick up typical designs with Pernambuco motifs, as well as gemstones in the more conventional style.

Barracão
Av. Boa Viagem, 5000
Phone 341-3088

Try Borracão for handicrafts and gifts near the beach in Boa Viagem. There is a large selection of inexpensive items, and browsers are welcome.

O Casarão
Artesanato
Casa da Cultura

This is an excellent choice for local artifacts, located within the Casa da Cultura.

Tapetes Olinda
Rua Bispo Coutinho, 492
Alto da Sé, Olinda
Phone 429-3109

Here you can pick up tapestries of local color and design. Prices are high.

Michel/Xtiano
Rua Bernardo Viera de Melo, 91
Phone 429-3099

Another fine spot for first-quality tapestries.

Recife Potpourri

Buses

Buses to Olinda from Recife run along Av. Cons. Aguiar and are identified by Casa Caiada—Piedade or Rio Doce—Piedade. The bus to the airport will read Aeroporto.

Racetrack

The Hipódromo runs at night. Located at Rua Carlos Gomes, 390, in Prado.

Railroad Station

In São José (phone 224-9229).

Post Office

On Rua Cons. Aguiar, 4995, in Boa Viagem; another is at Santo Antônio, downtown.

Schedules

The Casa da Cultura publishes a monthly program. The newspaper *Diario de Pernambuco* lists events for the day, covering nightlife, restaurants, movies, shows, etc.

Curitiba

A Taste of Europe

uritiba, the capital of the state of Paraná, is Brazil's fifth largest city, with a population of one million. A well maintained highway links Curitiba with Paraná's major attraction, Iguaçú Falls. Although the city has experienced a population explosion and accelerated growth in the past ten years, Curitiba has assimilated this growth without damage to the environment, and manages to maintain a more provincial pace than most large cities. Its large population of European immigrants—Germans, Italians, Poles, Ukrainians, Dutch, Portuguese, Spanish, French, and Swiss—have earned for Curitiba its reputation as a cosmopolitan city, with more Western influence than any other in Brazil.

Although virtually undiscovered by tourists, Curitiba's pleasant climate and relaxed pace of life make it worthwhile to visit. The city is not only a cosmopolitan community created from a unique blend of cultures, but a university town, with a large population of students and academic community. The pace of Curitiba is slower than in other Brazilian cities. People are very important here; it is very human.

Founded in 1693 by explorers following the rivers from the coast in search of gold, the city was originally called Nossa Senhora da Luz dos Pinhais. Due to its location on the route taken by cattle drovers from the south to the Sorocaba cattle fair, the city grew rapidly. Development of Curitiba as a center for the harvesting and trading of the maté herb spurred its growth even further.

The year 1830 marked a first wave of immigration, and in 1854 Curitiba was made capital city of Paraná. The city hasn't stopped growing since.

Curitiba's economy is based on the industries of metal-
lurgy, electronics, transportation equipment, lumber, furniture, paper pulp, and mechanical goods. Unlike most of
Brazil, agriculture plays a lesser role.

Getting There

Daily flights which connect Curitiba to Foz do Iguaçú
continue on from there to Asuncion, Paraguay, and Buenos Aires. Flights also link Curitiba with other Brazilian
cities. The Afonso Pena Airport is fifteen kilometers from
town. Flights also leave from Bacacheri Airport, a military
airport at Base Aerea.

Curitiba is located at the crossroads of five federal highways. BR 277 leads to Foz do Iguaçú, 659 kilometers
away, and to Paranaguá, 100 kilometers away. BR 116
may be taken to São Paulo, 408 kilometers from Curitiba,
or Porto Alegre, 722 kilometers away. The coffee road,
BR 376, leads to Florianópolis.

The Curitiba–Paranaguá railroad connects Curitiba with
Santa Catarina state and São Paulo state, as well as with the
coast of Paraná. The station, R.F.S.A, is located on Afonso
Camargo Avenue.

Buses leave from the station on Afonso Camargo Avenue for many other Brazilian cities.

Hotels

Curitiba is a city with an abundance of hotels. Rather than
include an extensive number, I have included by favorites
in the three- to five-star category.

Araucaria Flat Hotel 5* The hotel consists of 84 suites
Rua Dr. Faivre, 846 and is best for families. It is con-
Phone 262-3030 veniently located. Expensive.
Telex 041-5548

Caravelle Palace Hotel 4*
Rua Cruz Machada, 282
Phone 223-4323
Telex 041-5085

This hotel, right in the heart of town, has 87 regular hotel rooms plus suites. It's your best bet here. Moderate.

Hotel Iguaçú 4*
Rua Candido Lopes, 102
Phone 224-8322
Telex 041-6109

This 200-room hotel is convenient and moderately priced. Moderate.

Araucaria Palace Hotel 4*
Rua Amintas de Barros, 73
Phone 224-2822
Telex 041-5548

This modern hotel is under the same management as the Araucaria Flat Hotel. There are 110 rooms. Moderate.

Hotel Lancaster 3*
Rua Voluntarios da Patria, 91
Phone 223-8953
Telex 041-5514

If price is a consideration, this is a perfect choice. It is well located and offers fine service and all the necessary amenities. Inexpensive.

Restaurants

Because its population is large and ethnically diverse, Curitiba offers food of every type. Portuguese, French, German, Swiss, Chinese, and Japanese restaurants can be found.

Head to the Santa Felicidade section of town, where Italian immigrants have opened canteens and larger restuarants where delicious chicken, lasagna, and spaghetti can be had with sweet, homemade wine. Select one that suits your taste and pocketbook. The people of this section have isolated themselves and use horse-drawn carriages in adherence to the customs of the old country.

What to Do in Curitiba

The commercial center of town, Rua XV de Novembro is also called Rua das Flores. Curitiba's main street, it has a large pedestrian walkway. On Saturday mornings a large roll of paper is stretched along the pavement, and children come to paint and draw on it. Part of the street is called the Boca Maldito, or speaker's corner, where politicans, soccer fans, and men from various circles gather to "argue" their positions.

The commercial and social center of town is also its oldest section, where you will find the Casa Romário Martins, an eighteenth-century building that is now a research institute, and two colonial-style churches: the Church of the Third Order of St. Francis, built in 1737, and the Church of the Rosary, built in 1762. Also in this sector is the famous Relógio das Flores (Flower Clock) in the Praça Garibaldi. An art and handicrafts fair, well worth a visit, is held here every Sunday morning. The Civic Center, two kilometers from the center of town at the end of Av. Dr. Candido de Abreu, is the headquarters of the state and municipal governments. It includes impressive structures dominated by the Palácio Iguaçú.

Theaters

The city has several excellent theaters that present plays, ballet, and music. The Guaíra, inaugurated in 1974, seats 2,173 and has an international ballet troupe. Revues, plays, and free events are also presented here. The Teatro Paiol presents high quality shows on a daily basis.

Museums

The inhabitants of Curitiba place an emphasis on culture and leisure, and the city's many museums are testament to that.

The *Museu Paranaense*, Praça Generoso Marques, has a collection of 45,000 historical pieces. The building is of neoclassical design with art nouveau touches. Open every afternoon, admission is free.

The privately owned *Museu David Carneiro*, Rua Comendador Araújo, 531, displays 10,000 historical pieces and has a 6,000-piece library as well as a collection of paintings. It's open Saturdays from 2 till 4.

The *Museum of Contemporary Arts*, Rua D. Westphalen, holds 280 works of art by Brazilian and foreign artists. Closed Saturdays and Sunday mornings.

Two painters' houses are the *Guido Viaro Museum*, Rua São Francisco, and the *Casa Alfredo Andersen*, Rua Mateus Leme, 336, open Monday through Friday.

The Casa do Expedicionário (Rua da Paz, 187), showing artifacts from early expeditions, is also worth a visit.

Parks

With more green areas per inhabitant than most cities, Brazilian or North American, Curitiba has a long list of parks. The most popular of these is the Passeio Público, in the heart of the city. Designed and constructed by the Viscount of Taunay, the park has a lake with tiny islands, a series of canals with boats, a zoo, and an aquarium. On Sundays, free shows are presented on a floating stage. Closed Mondays.

Farther from the center of town, but with a total area that is sixty times larger than Passeio Público, is Parque Barigui, which has over 1,500,000 square meters. The park is filled with fruit groves, a lake with boats, and a pavilion.

São Lourenço is another popular park, five kilometers
from the center of town, with 230,000 square meters.
Here, in addition to a lake and sports facilities, there is a
creativity center where plastic arts are taught, mainly to
children.

Excursions

In addition to the attractions of the city itself, Curitiba is
the point of origin for trips to many small towns and
villages along the Paraná coast. Many of these towns are
quite old and still have churches and buildings dating from
the colonial period. The routes to these towns, either by
highway or railroad, lead through breathtaking mountain
scenery. A voyage southward from Curitiba will lead to
some of the following towns.

Morretes is an ancient river port at the foot of the Nhun-
diaquara river, which historically has been a point of access
to other points on the coast. The town is known for its
version of the typical dish of the Paraná coast, barreado, a
meat dish that is usually washed down with pinga
(firewater).

Antonina, a short distance from Morretes, has two beautiful colonial churches: Bom Jesus and Nossa Senhora do
Pilar. The town specialty is crab meat in the shell.

The oldest city in the state, Paranaguá is the point of
deparature for most of the other small coastal towns.
Among its oldest relics is a centuries-old fountain built in
1646. The cathedral, the Church of St. Benedict, built in
1710, and the Church of the Third Order of St. Francis, a
Baroque-style building dating from 1741, are all worth the
visit. Don't miss, also, the private colonial-style house
called Visconde de Nacar Palace.

Farther south, *Matinhos* and *Caiobáare* are both popular
resorts with urbanized areas. The most exclusive resort in
this area is Caiobá, where the most sophisticated hotels can
be found. There are two beaches; that on the northern side

of the hill is rough, while the beach on the southern side where the lighthouse is, is calm.

From Caiobá, one can take the ferry boat across Guaratuba Bay to Guaratuba, the southernmost town on the coast, and also one of the most popular. The service is round the clock. One can also pass through the town of Garuva on the Paraná-Santa Catarina border.

Routes

If you are driving to the coast, there are several routes you can follow. Graciosa Highway, constructed in 1873, starts from the Curitiba – São Paulo highway. Paved from end to end, it passes through the Serra do Mar mountains before reaching Antonina, Morretes, and Paranaguá. The winding highway is renowned for its beauty. Another route to take is BR-277, which connects Paranaguá to Foz do Iguaçú. Less interesting, it is probably safer to drive. The Curitiba – Joinville highway offers another way to reach the beach resort of Guaratuba, passing through Praia do Leste, Matinhos, and Caiobá on the way.

The Curitiba – Paranaguá Railroad is an interesting trip to coastal Paranaguá. Dating from 1885, it's considered a masterpiece of engineering. Its tracks climb to altitudes of over 1,000 meters and pass through dozens of tunnels. From the slopes of Marumbi peak, the train offers a magnificent view of the blue Atlantic, many miles below.

Shopping

The *Müller shopping center* is your best bet here. There are many shops to choose from. You'll find an H. Stern shop, featuring fine Brazilian gemstones and jewelry at the shopping center.

Pantanal

A Nature Lover's Delight

he Pantanal is a long plain, 80,000 square miles in area, that extends between the banks of two rivers in the Paraguay River basin in the states of Mato Grosso and Mato Grosso do Sul. The plain is regularly flooded by the rivers, causing salines and bogs to form, and earning for the region the name *pantanal,* which means "marshland." Scattered throughout the region are cordilheiras, (small hills) onto which all the wildlife of the region crowd at flood time, thus causing the extraordinary sight of jaguars, caimans, capivaras, and cattle cohabiting harmoniously.

Although not strictly a marshland, the pantanal's marshy environment creates a lush, watery paradise for vegetation, fish, water birds, and larger animals like the caimans and jaguars. It is also a fisherman's dream, especially from November to May when the plain is usually flooded and all species of fish abound. Unlike the jungle which, although it contains half the world's species, encloses them within an impenetrable cover of trees, the pantanal makes its natural wealth easily accessible.

The perennial floods, which often destroy cattle and require evacuation of entire towns, are also the source of the region's great fertility. Flood waters bring with them abundant fish that serve as a food source for the larger animals and water birds. The isolation caused by the flooding has also helped to insulate the area from the kind of progress that too often means the decimation of wildlife. The inhabitants of the pantanal have a special feeling for the region and protect the area zealously. All of this has helped make the region one of the largest natural ecological parks in the Americas.

371

The city of Cuiabá is the best kick-off point for visiting the pantanal, whether by boat or via the Transpantaneira Highway, which cuts across the region from Cuiabá to Porto Jofre. There are various towns within the pantanal and a few pousadas. Packaged tours into the region are also available.

History

Settled by pioneers from São Paulo, the pantanal has been greatly influenced by its proximity to Spanish America, and its location put it in the heart of the conflicts between Spain and Portugal over the acquisition of new lands. Most of its towns owe their existence to the discovery of gold nearby. The Tordesillas Treaty, signed in 1494, put Mato Grosso and Mato Grosso do Sul in Spanish-American territory. However, the boundaries established by the treaty, having little connection with geographic reality, soon proved inoperative, and conflict continued abroad and, most violently, in the area itself.

The return of the first exploring expedition into the region in 1525 with a cargo of silver sparked a host of gold-seeking expeditions, most of them originating in São Paulo. On the way, these fortune seekers fought off Spanish troops and Jesuit missionaries, and imprisoned many of the native Indians who, unable to withstand the onslaught of both Spanish and Portuguese conquerors at once, were soon decimated.

Discoveries of gold led to the founding of the village of Cuiabá. In 1748, King Dom João V created the captaincy of Mato Grosso to consolidate local power. In 1772, Cáceres was founded on the left bank of the Paraguay river to act as a strategic outpost for the region. Later, the fortress of Corumba was built to protect the region in the south.

As gold production decreased, cattle raising began to take over as the principal livelihood of the region, promoted by the isolation of the villages, originally built as strategic outposts. Large farms came into being, with as many as 500,000 head of cattle.

The isolation of the region is reflected in the way of life of its inhabitants. Farm owners generally dress and live unpretentiously, although they may be wealthy enough to own a private plane or commute from an urban area. Workers lead hard lives, moving from farm to farm as work becomes available. Workers' living conditions vary, and the farmhand may live near the farmhouse in relative comfort, or in a remote thatched hut. Farms have remained large, and an estate of less than 2,000 hectares is considered small.

The food of the region is usually quite simple—rice, manioc flour, beans, meat, and fish. The local palate, like music, dance, and folklore, has undergone considerable Paraguayan influence. One practice introduced by the Paraguayans is the drinking of the teire, a kind of cold constitutional that is taken at the same time every day, in the same way that gauchos drink their calabash.

The Transpantaneira Highway, begun in September 1973 and even now only partially finished, has begun to alleviate the isolation of the region's inhabitants by connecting towns to farms. Construction was halted because of the difficulty of the terrain, high costs, and ecological considerations. Full construction of the road according to the original plan may or may not take place. If it is completed, a direct route will have been established between the pantanal and the slaughterhouses of the big cities, thereby reducing weight loss by cattle in transit, and improving the region's economy.

Presently, the pantanal is in a state of flux; new technologies are expected to take hold as a result of greater access, and the Transpantaneira, if completed, is also expected to effect greater integration between the south and the north. In the wake of new economic development, the issue of what will become of the unique, fragile, and marvelous ecosystem of the pantanal is an important one.

Cuiabá

The usual route into the Pantanal is through Cuiabá, the capital city of Mato Grosso, with a population of 168,000. Cuiabá can be reached by air from Corumbá, São Paulo, Manaus, Campo Grande, Brasília, and Rio. There is paved road to São Paulo, and the route from Brasília to Porto Velho, BR-364, also passes through Cuiabá.

Cuiabá hosts the Geodesic Center of South America, as well as some fine old churches and government buildings. The University of Mato Grosso has an interesting Indian museum (closed weekends) and the Cultural Foundation gives a natural history of the region. Regional handicrafts are sold at the Casa do Artesão Handicraft Center, Rua 13 de Junho and Senador Maletto; they include wood, straw, leather, skins, Indian objects, Pequi liquor, crystallized caju fruit, and guarana fruit. You might also try Funai, the Indian Foundation, at Rua Joaquim Murtinho, 1134.

Hotels

The better hotels will be found on the Av. Getulio Vargas.

Santa Rosa Palace 3*
Av. Getulio Vargas, 600
Phone 322-9044

Pool and restaurant, and air-conditioned rooms.

Santa Rosa Excelsior 3*
Av. Getulio Vargas, 246
Phone 322-6322

Also with pool and restaurant.

Fenicia 3*
Av. Getulio Vargas, 296
Phone 321-5122

The Fenicia has no restaurant. Rooms are air-conditioned.

Mato Grosso 3* **Rua Comandante** **Costa, 2522** **Phone 321-9121**	Small and clean, this hotel is almost opposite the Fenicia, down a small side street.

Restaurants

Cuiabá's best restaurant is located at the *Casa do Artesão*. *Novo Mato Grosso*, on the Coxipó River, is another good one. There are two good churrascarrias: *Churrascaria Majestic*, Av. Coronel Escolastico, 585, and *Bierhaus*, Av. Isaac Povoas. There is also a floating fish restaurant at *Varzea Grande*.

Nightlife

Cuiabá is an early-to-bed town but it does have one good discotheque, *Disco Keda d'Agua* on Av. C.P.A.

Sights/Excursions

Chapada dos Guimarães

Sixty-eight kilometers from Cuiabá in the mountains is Chapada dos Guimarães, site of canyons and strange prehistoric rock formations. Here too is the *Véu de Noiva* (Bridal Veil), a beautiful waterfall that drops from seventy feet above in a thin spindle of white spray. In the town, see *Our Lady of Santana* the oldest church in Mato Grosso, built in 1779. As one descends from the highlands, gravity-defying magnetic forces are said to reduce the speed of moving vehicles. Along the way to the mountains are a few other sites worth visiting: *Salgadeira, Portão do Inferno,* and the falls of *Cachoeirinhas.*

Águas Quentes/Hot Springs

Eighty-seven kilometers from Cuiabá in roughly the same direction as Chapada dos Guimarães is Serra de São Vicente, where the hot springs of Águas Quentes are found. The water is quite hot (42 degrees centigrade), and is thought to be therapeutic. Water is so abundant that it is used in the swimming pools of the hotels in Águas Quentes.

Santo Antônio do Leverger

Twenty-eight kilometers in a southeasterly direction from Cuiabá are the lovely river beaches of Santo Antônio de Leverger, on the Cuiabá River. Santo Antônio de Leverger is also a gastronomical center for the region.

The Pantanal

There are several ways to visit the pantanal's wilds. One of them is to drive the Transpantaneira highway along its completed route—from Cuiabá to Porto Jofre. At Porto Jofre, you can stay at the Santa Rosa Pantanal Hotel. Excursions and fishing trips can be easily arranged for you. From Porto Jofre, you can only go south via plane or boat. Some boat pilots are willing to take you to Corumbá, the next closest southern city. But be warned that the trip takes three days.

Other small towns in the region are points of access as well. The principal one is Barão de Melgaco, where the Brazilian Institute of Forest Development (IBDF), staffed by scientists and naturalists who study the pantanal, may be visited with permission. Other towns in the region are Poconé, 100 kilometers from Cuiabá, and Porto Cerdo and Cáceres, 200 kilometers from Cuiabá.

Because of the pantanal's relative isolation, access via independent travel is somewhat difficult, and you should consider taking one of the package tours offered to the region. The Onlytur travel agency offers several, most of them based from their pousada, which is located on the San Lourenço River, and accessible from Barão de Melgaco. A seven-day trekking tour is available. One night is spent in tents, and the others in the pousada.

One five-day tour emphasizes fishing and photo safaris with all nights spent in the pousada, while another five-day tour includes two nights of camping. A third five-day tour that is based in Cuiabá visits the pantanal via the Transpantaneira, as well as local sights including Chapada dos Guimarães. For those who want to concentrate on a special interest, there are four-day fishing and birdwatching tours, based at the pousada. Tours leave from Cuiabá.

There are two more extensive tours that last for seven and eight days. One of these features a three-day cruise up the Paraguay and Cuiabá Rivers from Corumbá to Barão de Melgaco, where the agency's pousada is located. Three nights are spent in the pousada, with small exploring tours during the day. The other long tour covers Corumbá, Cuiabá, and Barão del Melgaco, with three nights at the pousada, and departs from Cuiabá.

Wildlife

Walking and boat tours will give you a good opportunity to see the pantanal's wildlife, but so will a drive across the Transpantaneira highway. Park rangers patrol this road, and are ever watchful for signs of poachers. Among the bigger animals, jaguars prefer to isolate themselves. Caimans, which look like fat, broad-snouted alligators, will often be seen sunning themselves on the side of the road. Farther off, herds of capivara may be seen grazing in the fields. Capivara are furred, square-snouted rodents that resemble huge guinea pigs (this is in fact their nearest ancestor). The marsh deer is one of the most prolific species of larger animals in the region. Usually alone, it is in the habit of bathing in the warm lagoons in the late afternoon.

Birdwatching

Seasonal flooding makes the pantanal an ideal environment for water birds. Symbolic of the pantanal is the tuiuiu, an arresting, five-foot tall white jabiru stork with a wingspan of eight feet. The macaca, a colorful bird that lets out a raucous scream when its territory is invaded, is plentiful. So are hyacinthine macaws, parakeets, and a host of water birds: the toucan, the great egret, the roseate spoonbill, the bull-necked ibis, green kingfisher, crested catacara, and many, many more. The greater rhea, often found near farms and easily tameable, is the pantanal's largest bird. When birdwatching, do not wear vivid colors, as these will scare most birds away. Remember to stick to beiges and tans.

Fishing

As might be expected, fish are especially abundant in the pantanal. The most popular species in fisherman's terms are the pirambucu, jau, pintado, and dourado, the golden-scaled fish. Other species include jurupoca, bagre, mandichorao, tuvira, pacu, pirputanga, papudinha, traira, and curimbata, along with the infamous piranha, which most fishermen throw back into the water, but which inlanders will cook and eat with pleasure.

Fishing with a trawl is strictly forbidden at all times of year, and only professional fishermen are allowed to use nets. Fishing is particularly good during the flooding season, December through March. During spawning time, fishing is suspended.

Porto Alegre

Land of the Gaucho

For a different view of Brazil, plan to visit Porto Alegre, a 250-year-old city, the capital of Rio Grande do Sul and the heart of the nation's southern industrial region. A city in a state of flux, Porto Alegre is booming.

On the banks of the Guaiba River, with access to the sea through the Lagoa dos Patos (Lake of the Ducks), the city is surrounded by hills that give it an alpine look. This feeling is enhanced by the fair-skinned descendents of the Portuguese, Germans, and Italians who settled this area. Although the city retains flavors of these cultures, it has been most heavily influenced by its proximity to Uruguay and Argentina. In fact, Porto Alegre is more closely akin to Montevideo and Buenos Aires than it is to Rio and Salvador. The biggest influence on the city, and its distinctive feature, is the gaucho, a legendary figure who still roams the plains beyond the city's hills.

Gauchos, rather like the stalwart cowboys in the days of the Old West, stand out by their typical dress, which includes a flat, wide-brimmed hat, baggy trousers, sheepskin vest, and high leather boots with spurs. The word gaucho first appeared in the late eighteenth century when it was used by both the Spanish and Portuguese who were fighting for control of the strategic area around the estuary of the Rio de la Plata. It was a derogatory term, however, and denoted cattle rustlers and other unsavory varmints. Eventually, the term was given to a special breed of excellent horsemen who became known for their skill, hard work, and incredible hospitality.

Today's gaucho loves his beer, his pasta, and bocce, and the beef he produces is the finest in the country. You'll definitely want to try it (it is sold throughout Brazil as well), and you'll also want to try a non-beef traditional gaucho dish, galletto al primo canto (a roasted small rooster).

What to Do in Porto Alegre

Stroll along Rua dos Andradas, the city's bustling pedestrian-only street. Running for one and a half miles, it is lined with boutiques for leather goods, lots of shops, restaurants, and bars. It's a good place to see the Porto Alegrian at work and play. Spend a quiet afternoon at Parque Farroupilha, a popular park with bikes and rowboats to rent and an ice-skating rink as well. If it's a Sunday, look for the outdoor market where you can buy gaucho handicrafts and souvenirs. Do try chimiarrão, a strong tea made with maté leaves. To view Porto Alegre's beautiful people (some consider the women here the loveliest in all of Brazil), head to Parque Moinhos de Vento, which is in a lovely part of town. The city has several museums and one, the Varig Airlines Museum at Rua 18 de Novembro 800, has a collection of miniature airplanes. Visit the Palacio Piratini, built in 1890 by a French architect. It now houses government buildings. Nearby is the city's cathedral in neo-classic Renaissance style.

Where to Stay

Porto Alegre has a lot of hotels, in all price categories, and we have listed only a few below. All are moderate in price.

Plaza São Rafael 5*
Av. Alberto Bins, 514
Phone 21-6100
Telex 051-1339
Moderate

This 287-room hotel has an excellent restaurant called Bon Gourmet, a sauna and bar, and first-class service. The 16-story modern edifice is a landmark in town.

Center Park Hotel 4*
Rua Al Frederico,
Linck 25
Phone 21-5388
Telex 2737 VIVA
Inexpensive

A small 48-room hotel in the center of town. The low prices make this a great stop.

Embaixador Hotel 4*
Rua Jerinimo Coelho,
354
Phone 26-5622
Telex 051-1527
Inexpensive

This fine 182-room hotel has a good location, offers helpful service and low prices. This is another good choice.

Hotel Plaza 4*
Rua Senhor dos Passos,
154
Phone 26-1700
Telex 051-1339
Inexpensive

Housed in another attractive yellow and white building, our final choice has 174 rooms with yellow furnishings. A coffee shop, restaurant, and bar are on the premises.

Where to Dine

Restaurants here feature huge portions of beef, fine local wines, and spit-grilled chicken. One local delicacy is *arroz de carreteiro,* a salty dry beef called charque, which is stewed with rice. Many German and Italian restaurants are popular, too.

Try *Quero-Quero* (downtown at Otanio Rocha Plaza 47) for beef and grilled meats. Another excellent churrascareria is *Capitão Rodrigos* in the Hotel Plaza São Rafael. Gauchos call the food here "fresh churrasco" because it is served with a salad. *Bone Gosto* serves rodizio style where waiters circulate offering meats cut from a skewer. *Don America* is owned by a charming Uruguayan who often plays the guitar during dinner. Seafood and French specialties here. *Ratskeller* is a fine German eatery. Try the cutlet with sour cream. For posh dining, try the *Hotel Center Park*, which serves Brazilian food amid elegant surroundings.

Nightlife

There are many small clubs in the city and most cater to a young crowd. *Villa* in the Parque Moinhos de Vento is very popular and is often filled with revelers. More sophisiticated, *Le Club* features shows and dancing to live music.

Index

Continent-sized Brazil is a country of vast contrasts. With a VARIG AIRPASS you can see the lush beauty of Brazil's tropical rain forests, grassy savanahs, mountain vistas and white, powdery beaches. Experience the excitement of such cosmopolitan cities as industrious Sao Paulo or fabled Rio de Janeiro. And meet an international mix of truly handsome and gracious people.

A VARIG AIRPASS makes all of Brazil a travel bargain. For instance, with AIRPASS I, you get 21 days of unlimited mileage and stopovers for $330. With AIRPASS II, you will have 14 days of unlimited mileage and 4 stopovers in addition to the gateway city for $250.

Just be sure to purchase your VARIG AIRPASS at the same time you buy your international ticket since the AIRPASS may only be sold outside of Brazil.

*Contact your travel agent or VARIG office for complete details.

LANGUAGE AND TRAVEL BOOKS
FROM PASSPORT BOOKS

Dictionaries and References
Vox Spanish and English Dictionaries
Harrap's Concise Spanish and English
  Dictionary
Harrap's French and English Dictionaries
Klett German and English Dictionary
Harrap's Concise German and English
  Dictionary
Everyday American English Dictionary
Beginner's Dictionary of American
  English Usage
Diccionario Inglés
El Diccionario del Español Chicano
Diccionario Básico Norteamericano
British/American Language Dictionary
The French Businessmate
The German Businessmate
The Spanish Businessmate
Harrap's Slang Dictionary (French and English)
English Picture Dictionary
French Picture Dictionary
Spanish Picture Dictionary
German Picture Dictionary
Guide to Spanish Idioms
Guide to German Idioms
Guide to French Idioms
Guide to Correspondence in Spanish
Guide to Correspondence in French
Español para los Hispanos
Business Russian
Yes! You Can Learn a Foreign Language
Everyday Japanese
Japanese in Plain English
Korean in Plain English
Robin Hyman's Dictionary of Quotations
NTC's American Idioms Dictionary
Passport's Japan Almanac
Japanese Etiquette and Ethics in
  Business
How To Do Business With The Japanese
Korean Etiquette And Ethics In Business

Verb References
Complete Handbook of Spanish Verbs
Spanish Verb Drills
French Verb Drills
German Verb Drills

Grammar References
Spanish Verbs and Essentials of Grammar
Nice 'n Easy Spanish Grammar
French Verbs and Essentials of Grammar
Nice 'n Easy French Grammar
German Verbs and Essentials of Grammar
Nice 'n Easy German Grammar
Italian Verbs and Essentials of Grammar
Essentials of Russian Grammar

Welcome Books
Welcome to Spain
Welcome to France
Welcome to Ancient Greece
Welcome to Ancient Rome

Language Programs
Just Listen 'n Learn: Spanish, French, Italian,
  German and Greek
Just Listen 'n Learn Plus: Spanish, French,
  and German
Japanese For Children
Basic French Conversation
Basic Spanish Conversation

Phrase Books
Just Enough Dutch
Just Enough French
Just Enough German
Just Enough Greek
Just Enough Italian
Just Enough Japanese
Just Enough Portuguese
Just Enough Scandinavian
Just Enough Serbo-Croat
Just Enough Spanish
Multilingual Phrase Book
International Traveler's Phrasebook

Language Game Books
Easy French Crossword Puzzles
Easy French Word Games and Puzzles
Easy Spanish Crossword Puzzles
Easy Spanish Word Games and Puzzles
Let's Learn About Series: Italy, France,
  Germany, Spain, America
Let's Learn Coloring Books In Spanish,
  French, German, Italian, And English

Humor in Five Languages
The Insult Dictionary: How to Give 'Em
  Hell in 5 Nasty Languages
The Lover's Dictionary: How to Be
  Amorous in 5 Delectable Languages

Technical Dictionaries
Complete Multilingual Dictionary of
  Computer Terminology
Complete Multilingual Dictionary of
  Aviation and Aeronautical Terminology
Complete Multilingual Dictionary of
  Advertising, Marketing and Communications
Harrap's French and English
  Business Dictionary
Harrap's French and English
  Science Dictionary

Travel
Nagel's Encyclopedia Guides
World at Its Best Travel Series
Runaway Travel Guides
Mystery Reader's Walking Guide: London
Japan Today
Japan at Night
Discovering Cultural Japan
Bon Voyage!
Business Capitals of the World
Hiking and Walking Guide to Europe
Frequent Flyer's Award Book
Ethnic London
European Atlas
Health Guide for International Travelers
Passport's Travel Paks: Britain, Italy,
  France, Germany, Spain
Passport's China Guides
On Your Own Series: Brazil, Israel
Spain Under the Sun Series: Barcelona, Toledo,
  Seville and Marbella

Getting Started Books
Introductory language books for Spanish,
  French, German and Italian.

For Beginners Series
Introductory language books for children
  in Spanish, French, German and Italian.

PASSPORT BOOKS

Trade Imprint of National Textbook Company
4255 West Touhy Avenue
Lincolnwood, Illinois 60646-1975 U.S.A.